THE STUDENTS' GUIDE
WESTERN CALLIGRAPHY

THE STUDENT'S GUIDE TO

WESTERN CALLIGRAPHY

AN ILLUSTRATED SURVEY

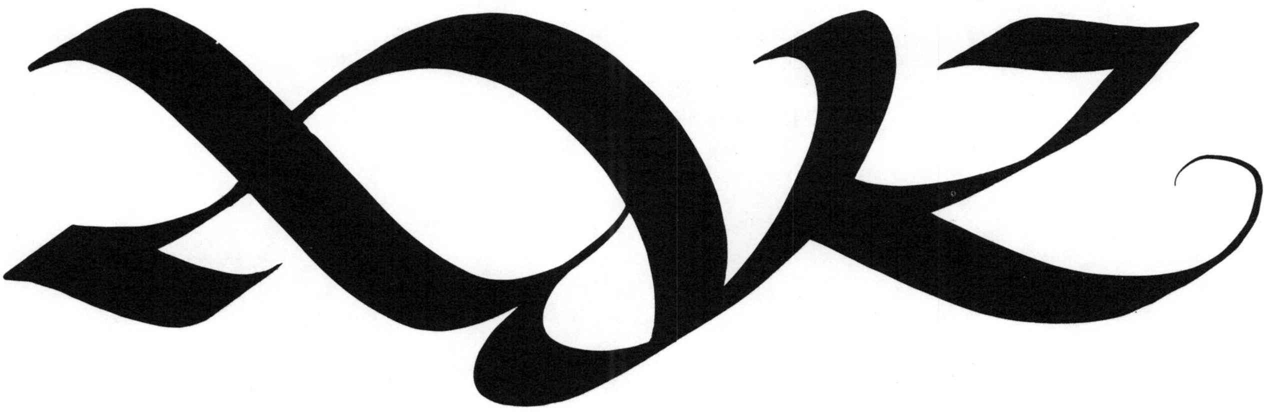

BY JOYCE IRENE WHALLEY

SHAMBHALA/Boulder & London, 1984

SHAMBHALA PUBLICATIONS, INC.
1920 13th Street • Boulder, Colorado 80302

9 8 7 6 5 4 3 2 1
First edition
Distributed in the United States by Random House and in Canada by Random House of Canada Ltd. Distributed in the United Kingdom by Routledge & Kegan Paul Ltd., London and Henley-on-Thames.
Printed in the United States of America.

LIBRARY OF CONGRESS CATALOGING IN PUBLICATION DATA

Whalley, Joyce Irene.
The student's guide to Western calligraphy.
Bibliography: p. Includes index.
1. Calligraphy—History. 2. Penmanship—Copy-books.
3. Paleography—Handbooks, manuals, etc. I. Title.
Z43.W53 1983 745.6'197'09 83-42805
ISBN 0-87773-239-6
ISBN 0-394-72189-6 (Random House).

THE author and publisher wish to express their thanks to the following institutions which have kindly given permission for the photographic reproduction of objects in their collections:

The Bodleian Library, Oxford

The British Library, London

The Philadelphia Museum of Art

The Victoria and Albert Museum, London

CONTENTS

PREFACE

THE main purpose of this book is to enable those interested in the history of calligraphy to have before them a wide range of examples showing the development of the various scripts from the Roman period up to the present time. It is therefore primarily a picture book, but each group of illustrations has an introductory text which sets the general background to the period. Since it is both annoying and time-consuming to hunt for explanations of the pictures in the text, each illustration is accompanied by a detailed caption, so that it is to some extent self-contained and self-explanatory.

It is hoped that one result of looking at the pictures in this book will be to encourage the reader to try his or her hand at calligraphy. There is no substitute for personal teaching, but if you cannot attend a class in calligraphy, the next best thing is to buy yourself one of the many excellent manuals that are now being published. This book is not a manual on how to write, but it does portray the various kinds of scripts that have evolved over the centuries, and the illustrations are for the most part clear enough to be copied. If they are not always as clear as the would-be scribe might wish, remember that many of the copybooks and manuscripts are very old, and the pages have become somewhat dim and worn.

Do not be despondent if your writing is not up to the standard of the examples portrayed here. Most of the manuscripts and books chosen for inclusion were selected because they were the best of their kind. Not everyone in the past wrote so well, nor did every scribe write so beautifully all the time. Try your hand at as many different styles as possible, but at the same time remember that each script is linked to the social and economic conditions—and the art—of its time, and that goes for your own writing too!

THE STUDENTS' GUIDE TO WESTERN CALLIGRAPHY

FIGURE 1: Part of a Roman school grammar found at Karanis Egypt after 172 A.D.

This shows a papyrus fragment in rustic capitals. It will be noted that there is no punctuation and no separation of words. These began to appear only in about the seventh century.

REPRODUCED BY PERMISSION OF THE BRITISH LIBRARY PAPYRUS 2733 (verso)

From Roman Times to the Early Middle Ages

HOW often do you write? I am not referring to correspondence, but to actual pen-in-hand writing. Today few of us need to write very much or very often, the typewriter and the telephone having largely taken over the rôle of communicators. But it is a strange quirk of human nature that we often only come to value things as they begin to disappear, and handwriting was scarcely given a notice until we ceased to need it. However, in recent years the study and practice of writing has increased considerably, especially that branch of writing known as calligraphy.

Calligraphy is the art (or craft) of fine writing, and the word derives from two Greek ones meaning "beauty" and "to write." Not all writing is fine writing. Most of us use a different style of writing for different occasions—a mere scribble when we write out a shopping list, and something rather better when we are applying for a job (that is, if we don't type the application!). In making this simple distinction we are in fact following a centuries-old practice, for writers in the past also had this same attitude to the kind of script required for different occasions—though these were not usually either shopping lists or job applications, of course. The writing we use today can trace its development right back to Roman times, and is the result of the constant battle between beauty and legibility on the one hand, and speed and convenience on the other. This book aims to show the development of modern scripts from their Roman origins, and to explain some of the reasons for the change in styles of handwriting from one century to another.

The single most important factor affecting any script is the method used to produce it. If you decide to show your support for some cause by writing a slogan on the nearest blank wall, you can do it in two ways. You can write it with paint or an aerosol spray; this is usually the easiest way. Or you can take a sharp tool and scratch the letters into the surface. This is slower and more difficult, but it is also more difficult to erase. And when you have tried both, you will notice that the shapes of the letters you have drawn differ according to the instrument you have used and the surface on which you have written them. As with graffiti on walls, so with early writing.

For most people, Roman "writing" is represented by inscriptions, such as can be seen on monuments scattered about the countries that once formed part of the old Roman Empire, or on gravestones and similar remains to be found in museums. But such things formed only a part of Roman methods of communication, though by reason of their nature they have proved among the most durable. The letters that we find carved on Roman monuments (usually capital letters or "majuscules") are some of the finest that have ever been devised, though of course they do vary in quality, since not every craftsman was equally skilled at the work. But these fine square capitals did provide models for Roman writing, even if in practice the results fell far short of the best. While these grand inscriptions offered a suitable record of important events or people, they were obviously not the things to use for conducting business affairs, or even communicating with friends. For this purpose the Romans used completely different materials, and so, not surprisingly, they also had a different script. For their business and personal letters they used a kind of paper made from the pith of the papyrus reed, which grows in the eastern Mediterranean. They wrote on the papyrus with a reed pen, which was less likely to pierce the sheets than a metal pen or stylus might do. With this reed pen they wrote a quick and cursive script, one which today we find very difficult to read, even though the letters derive from the very clear inscriptional alphabet. A certain amount of their personal and business correspondence has survived, preserved in the dry atmosphere of Egypt, so that we do have quite a good idea of what informal Roman handwriting looked like.

The Roman papyrus letter was the main means of communication throughout the Empire during the first centuries of the Christian era, and only began to disappear as the sea and land routes that transported it began to succumb to the attacks of invaders. The Roman "book," which was also written on papyrus, was in the form of a scroll or roll, with a title tag hanging from one end to identify it. The scroll had certain disadvantages, and one of them was that it was not easy to refer to a passage in the middle of a roll for example, since it was necessary to unwind part of the scroll with one hand and wind it up with the other until the desired passage was traced. This disadvantage became even more noticeable with the formal acceptance of Christianity as the official religion of the Roman Empire in the fourth century A. D. The Christians placed great emphasis on the Bible and on the commentaries and other writings associated with it, and their teachers needed to make frequent reference to the Word of God as thus revealed. It therefore became much more convenient to use another form of book which was already in existence, namely the "codex," which was the forerunner of the modern volume. Such a format was certainly a great improvement when it came to looking up specific passages in a text. Another factor also helped to change the style and type of book in use during the early Christian centuries. This was the increasing difficulty of obtaining supplies of papyrus, as the Mediterranean sea routes were attacked and fell into hostile hands. Instead, the use of vellum or parchment increased, and this accorded well with medieval economy. Vellum is made from the skins of animals—sheep, goats, or cows. Not only were there plenty of these animals around, but the lack of overwintering feedstuffs throughout the Middle Ages necessitated the autumn slaughter of cattle, and so provided a plentiful supply of skins for vellum production. Vellum is tough and durable, but it needs a considerable amount of preparation before it can be written upon. Moreover, although it was possible to write with a reed pen on vellum, it was better to use something that would have a firmer point, and could be used with a stronger ink. For this purpose the quill pen proved not only suitable but economically sound. The quill was made from the feathers of a bird (Latin *penna*—a feather), usually goose or crow. Every village had its flock of geese in order to provide fresh meat for the community, and so supplies of feathers were assured. The quill pen was a very flexible instrument, and could be shaped and sharpened to suit the needs of individual scribes. But of course it did need frequent attention to keep it in good trim.

The changes in writing materials affected the style of writing for which they were used. And times had changed, too. With the breakup of the Roman Empire, Europe was in turmoil. A period frequently referred to as "The Dark Ages" had begun, when settled life and business was liable to the attention of hostile forces throughout the European continent. Only in the monasteries was the lamp of learning kept burning, and even here it was liable to extinction at the hands of non-Christian invaders. In such conditions, only essential work could proceed, and naturally enough this work was confined to the copying of religious texts. In these days of the multiplicity of books and the regular supply of newspapers, we find it hard to imagine what it must have meant to a community when everything had to be handwritten. If you wanted a book to read or to study, you had first to locate a copy, then persuade the owner to lend it to you while you laboriously copied out the text. Even when you had finished the copying, which might take months—especially during the short dark days of winter—you still only had one further copy of the work. In order to share the knowledge it contained with your fellows, it would have to be read out loud, unless you lent your precious copy (of a copy) to someone else. This was the only way in which learning could be passed on before the invention of the printing press in the fifteenth century.

As a result of all this, writing changed considerably. Two strands of development are discernible. There was the production of the fine large religious volumes, some of which have survived to show us what the Dark Ages could provide. Copying out the Bible or other religious texts was considered to be a work highly pleasing to God, and the best vellum, the best scribes, and the best scripts and decoration were used, especially when the volume had been commissioned for some great religious foundation. Scripts were large and splendid. One used during this period, the uncial script, is still considered by some to be the most beautiful ever devised. This script shows how gradually the square capitals of the Romans became rounded as they were written with a quill pen on a vellum surface. The Romans themselves had already given the handwritten letters a certain curve, in the alphabet known rather unfairly as "rustic." Rustic capitals continued to be used throughout the early Middle Ages, usually in headings. The uncial hand, which was far more rounded than the rustic, was a majestic hand, slowly written—not at all suitable if you wished to copy a text quickly for your own use. Hence for personal use a more cursive hand, or half-uncial might be employed, an indication of the second strand in the evolution of scripts. But the trouble with all cursive scripts is that they tend to deteriorate, especially when written at speed (consider your own writing!). By the eighth and ninth centuries the scripts written in most western European countries were both ugly and difficult to read. Something neater and more economical of space was needed. For one has to remember that however many animals were killed to provide a supply of vellum, the amount of skin on each animal that could actually be used to provide suitable writing material was very limited. And, as we have seen, the large uncial letters were uneconomical in their use of vellum.

In fact, most of the scripts described so far have been majuscule scripts—i.e. composed of capital letters—slow to write and space-consuming. The great contribution of the reign of the Emperor Charlemagne (742–814) was the minuscule or small letter script, known from the court at which it received so much encouragement, as the "Carolingian minuscule." Minuscule or small letters are something we take for granted as we read the print of the present book, but nevertheless they were a form not used widely until the eighth or ninth century. The Carolingian minuscule as written by the scribes at the court of Charlemagne was an extremely elegant hand, fast to write yet spacious in appearance, and easily read. Its suitability ensured its rapid adoption in most western European countries, although in the British Isles it was much slower to replace the existing insular, or Anglo-Saxon, minuscule. With the development and spread of the Carolingian minuscule all the ingredients for the future development of handwriting had been evolved. This makes the decades on either side of the year 1000 A.D. a suitable place to move from the study of the hands of the early Middle Ages to those that were to hold sway during the later period, until the invention of printing from movable types in the middle of the fifteenth century was to effectively proclaim the end of the medieval era and the beginning of the modern.

FIGURE 2: Edward Johnston: Manuscript & inscriptional letters for schools and classes & for the use of craftsmen   London 1928

This is an illustration from a teaching portfolio by Edward Johnston, the twentieth-century scribe, in which he has written out various early scripts. They show, better than photographs of originals, the way in which the letters were formed; Johnston has also added examples of his own for those letters which did not appear in the Latin alphabet. The way in which rustic capitals developed from square capitals of the inscriptional kind is very clearly displayed.

AUTHOR'S COLLECTION

ABCDEFGHILMN

special positions

Normal pen position

OPQRSTVXY AJKUWZ

Suggested modern A & JKUWZ forms

"SQUARE CAPITALS" freely copied with a pen from a photograph of a 4th. or 5th. Century MS. (Vergil) – abt. 2ce. the height of originals

ACCEDENS AVTEM TRIBVNVS, DIXIT ILLI: DIC MIHI SI TV ROMANVS ES? AT ILLE DIXIT: ETIAM. ET RESPONDIT TRIBVNVS: EGO MVLTA SVMMA CI-VILITATEM HANC CONSECVTVS SVM.

Example of (modern) Writing. Note: the words are 'packed' and separate now: in the early MSS. there was no such division. (Actus Apostolorum xxii.27.)

ABCDEFGHILMNOPQ

for thin stems (varies)

Normal pen position for thicks

RSTVXY·AHJKUWZ

Suggested modern A, H, & J, K, U, W, Z forms to match.

"RUSTIC CAPITALS" freely copied with a pen from a photograph of a 3rd. or 4th. Century MS. (Vergil) – abt. 2ce. the height of originals.

PLATE 2.—"SQUARE" & "RUSTIC" CAPITALS the two great Book-hands of the 3rd to the 5th century A.D. CONSTRUCTION: The Square capitals followed the inscriptional forms (cf. Pl. 12): the Rustic variety was more easily written. Both are written with a "slanted-pen," i.e. a pen so held or cut that the thin stroke is oblique ⁄ : cf. "*straight pen*" (Pl. 4), the *Square* with a slight slant ⁄, the *Rustic* with a great slant /. In either case the position is generally uniform, but the slant is increased for all *thin stems* and the nib moves on to one of its "points" in making some of the terminals. USE: The *Square* MS. makes a *beginning book-hand*; the *Rustic an occasional hand & a basis for ornamental forms* (W.&L., p. 297.)

2 *School Copies and Examples, No. 2. Sir Isaac Pitman & Sons, Ltd., Parker Street, Kingsway, W.C.2*

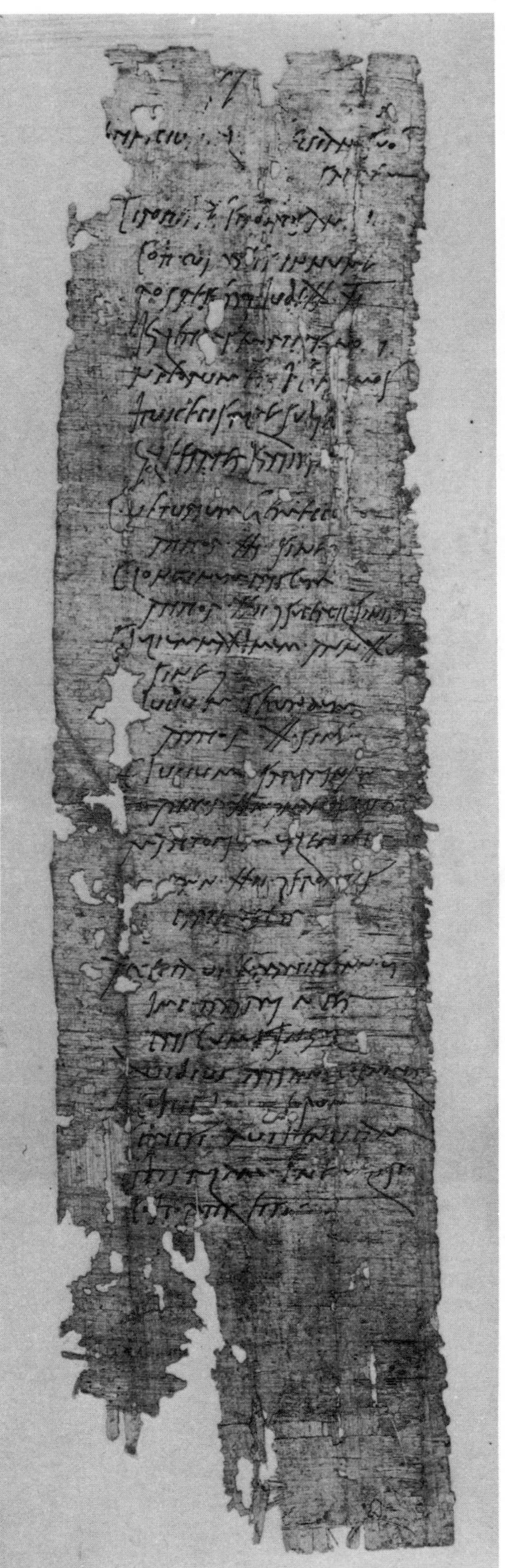

3

FIGURE 3: Letter from a Roman officer, found at Oxyrhynchus in Egypt A.D. 103

This shows an example of the Roman cursive hand, and is written on papyrus. This hand had a long life, from at least the second century B.C. until the seventh century A.D. It was this style of hand which was to influence medieval writing. Today we find it almost impossible to read, though it cannot have been so difficult for the original recipient. The letter itself concerns the enrollment of six new recruits.

REPRODUCED BY PERMISSION OF THE BRITISH LIBRARY PAPYRUS 2049

FIGURE 4: Ecclesiastical Canons Italian? sixth/seventh century

This is a good example of the uncial script, spacious and rounded. It will be noted that the words are still not separated one from another. Can you identify the various letters?

REPRODUCED BY PERMISSION OF THE BODLEIAN LIBRARY OXFORD MS E MUS 100 f.7v 26 × 18.5

ea capitula quae in commonito
rio praesente fratre et coepisc
nostro Faustino sede et praes
byteri Philippus et Asellus secu
adtulerunt collecta synodus
de hoc in secundo tractauimus
ut ea ut ibidem reperta a nobis fir
mabuntur aut si non inuenta
fuerint silebunt
Danihel notarius recitauit
Nicaeni concilii fidei professio
uel eius statuta ita se habent
ut superius lectum est tituli xx
quos in ordine recitauit
et cum recitaret
Aurelius episc d haec ita apud nos
habentur exemplaria statutorum
quae tunc patres nostri de con
cilio Nicaeno secum detulerunt
cuius formam seruantes haec
quae secuntur constituta a nobis
custodiuntur
de trinitate
Uniuersum concilium d do pro
pitio pari professione fides
ecclesiastica quae per nos traditur

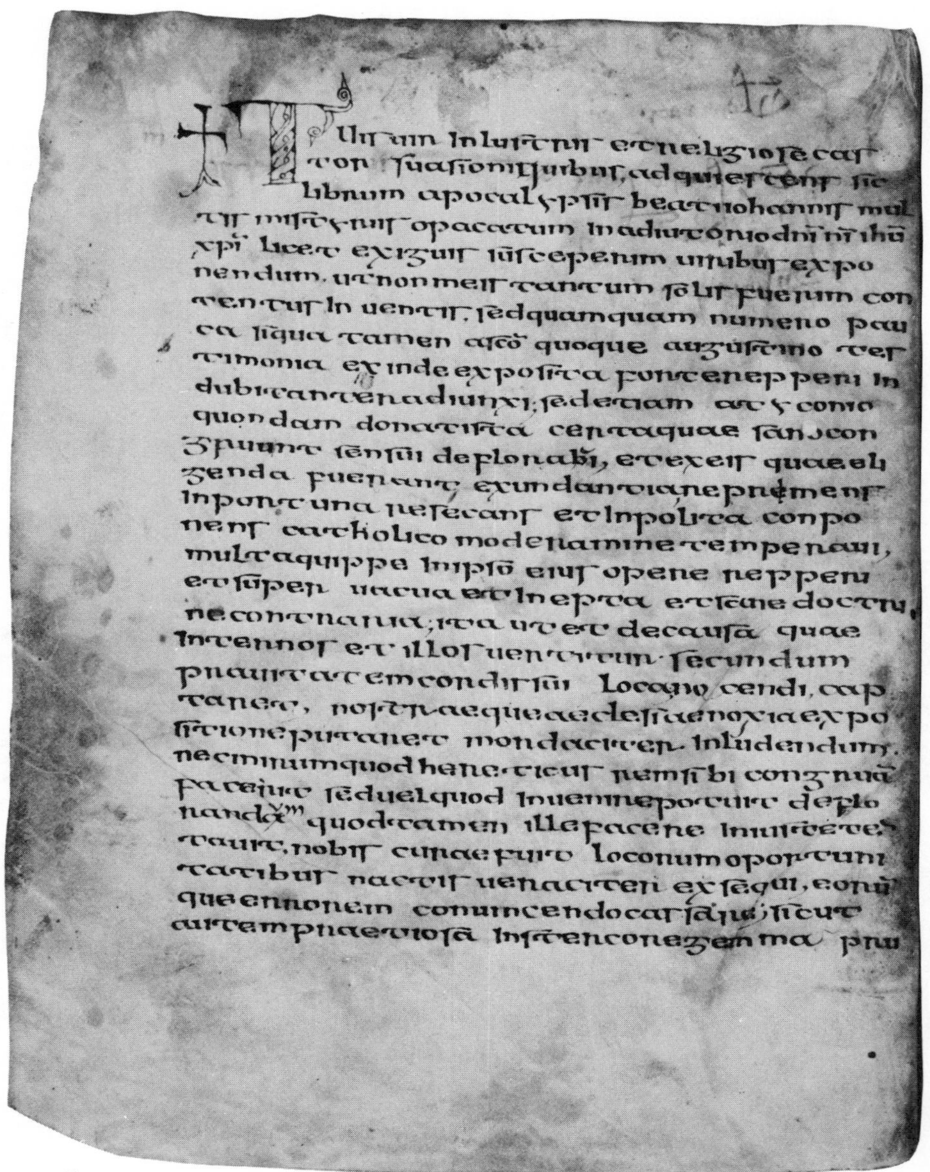

5

FIGURE 5: Primasius in Apocalypsim English? seventh/eighth century

This version of the half-uncial was written in England, though probably based on French models. It is well on the way to being a true minuscule hand. In the original, the initials are filled in with red and yellow.

REPRODUCED BY PERMISSION OF THE BODLEIAN LIBRARY OXFORD MS. DOUCE 140 f.1v 24 × 18.5

FIGURE 6: The Canterbury Gospels English eighth century

This is a very elegant example of the Anglo-Saxon script written in the south of England. The manuscript was known to be in Canterbury by the fourteenth century, hence its name.

REPRODUCED BY PERMISSION OF THE BRITISH LIBRARY ROYAL MS. 1EV1 f.14r 47 × 34

In illo tempore respondens ihs
dixit. Confiteor tibi pater dñe
caeli et terrae quia abscondisti
haec a sapientibus et prudentibus
et revelasti ea parvulis. Ita pater
quoniam sic fuit placitum ante te.
Omnia mihi tradita sunt
a patre meo.
Et nemo novit filium nisi pater
neque patrem quis novit nisi filius.
et cui voluerit filius revelare.
Venite ad me omnes qui laboratis
et honerati estis et ego reficiam vos
Tollite iugum meum super vos
et discite a me quia mitis sum
et humilis corde et invenietis
requiem animabus vestris.
Iugum enim meum suave est
et honus meum leve est.
2. In illo tempore abiit ihs sabbato
per sata discipuli h eius esurientes
coeperunt vellere spicas.
et manducare.
Pharisaei h videntes dixerunt ei
Ecce discipuli tui faciunt quod non
licet eis facere sabbatis.
At ille dixit eis Non legistis quid
fecerit david quando esuriit
et qui cum eo erant.
Quomodo intravit in domum dei
et panes propositionis comedit
quos non licebat ei edere.
neque his qui cum eo erant
nisi solis sacerdotibus. aut non
legistis in lege. quia sabbatis
sacerdotes in templo sabbatum
violant et sine crimine sunt
Dico h vobis quia templo maior est
hic. Si h sciretis quid est miseri
cordiam volo et non sacrificium
numquam condemnassetis inno
centes. dñs est enim filius hominis etiam sab
bati.

Et cum inde transisset venit
in synagogam eorum et ecce homo
manum haridam habens
Et interrogabant eum dicentes
Si licet sabbatis curare ut accusarent
eum. Ipse h dixit illis
quis erit ex vobis homo qui habet
ovem unam et si ceciderit haec
sabbatis in foveam. nonne tene
bit et levabit eam. quanto magis
melior est homo ove. Itaque licet
sabbatis bene facere.
Tunc ait homini extende manum
tuam et extendit et restituta est
sanitati sicut altera.
Exeuntes h pharisaei consilium
faciebant adversus eum quomodo
eum perderent.
Ihs h sciens recessit inde et secuti sunt
eum multi et curavit eos omnes
et praecepit eis ne manifestatum
eum facerent. Ut adimpleretur
quod dictum est per esaiam prophetam
dicentem Ecce puer meus quem
elegi. dilectus meus in quo bene con
placuit animae meae.
Ponam spm meum super eum.
et iudicium gentibus nuntiabit
Non contendet neque clamabit neque
audiet aliquis in plateis vocem eius.
Harundinem quassatam non confrin
get et linum fumigans non extinguet
donec eiciat ad victoriam iudicium
et in nomine eius gentes sperabunt
Tunc oblatus est ei homo daemonium
habens. caecus et mutus et curavit
eum ita ut loqueretur et videret.
Et stupebant omnes turbae et dice
bant. Numquid hic est xps filius
david.
Pharisaei autem audientes dixerunt
hic non eicit daemonia.

Quae in nobis completae
sunt rerum
Sicut tradiderunt nobis
qui ab initio ipsi uiderunt
et ministri fuerunt
sermonis
uisum est et mihi
adsecuto a principio omnia
diligenter ex ordine tibi
scribere optime theophile
ut cognoscas eorum
uerborum de quib:
eruditus es ueritatem

FUIT IN DIEBUS
herodis regis
iudaeae sacerdos
quidam nomine
zacharias de uice abia
et uxor illi de filiab: aaron
et nomen eius elisabeth
Erant autem iusti ambo
ante dm

incedentes in omnibus
mandatis et iustificatio
nib: dni sine querella
Et non erat illis filius eo
quod esset elisabeth
sterelis
Et ambo processissent
in dieb: suis
Factum est autem cum
sacerdotio fungeretur
in ordine uicis suae
ante dm
Secundum consuetudinem
sacerdoti
sorte exiit ut incensum
poneret ingressus
in templum dni
Et omnis multitudo erat
populi orans foris
hora incensi
Apparuit autem illi
angelus dni stans
a dextris altaris
incensi

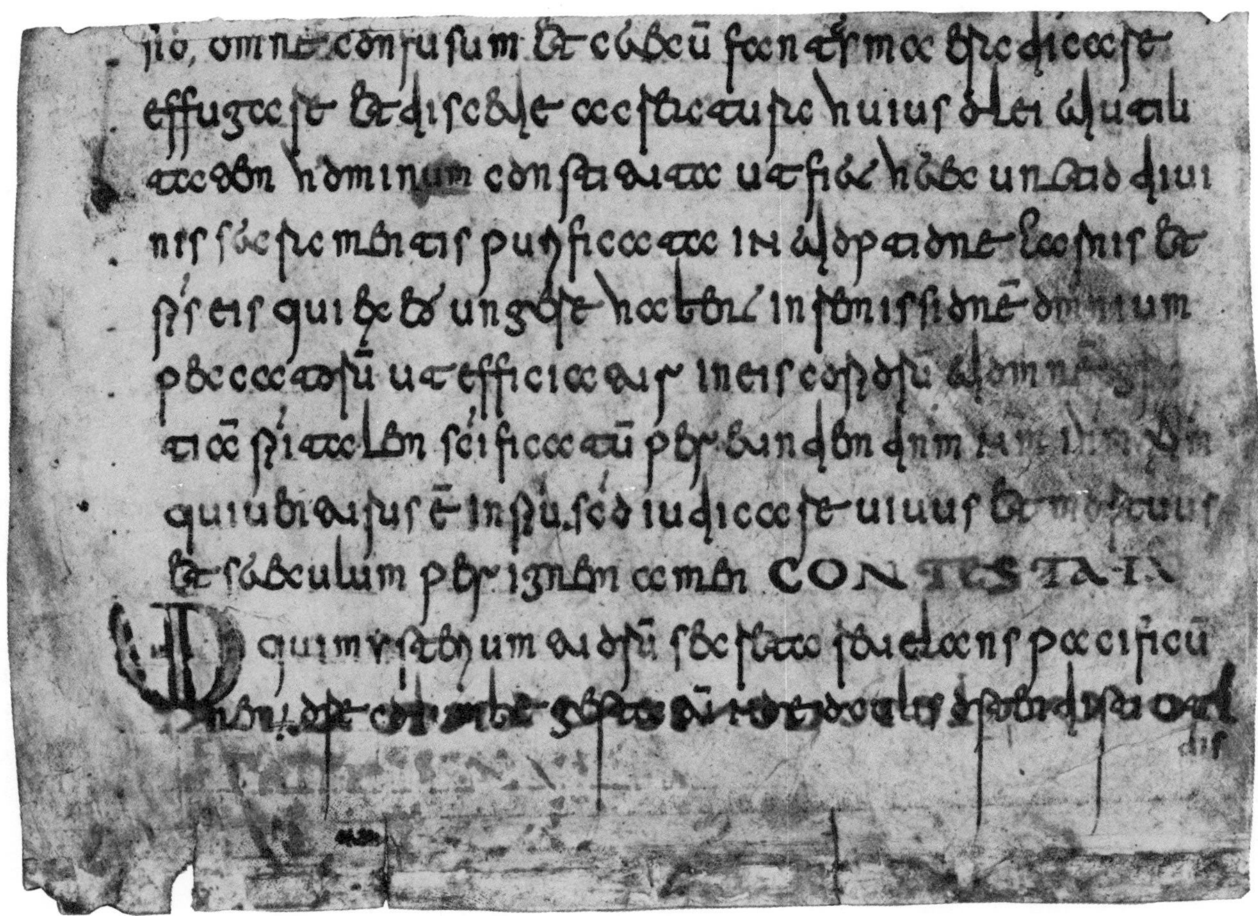

8

FIGURE 7: The Lindisfarne Gospels English eighth century

This is a well-known early manuscript, but illustrations usually concentrate on the decorated pages. Here we are looking only at the script in which it is written—according to the colophon by Eadfrith, Bishop of Lindisfarne (698–721). The main text is in Anglo-Saxon majuscules, while the interlinear gloss of the tenth century is in Anglo-Saxon minuscules. Under the text we can see the shadowy traces of the decoration on the next page showing through the vellum.

REPRODUCED BY PERMISSION OF THE BRITISH LIBRARY COTTON NERO D.IV f.139v 34 × 24.5

FIGURE 8: Sacramentum Gelasianum French eighth century (second half)

This fragment, which was removed from a binding, shows the kind of script in use in France before the reform of Charlemagne; it is known as the Merovingian script. It is very difficult to decipher!

REPRODUCED BY PERMISSION OF THE BODLEIAN LIBRARY OXFORD MS. DOUCE f.1v 15.5 × 21

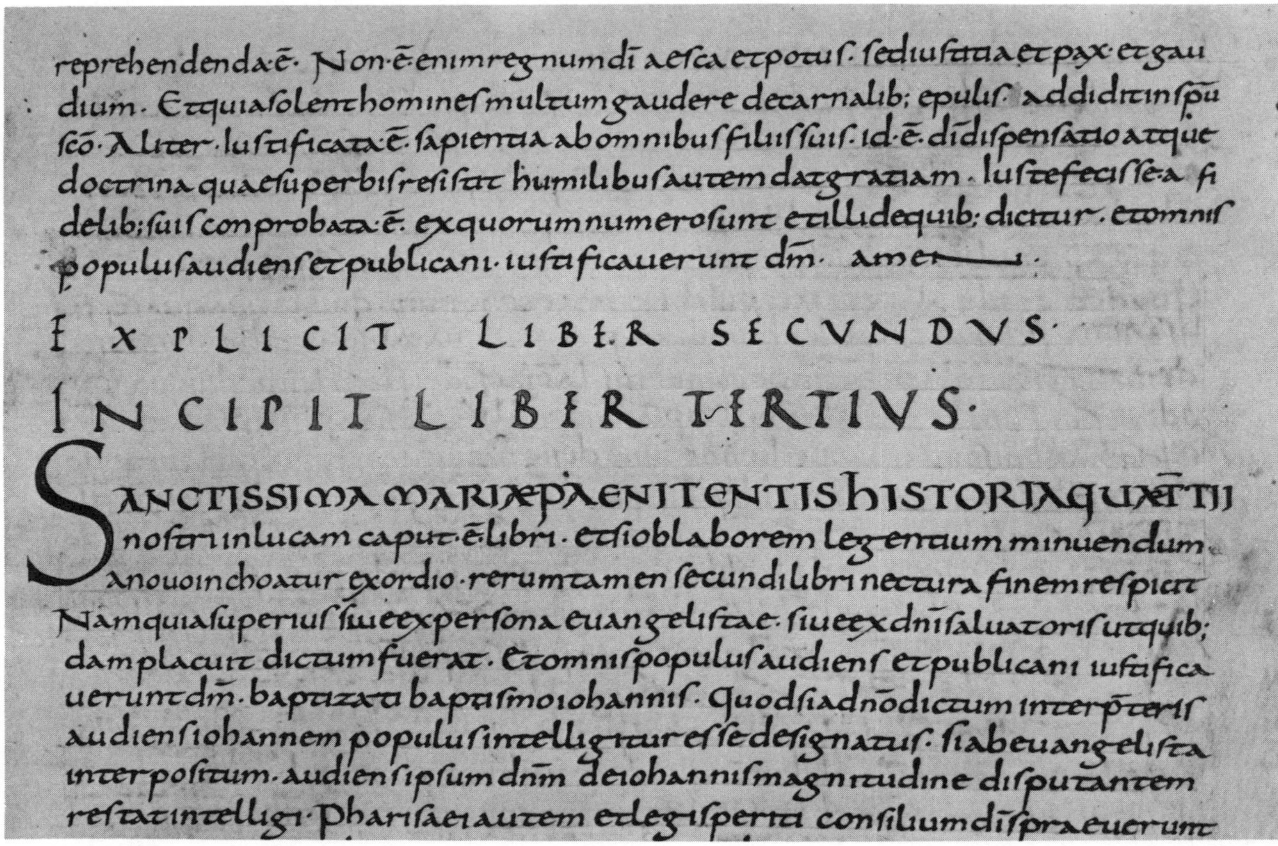

9

FIGURE 9: Bede: Expositio in Lucam French (Tours) c.820, with late 10th-century additions.

This fine Carolingian manuscript emanates from the scriptorium of Tours, which became famous for the quality of the manuscripts it produced. The passage shown here is a good example of what became known as the "hierarchy of scripts." The idea of the relative importance of the various scripts (square capitals, rustic, uncial etc.) indicates an awareness of their antiquity. In this example the "explicit" and "incipit" lines are in rustic capitals and the first line beginning "Sanctissima" is in uncials.

35.5 × 25

FIGURE 10: Evangelia "Gospels of MacRegol" Irish eighth/ninth century

This is an example of the late Irish majuscule script and it was written in part at least by MacRegol (identified as "scribe and Bishop"), abbot of Birr, who died in 822. Note the decoration of the first six lines: the capital letters are in colored inks and surrounded with red dots. In the tenth century an Anglo-Saxon interlinear gloss was added so that we can see the two different hands on the same page.

35 × 27

Qui fuit arfaxat Qui fuit iareth
Qui fuit sem Qui fuit malelel
Qui fuit noe Qui fuit cainan
Qui fuit lamech Qui fuit enos
Qui fuit mathusale Qui fuit seth
Qui fuit enoc qui fuit adam
Cap: 4. IHS autem plenus spu (qui fuit dī
sco regresus est a iordane & agebatur in spu
2 in desertum diebus XL· & temptabatur a diabu
lo & nihil manducauit in diebus illis & consum
3 matis illis essuriit dixit autem illi zabulus
Si filius dī es dic lapidi huic ut panis fiat
4 & respondit ad illum ihs scriptum est enim
quia non in pane solo uiuit homo sed in om
5 ni uerbo dī & duxit zabulus & ostendit illi omnia
6 regna orbis terrae in momento temporis & ait
ei tibi dabo potestatem hanc uniuersam & glori
am illorum quia mihi tradita sunt & cui uolu
7 ero do illa tu ero si adoraueris coram me
8 erunt tua omnia & respondens ihs dixit
illi scriptum est dnm dm tuum adorabis & illi
9 soli seruies & duxit eum in hierusalem & statuit

bores eorum introistis .·. Ex ciuitat
e autem illa multi crediderunt
in eum samaritanorum . propter
uerbum mulieris testimonium
perhibentis . quia dixit michi
omnia quaecumque feci .·. Cum uenis
sent ergo ad illum samaritani .
rogabant eum ut ibi maneret .
et mansit ibi duobus diebus .·.
Et multo plures crediderunt propter
sermonem eius . et mulieri
dicebant . quia iam non propter
tuam loquelam credimus . ipsi
enim audiuimus et scimus . quia
hic est saluator mundi .·.

Ioa. C. 8. V. 1

In ill. temp. Perrexit ihs
in montem oliueti . et
diluculo iterum uenit

12

FIGURE 11: Gospel Lectionary Dalmatia (Zadar) late eleventh century (1081–86)

This is an example of the Beneventan script that remained in use in southern Italy for nearly five hundred years. Although it looks attractive on the page, it is by no means easy to read. Try to pick out the letters e *and* a, *for example.*

REPRODUCED BY PERMISSION OF THE BODLEIAN LIBRARY OXFORD MS. CANON. BIBL. LAT. 61 f.50v 28.5 × 18.5

FIGURE 12: Pontifical from Exeter English before 1072

This fine manuscript was written in the English version of the Carolingian minuscule, which reached England about 950, although the Anglo-Saxon hand continued to be used for some time after this.

REPRODUCED BY PERMISSION OF THE BRITISH LIBRARY ADDL. MS. 28188 f.73v/74r 18 × 12.5

13

FIGURE 13: Bible, written in the nunnery of Diepenveen, Holland. Netherlandish c.1450–53

An enlarged miniature from the Diepenveen Bible which shows the monkish scribe using a pen knife to mend his quill pen, which he holds in his left hand. In front of him stands a desk with two sheets of vellum on it—the scribe is obviously about to start work.

VICTORIA & ALBERT MUSEUM REID MS.23

Gloria.

Maiestatem tuam Sci Andree apli.
dne suppliciter exoramus.
ut sicut ecclie tue beatus
andreas apls extitit predi
cator et rector. ita apud te sit p nobis
ppetuus intercessor. p dnm. Secretu.
Sacrificium nrm tibi dne qs beati andree
apli tui precatio sca conciliet. ut cui
honore solempnit exhibetur. eius meritis
efficiatur acceptu. p. pf. Te dne supplicit.
Sumpsimus dne diuina misteria pco.
beati andree apli tui festiuitate le
tantes. que sicut tuis scis ad glam. ita
nobis qs ad ueniam pdesse pficias. p.
Sci Nicholai epi et conf. Colla.
Ds qui beatum nicholaum
pontificem tuum innume
ris decorasti miraculis. tri
bue nobis qs. ut ei meritis et pcib; a ge
henne ignis incendiis liberemur. p. Secr.
Scifica qs dne munera que in uene
ratione sci antistitis tui nicholai

THE LATER MIDDLE AGES AND THE RENAISSANCE

WITH the establishment of the Carolingian minuscule in most countries of western Europe, there was little further development over the next few centuries. A certain refining of the various strokes of the individual letters took place, together with modifications brought about by the influence of national hands on the imported script. The twelfth century saw the production of some of the grandest examples of the Romanesque book, works on a large scale with well-proportioned margins and elegant script. But the artistic style of Europe was changing, and in building, for example, the Romanesque rounded arch was beginning to give way to the pointed Gothic arch. In calligraphy, too, a change was taking place, as an urge towards lateral compression caused letters to become more angular and pointed—Gothic, in fact. By the fourteenth century the letters had become so compressed that in many instances they appeared more like a series of straight lines. The angularity and compression of the Gothic or "textura" script is especially characteristic of the grander larger volumes—the great Bibles and Psalters of the period, for example. But another trend had become noticeable during the thirteenth century, when the popularity of the lectures at the University in Paris had stimulated the demand for small portable Bibles. At all times it has proved difficult to produce the complete Biblical text in a compact yet legible form, and this was as true of the thirteenth century as it is today. A number of quite small, finely written Bibles survive from this period, usually with the text written

FIGURE 14: Missal of Lesnes Abbey   English   c. 1200

This manuscript was written during the transitional period of English art, between Romanesque and Gothic. The Romanesque tradition lingers to give the text a spacious and pleasant appearance on the page, but the actual letters already show Gothic tendencies by becoming more angular.

VICTORIA & ALBERT MUSEUM   MS.L.404–1916   f.113v   33×22.5

in double columns and often containing a number of contractions. Contractions have always been the scribe's friend, especially if he is copying for himself or for someone who knows the subject well. We ourselves make great use of contractions, as when we talk about the U.S.A. or UNESCO, for example. The scribe could do the same, provided the contractions could be easily understood by the reader. Usually they were. In fact, there was a certain standardization about them, which meant that the doctor or lawyer or merchant, for example, could easily supply the missing words or letters for himself. And the use of contractions meant a great economy in both time and space.

But all this use of contractions, double columns, and small writing only helped to emphasize the inadequacies of the existing system of writing and bookmaking. Political and economic conditions further underlined the problem. Although there were still wars, both civil and international, on the whole life was becoming more stable. Towns were developing and trade increasing. A class of people was coming to the fore who were neither great military landowners nor clergy—the "middle class." They needed to read and write in order to carry out their business; as they prospered they wanted to own their own books and do the things that they saw being done by the wealthier or noble classes. It was now no longer a question of the monk in his cell writing out a religious text to the greater glory of God. By the fifteenth century, book production had become something of a mass-produced effort. Large numbers of scribes were employed in workshops to copy out different parts of a text that could then be assembled and bound elsewhere. Such texts might consist of chronicles, folk tales, legends of the saints, and other such popular works. It is to this period that we owe the many *Books of Hours* that have survived in large numbers today in public collections. *Books of Hours* were prayer books for the use of the laity in their private devotions, and were the "best sellers" of their day. So by the middle of the fifteenth century, ever more books were being demanded, and more and more people were engaged in providing them. But they were all still hand-copied, and so laborious to produce.

The changes in the social scene had produced changes in handwriting, just as they had done before. The search, as always, was for a speedier and simpler form. In their business and private affairs people wrote a cursive informal hand which differed considerably from the formal book hands of the period. It was speedy and small, with many of the letters joined together, and it was much rounder than the prevailing Gothic script. Inevitably people accustomed to writing both scripts would often mix the two styles, and so towards the end of the fifteenth century this mixed hand or "bastarda" had become quite common. As so often happens, what began as an informal hand was gradually elevated to a formal book hand, so that eventually we can find entire volumes written in bastarda, especially where secular texts were involved. However, like most cursive scripts, bastarda too could easily deteriorate, especially when written quickly, so that it was never seriously considered as a model when printing was invented in the middle of the fifteenth century.

In tracing the development of scripts from the Roman to the early medieval period, and then through the Romanesque to the Gothic and bastarda, we have in fact been largely concerned, in the later centuries, with countries north of the Alps. In Italy, however, writing developed along somewhat different lines, and that difference was to prove important in the context of later scripts—not least in the form of printing, such as that which you find in the present book. Italy never completely escaped from the influence of the Roman Empire, traces of whose civilization lay around throughout the Middle Ages. Buildings and sculpture survived in town and countryside, with the results that can be clearly seen in the classically influenced work of a sculptor like Giovanni Pisano in the thirteenth century. Gothic, with its pointed arches and elongated windows giving rise to mysterious shadows, never really caught on in Italy, where the lightness and roundness of the Romanesque style remained fashionable. The medieval script of Italy followed the same trend: it is known as rotunda, which indicates its prevailing characteristic. At first sight it appears to be completely rounded and spacious, but a closer inspection reveals that in fact the individual letters have considerable angularity, with a differentiation between the thick and the thin strokes such as we find in Gothic scripts. The rotunda script continued to be used in Italy for liturgical works until the sixteenth century, long after it had been abandoned for secular texts, and it certainly gave a majestic appearance to those pages where it was used.

Italy was the birthplace of that movement which we call the Renaissance, one aspect of which was a revived interest in classical learning. The literature of classical antiquity had never been without some students throughout the Middle Ages, and copies of works of the Greek and Roman writers had been preserved in monasteries all over Europe. The Renaissance encouraged the search for these much-neglected works, and also the reconsideration of both their form and content. Scholars and aristocrats alike joined in the hunt for everything that could be associated with the classical world, from sculpture to texts. When found, early manuscripts were eagerly copied. Many of them survived in the form of copies made during the period of the Carolingian Renaissance, and were therefore written out in the fine script of that period.

This in turn led the humanist scholars, who were copying out these works for their own use, to adapt their own script to something approaching that of the original manuscripts. This new hand was an elegant form of writing known as *littera antiqua,* from its association with these early manuscripts which acted as a model. It was a neat minuscule script, and one that could be written with some speed. From it there gradually developed an even speedier and more cursive sloping script, which we know as italic, from its country of origin. This style of writing owed much of its popularity to its widespread dissemination through the scriptors of the Papal Chancery; hence in Italy it was known as *cancellaresca.* It could be written at speed, since it was made up of linked or joined letters, and it could also be compressed and yet remain legible—an important factor when a scholar was considering the cost of writing out a long classical text. By now vellum had been largely superseded in everyday affairs by the use of paper, which became much less costly as more and more paper mills were set up in Europe in the late Middle Ages, to cope with the increasing demand for books. But in spite of the improvements in the transmission of learning brought about by changes in scripts and materials, the real impetus to the Renaissance came from quite a different source. This was the invention of printing from movable types, which took place in Germany in the middle of the fifteenth century, and by the end of that century had spread to most of Europe, with far-reaching results for all of us.

FIGURE 15: Leaf from an antiphoner Flemish c. 1300

This leaf is taken from the choral part of the Mass. It is written in a very angular script, and contains an illuminated initial D (Dum) in which we see the Descent of the Holy Spirit. Outside the initial kneels the Abbess, and her name "Domina Abbatissa Soror Heylwigis" is written in an abbreviated and much less formal script at the bottom of the page.

VICTORIA & ALBERT MUSEUM MS. 8997.1

15

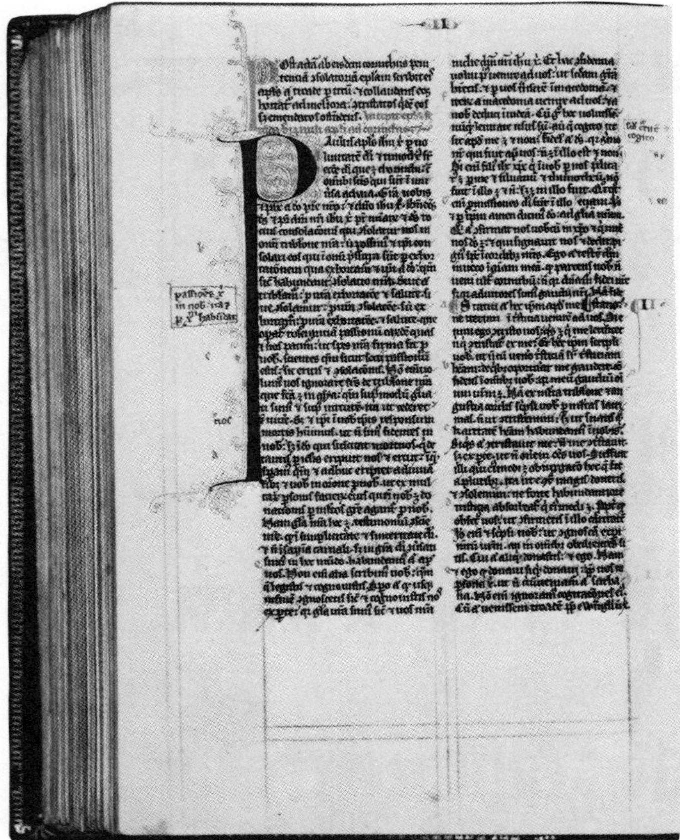

16

17

FIGURE 16: Biblia Sacra English? thirteenth/fourteenth centuries

This little Bible is typical of its period, when the increased interest in the universities led to a greater demand for Bibles. It is always difficult to get the whole Biblical text into one small volume, and in this one great use has been made of contractions; the writing is small and written in two columns, and the vellum is very thin and smooth. The result is a very personal, portable Bible, far removed from the larger service books of the previous century.

VICTORIA & ALBERT MUSEUM
REID MS. 21 16 × 11

FIGURE 17: Missal of St. Denis Abbey, Paris French c. 1350

It is unusual to find a Missal as fully illuminated as this one, and the compressed and cramped appearance of the text compares unfavorably with the spaciousness and decoration of the margins. The scribe and the decorator were of course two different people, while the miniatures were probably painted by yet another artist.

VICTORIA & ALBERT MUSEUM
REID MS. 51 15 × 12

FIGURE 18: Psalter English c. 1420

This is typical of the quite large Psalters (or books of psalms) which were popular in the fifteenth century. The Gothic script is not always very legible, although the page looks very attractive and clear. In the original manuscript each page is colorfully illuminated.

VICTORIA & ALBERT MUSEUM
REID MS. 41 38 × 27

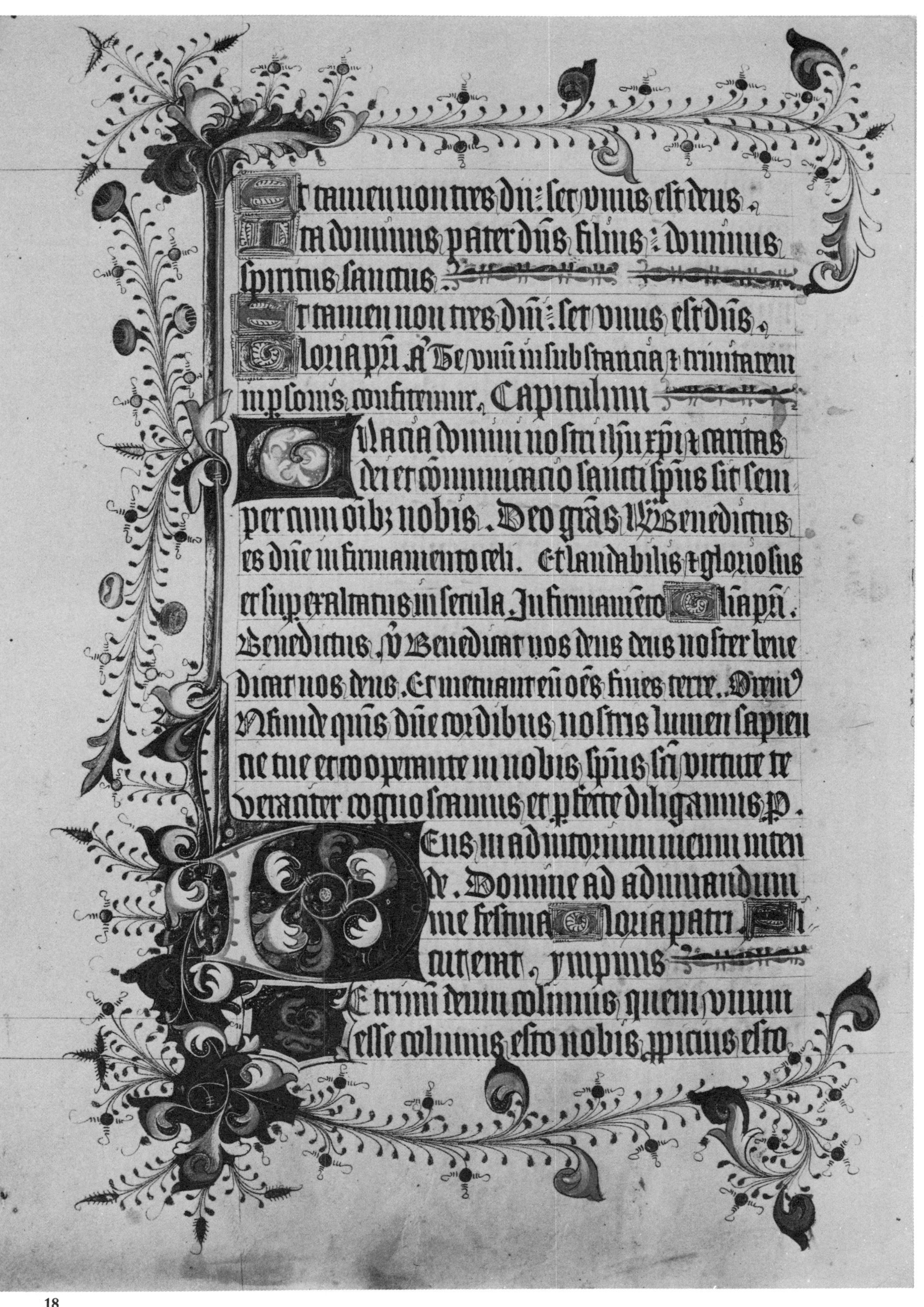

19

20

FIGURE 19: Diepenveen Bible Netherlands c. 1450–53

This Bible was written out in Gothic script by an anonymous nun in a house of the Canonesses of the Congregation of Windesheim, near Deventer. She has dated her work as she progressed. As often with Biblical manuscripts, the text is in double columns. This particular page emphasizes the preciousness of vellum. There were faults in the sheet but the scribe could not afford to waste it, so she has neatly written round the holes, and then incorporated them into the page by putting a line around them! The pricking, seen on the left-hand margin of this page, was for the guidelines, which can be clearly seen under the words of the text.

VICTORIA & ALBERT MUSEUM REID MS.20
f.112v 35 × 21.5

FIGURE 20: Missal (Use of Salzburg) Austrian c.1450

The manuscript contains a variety of scripts, but this passage, in the Canon of the Mass, is written in a large black Gothic hand. The letters are written with a thick pen and end with heavy wedge-shaped serifs. The use of contractions and the lateral compression of the letters make it very difficult to decipher. Its importance lies in the fact that it was this type of script which the early printers attempted to reproduce.

VICTORIA & ALBERT MUSEUM REID MS. 39
22.5 × 16.5

FIGURE 21: Calendar, alphabet, prayer, and hymns for private devotions French last quarter of the fifteenth century

Among other items, this manuscript contains a clearly written out Gothic alphabet. For some letters (a, r, and s, for example) more than one version is given. Below the alphabet, the beginnings of the Lord's Prayer (Pater Noster) enables us to see the letters in context. The coat of arms displayed in the bowl of the letter P are those of Guillaume d'Orgemont.

REPRODUCED BY PERMISSION OF THE BODLEIAN LIBRARY OXFORD MS. RAWL. LITURG. 40 f.40

A.a.a.b.c.d.
e.f.g.h.i.k.
l.m.n.o.p.q.r.ꝛ.ſ.
s.t.v.u.x.y.z.⁊.ꝯ.
ꝫ.t.t̃.t̃.t?.&.ꝶ.

Pater
noster
qui es
in ce
lis sanctificetur no

21

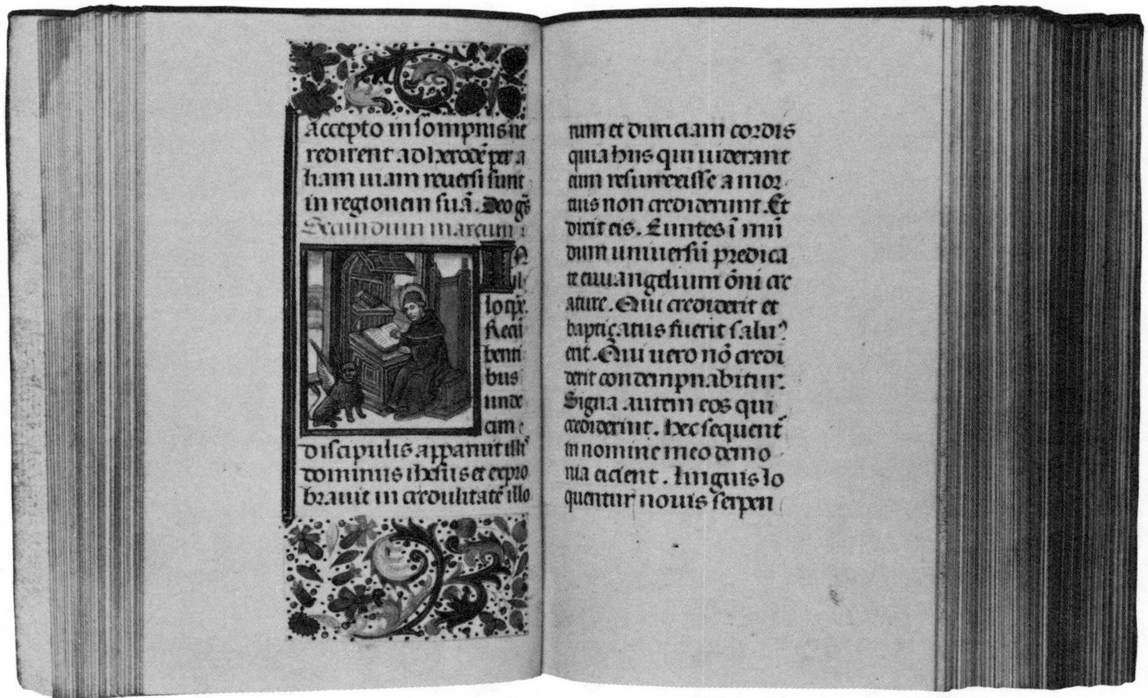

22

23

FIGURE 22: Book of Hours (Use of Rome), known as the Hours of Cardinal Hohenembs   Netherlands   c. 1475

Manuscripts like this were very portable objects, and were one of the ways in which artistic styles spread from one country to another. This elegant little volume is written in a fine even rotunda script, which would be more at home south of the Alps, until we realize the importance of Bruges as a trading centre at that time. The miniature shown here depicts St. Mark at work on his Gospel.

VICTORIA & ALBERT MUSEUM   SALTING
MS. 4478   f.43v/44r   11 × 7.5

FIGURE 23: P. de Crescentiis: Ruralium commodorum, libri XII   German   c. 1460

This manuscript is written out in bastarda script, with the initials at the beginning of the paragraphs in red. The use of contractions and the cursive nature of the script all suggest that the work was copied out for personal use. The Victoria and Albert Museum Library has a printed version of the same work dated 1471. A comparison of the two emphasizes the labor involved in copying such texts, compared with the relative ease with which multiple copies could be produced from the printing press.

VICTORIA & ALBERT MUSEUM   MS.L.98-1945
28 × 20

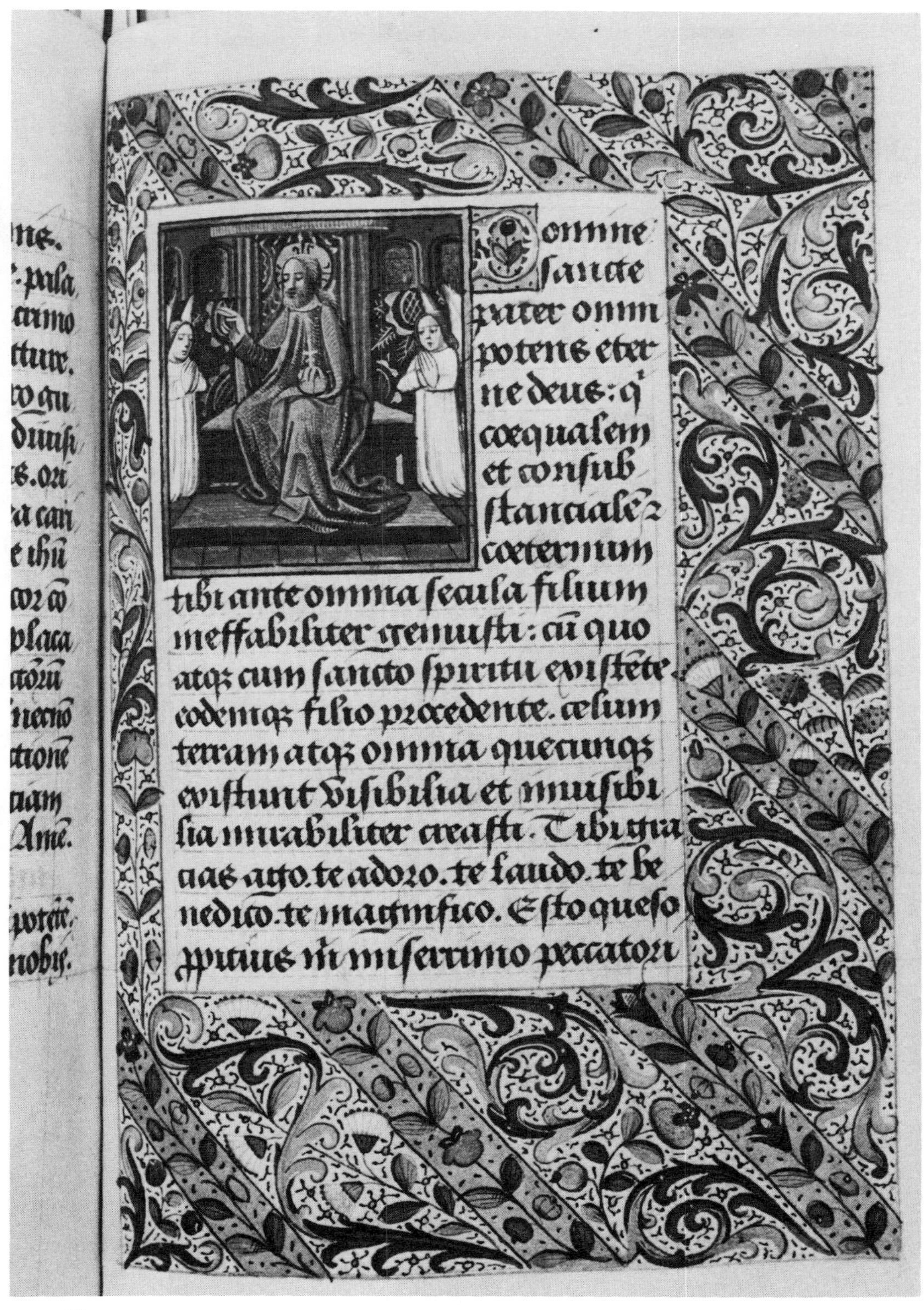

24

FIGURE 24: Book of Hours (Use of Sarum) Known as the Playfair Hours French late fifteenth century

At first sight the script of this manuscript looks very Gothic, but then we notice the long s *so characteristic of the bastarda hand. The letters are closely joined, but the text remains quite legible.*

VICTORIA & ALBERT MUSEUM MS.L.475-1918 f.149 22.5 × 12

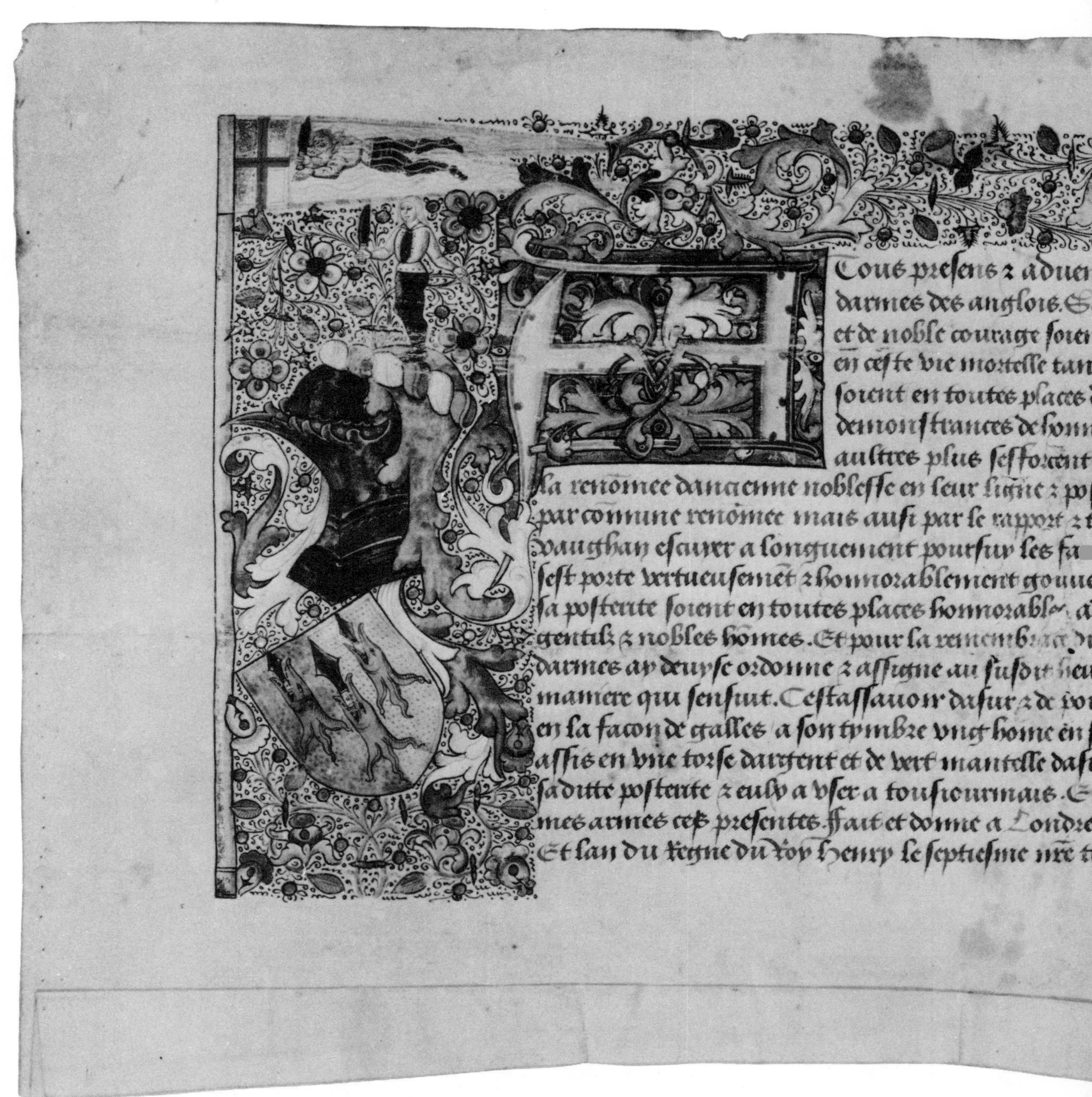

FIGURE 25: Grant of arms by John Wrythe, Garter King of Arms, to Hugh Vaughan 1492

Legal documents have always provided a source of income for scribes. This one is written in a fine bastarda script—and in French, which is surprising at so late a date. The characteristics of the bastarda script are very evident, especially the tapering descenders and the long s.

VICTORIA & ALBERT MUSEUM
MS.L.4362-1948

pntes lettres verront ou orront Johan Wrythe aultrement dit Jartier Roy
humble Recomendacion Equite veult z raison ordonne que les homes vertueux
s merites z bonne renomee remunerez et non pas seulement leurs personnes
z transitoire. Mais apres eulx ceulx qui de leurs corps yssiront z seront procreez
honneur perpetuellement avec aultres reluysans par certaines enseignes z
oblesse cestassavoir de blason heaulme z tymbre affin que a leurs exemple
rammet user leurs iours en faitz darmes z oeuvres vertueuses por aquerir
pource Je Jartier Roy darmes des angloys dessusdit qui non pas seulement
aige de plusieurs dignes de foy suis pour vray adverty z informe que heugh
z de armes tant par terre que par mer. z tant en ce que aultres ses affaires
nent quil a bien desservy z est digne que doresenavant perpetuellement luy z
omez comptez nombrez z receuz ou nombre et en la compaignee de aultres
blesse par vertu de lauctorite z pouoir annexe z atribue a mondit office de Roy
uy z sa posterite avec leur difference deue le blason heaulme z tymbre en la
y par pall a trois testes de luces (rasees) dor engueulans trois fers de lances darget
mit dargent ses chausses de sable tenant ung cousteau en sa main dextre
dargent si come la picture cy devant se demonstre a avoir z tenir pour luy z
g de ce Je Jartier Roy darmes dessusdit ay signe de ma main z seelle du seel de
e saint Ambroise. Lan de mreSr mille quatre cens quatre vingtz z douze
e z souverain seigneur le septiesme.

Jartier Roy darmez dez Angloys

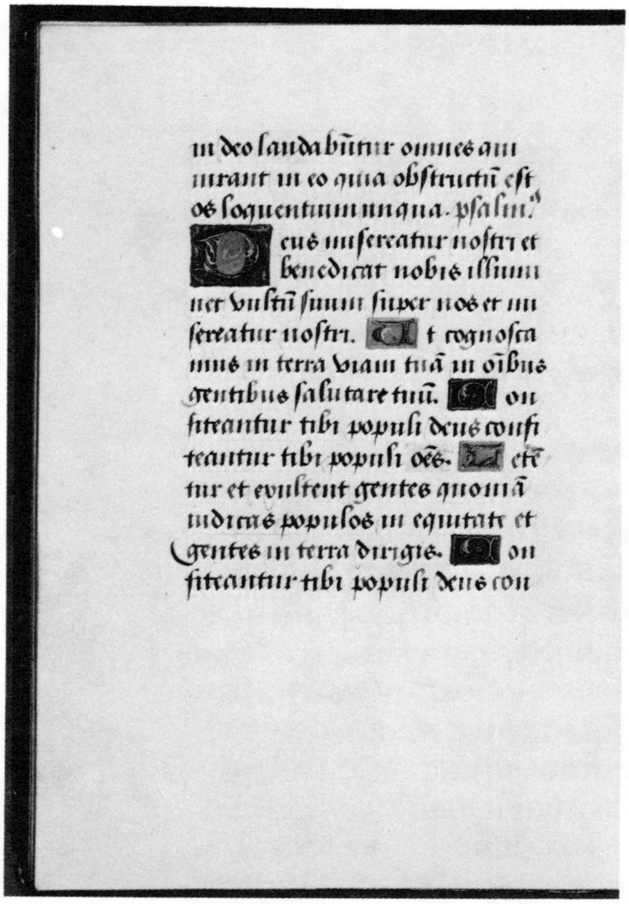

26

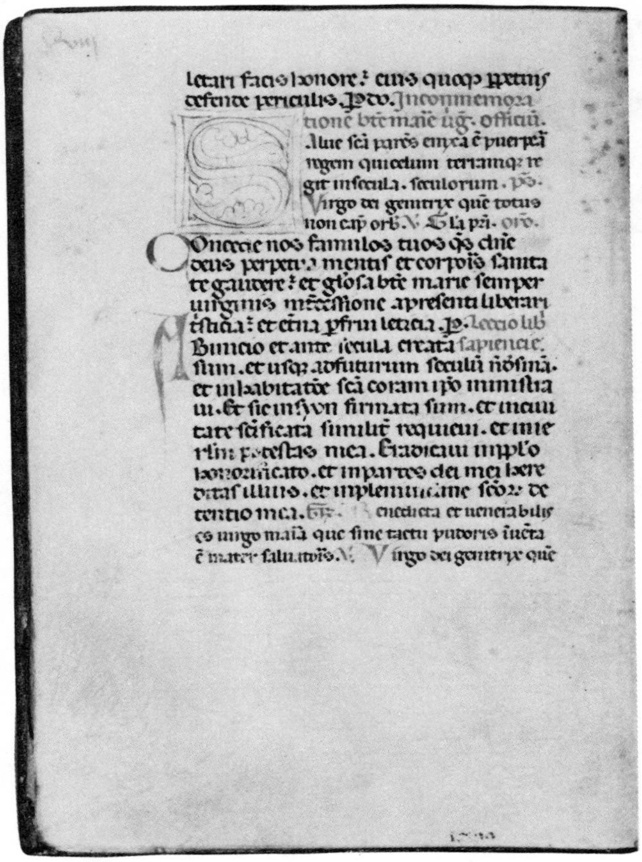

27

FIGURE 26: Book of Hours (Use of Rome) Flemish c. 1480

This manuscript is written in bastarda script, a mixture of the cursive informal hand and the Gothic. The descenders, especially the characteristic long s, *taper away and reveal a slight slant. The general effect is quite pleasing to the eye, and shows how an informal script could be satisfactorily elevated into a book hand with considerable grace.*

VICTORIA & ALBERT MUSEUM REID MS.31
16.5 × 11

FIGURE 27: Missal (Roman)
North Italian c. 1300

This manuscript provides a good example of the form taken by the Gothic script in Italy, where the "rotunda" script placed greater emphasis on roundness and lightness. This particular manuscript is incomplete, and interesting in that it shows us how the work of the scribe and decorator were carried out: here one of the larger initials remains in outline only, still awaiting the gold and colors of the illuminator.

VICTORIA & ALBERT MUSEUM REID MS.65
8.5 × 13

FIGURE 28: Egidio Colonna, Romano, Archbishop of Bourges: Libro . . . que trata del regimiento de los principes
Spanish c. 1470–80

This is a very unusual manuscript. The main text, in the center of the page, is written out in a formal hand, but it is surrounded by a commentary in a much more cursive style, in a script that seems to fall between Gothic and bastarda. The result on the page is quite attractive, but the additional text probably explains why the volume is extremely large and heavy!

VICTORIA & ALBERT MUSEUM
MS.L.2463-1950 41 × 21

Aqui se comiença la segunda parte del tercero libro del governamiento delos principes en que pone la opinion de aristotiles quanto al governamiento del regno e dela cibdat. Et muestra espresa mente qual fue el arte e la sabiduria que dio aristotiles para governar bien el regno e la cibdat en tiempo de paz por buenas leyes e por buenas costumbres antiguas e aprovadas que han fuerça de leyes asi en tiempo de guerra que se deve defender por armas. Onde tales son las armas en tiempo dela guerra para governar la cibdat como las leyes en tiempo de paz. Et asi mesmo que la cibdat e el regno se deve governar en tiempo de paz por leyes derechas e por costumbres buenas e aprovadas. Paresce que toda la entençion desta segunda parte es en mostrar quales e quantas cosas son menester para governar el regno e la cibdat en tiempo de paz. Et esto es el primero capitulo que pone toda la entençion desta parte que esta en fablar de quatro cosas que son menester para bien governar la cibdat e estas son segund que dise el filosofo en el tercero delas politicas: el rey o el principe. Et el consejo e el alcaldia e el pueblo que ha de ser governado. Et destas quatro cosas fabla en toda esta segunda parte. Del principe fabla en los quinse capitulos primeros. Et del consejo e delos consejeros fabla en los otros quatro capitulos que se siguen. Et del alcaldia e delos alcalles e delas leyes e del juysio fabla en los otros .xii. capitulos que se siguen adelante. Et del pueblo e dela cibdat e del regno fabla en los cinco capitulos postrimeros.

Capitulo primero en qual manera se ha de governar la cibdat en tiempo de paz e quales quatro cosas son de pensar en tal governamiento etc.

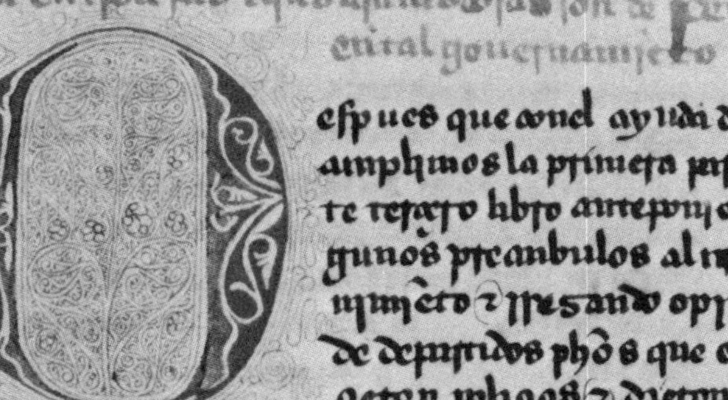

Despues que con el ayuda de dios acabamos la primera parte deste tercero libro anteponiendo algunos preanbulos al nuestro proponimiento e rresando opiniones de departidos philosophos que establescieron policias e dieron arte del governamiento dela cibdat e del regno. Finca nos de desir delas otras dos partes conviene a saber del governamiento dela cibdad e del regno en tiempo de paz. Et del governamiento dela cibdat e del regno en tiempo de guerra. Pues que asi es conviene de saber que asi como en tiempo de guerra es de defender la cibdat por armas. Asy en tiempo de paz es de governar por leyes derechas e por costumbres aprovadas que han fuerça de leyes. Et por ende asi se an las armas en tiempo de guerra como las leyes al tiempo de paz. Et pues que asy es visto que en el tiempo dela paz es de governar la cibdat e el regno por leyes derechas e por costumbres aprovadas de ligero puede paresçer quales cosas e quantas son de pensar en el governamiento del regno e dela cibdad. Mas el philosopho en el tercero libro delas politicas tanne quatro cosas que son de pensar en el governamiento dela cibdat e del regno. Et estas son el principe e el consejo e el alcaldia e el pueblo. Et por podemos de aquellas cosas

Pues que asi es quanto al primer capitulo prueva el philosopho por dos rasones que todo ome que quisiere bien governar regno o cibdat deve saber estas quatro cosas sobredichas. La primera rason se toma de parte delas leyes. Ca para que sea bien governado el regno o la cibdat por las leyes quatro cosas son menester. Lo primero que las leyes sean bien guardadas por el poderio real. Lo segundo que para que las leyes sean buenas que sean falladas por los sabios e puestas en la cibdat por el consejo dellos. Lo tercero que por los juesces e por los alcalles sean las obras delos omes judgadas segund las leyes puestas e ordenadas. Lo quarto que todo el pueblo e los cibdadanos para que ayan paz entre si que guarden bien los mandamientos delas leyes. Lo primero pertenesce al rey o al principe. Lo segundo al consejo e alos sabios. Lo tercero pertenesce alas alcaldias e alos alcalles. Lo quarto pertenesce al pueblo e alos cibdadanos. Et asi paresce que todo buen governador deve saber todas estas quatro cosas sin las quales non se puede dar arte del governamiento del regno. La segunda rason se toma de parte dela fin que deve ser entendida en las leyes. Ca el que pone la ley deve entender que por las leyes alcançemos el bien e fuyamos del mal e por ellas fagamos derecho e escusemos de faser tuerto. Otrosi que por ellas podamos alcançar loor e onrra e fuyr de denuesto e de desonrra. Et del bien e del mal es el consejo. Et del derecho e del tuerto es el consejo juysio e el alcaldia. Del loor e dela onrra o del denuesto o dela desonrra es la punicion o la conpunçion que deve ser fecha al pueblo. Et asi paresce que el que quisiere mostrar en qual manera es de governar la cibdat en tiempo de paz que sepa qual deve ser el principe que deve poner las leyes e quales deven ser los consejeros que han de conoscer qual es el bien e qual es el mal e qual cosa es provechosa ala cibdat e qual empesçible. Otrosi conviene le de saber quales deven ser los alcalles a quien pertenesce de judgar qual es el derecho e qual es el tuerto. Otrosi le conviene de saber qual deve ser el pueblo que es de enformar o de seguir lo que es de loar e es apuesto de escusar lo que es de denostar e lo que es feo. Et asy paresce que destas quatro cosas es la policia e el governamiento dela cibdat. Et aqui podemos annader otras dos rasones. La primera es que con todas las artes deve el maestro fablar e tractar de todas aquellas cosas que pertenescen a aquella arte asi como el governador dela nave conviene que sepa quales son las ancoras e quales los arbles e quales los remos e qual la vela e asi de todas las otras cosas. E como pertenesce a esta arte del governamiento del regno e dela cibdat saber que cosa es principado e principe e que cosa es consejo e sabio. Et que cosa es alcaldia e alcalle e que cosa es pueblo o cibdadano conviene al que quisiere dar sabiduria de governamiento de cibdat que sepa todas estas cosas e que de todas fable enteramente. La segunda rason es que quando se da conoscimiento de algunas cosas a que se pueden reduzir todas las otras conplida mente se da en general conoscimiento de todo aquello que fase menester en aquella arte. Et cierto es que al principado e al consejo e al alcaldia e al pueblo se pueden reduzir todas las cosas que

In diebus illis: Vidi
sup montem sy
on agnum stan
tem et cum eo cen
tum quadraginta
quatuor milia haben
tes nomen eius et
nomen patris eius
scriptum in fronti
bus suis. Et audiui
uocem de celo tamquam
uocem aquarum
multarum. et tam
quam uocem tonitrui
magni. Et uocem
quam audiui: sicut
cytharedorum cy
tharizantium in cy
tharis suis. Et can
tabant quasi canticum
nouum ante sedem
dei: et ante quatuor
animalia et seniores.
Et nemo poterat di
cere canticum: nisi
illa centum quadra
ginta quatuor milia.
qui empti sunt de ter
ra. Hii sunt qui cum
mulieribus non sunt
coinquinati: uirgi
nes enim sunt. Hii se
quuntur agnum: quo
cumque ierit. Hii emp
ti sunt ex omnibus pri
micie deo et agno:
et in ore ipsorum non
est inuentum men
dacium. Sine ma
cula sunt: ante thro
num dei. In sci tho
me. mr. Ad hebreos

29

FIGURE 29: Epistle Book Italian 1368

This manuscript shows the form taken by the Gothic script in northern Italy. The letters have the angularity expected of textura, and the joining strokes of the minims (in u, m, *and* n*) tend to disappear, but the general appearance still remains one of roundness, with the words clearly separated from one another.*
VICTORIA & ALBERT MUSEUM MS. 25.i.1861 33.5 × 25

FIGURE 30: Dominican Gradual North Italian late fifteenth century

The Gradual was a large choir book containing the choral parts of the Mass. It would have been placed on a lectern around which the monks could gather. The letters that are shown here are much larger than any others in this book, even as the manuscript itself is larger. One can imagine that such writing could be easily read even at a distance.
VICTORIA & ALBERT MUSEUM MS.L.3691-1963
f.79v 56.5 × 40.5

FIGURE 31: Book of Hours (Use of Rome) North Italian c. 1470

This is one of the few medieval manuscripts where we actually have the name of the scribe who wrote it. On the left-hand page, in the third line, we read "Per me ni/colaus hanrici sciptū." *Nothing further is known about Nicolaus Henricus, but he certainly wrote a nice rotunda script.*
VICTORIA & ALBERT MUSEUM REID MS.62
f.109v/110r 9 × 6.5

30

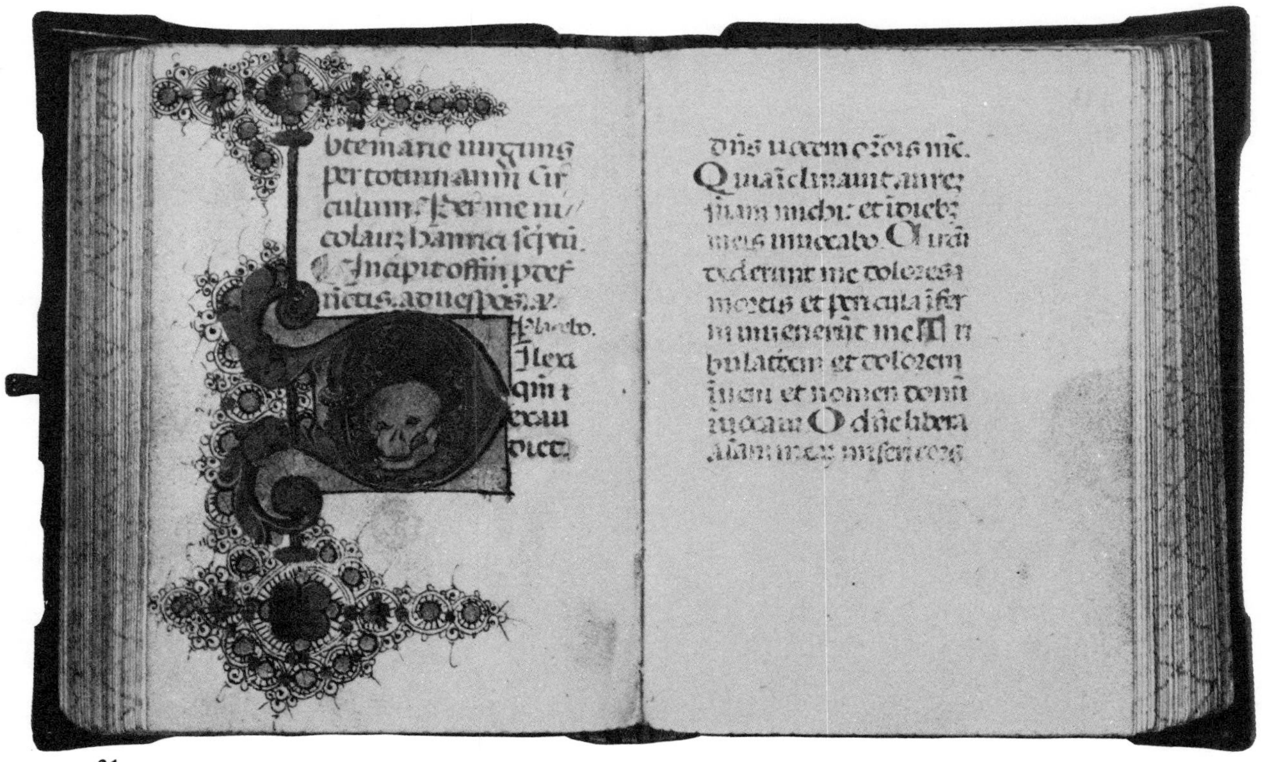

31

32

FIGURE 32: Book of Hours (Use of Rome), known as the Hours of Alfonso of Aragon   Neapolitan   c. 1480

This is a magnificent manuscript with splendid illuminations. Here we see only a detail from one of the pages, showing an historiated initial (the letter D*) containing an illustration of the Visitation. An enlarged detail like this enables us to study the individual letters more closely and the way in which they were integrated with the decoration.*

VICTORIA & ALBERT MUSEUM
SALTING MS.1224   25×27

FIGURES 33 & 34: Book of Hours (Use of Rome) known as the Bentivoglio Hours   Bologna   c. 1500

This manuscript is written in the humanist antiqua script and is a good example of a sumptuous book produced for a noble owner; it is lavishly decorated in bright colors. A detail from the same manuscript (but not from the same page) is also illustrated, thus permitting a closer study of the letter forms.

VICTORIA & ALBERT MUSEUM
REID MS.64   f.103r   21×15

33

E
to
in
m
ua
sti
pa

CRucifige crucifig
hora tertiarum : il
tur ueste purpurarum : c.

uō suasionis illecebras renuere in nobis est cur tu materiam abscidis corona
rum industrieq; et probitatis occasionem tollis. Ad hec si illum sciens fore
insuperabilem cunctosq; deuicturum ita illum dimisisset deus: nec sic qui
dem ista hesitatio locum habuisset. Nam tum quoq; quod ille obtineret
quod uinceret non reluctantes: sed sponte sibi cedentes atq; succumbētes
a nobis profecto manasset. Quod si plurimi quidem illius potentiam ac
uires frangunt complures item posthac illum superaturi sunt: quid tu
futuros probatissimos clarissimaq; uictoria insignes tanto priuas honore?
Idcirco enim eum dimisit ut illum deuicant qui fuerant ab eo superati q̄d
illi omni supplicio grauius ac dirius est. At non omnes inquies illum supe
raturi sunt. Quid hoc ad rem. Profecto enim multo melius multoq; con
uenientius est iustis occasiones suppeditari. quibus ad uirtutem se exer
ceant uoluntatemq; ostendant suam. Eos uō qui non sunt huiusmodi
ex propria puniri negligentia q̄ istorum causa illis etiam coronas suas adi
mi. Nam modo is qui malus ac uecors est: non aduersarii uiribus sed suo
potius torpore superatur: quod indicat uincentium illum multitudo
tunc uō studiosi quiq; atq; alacres malorum causa meritis honoribus
fraudati fuissent non habentes ubi uires exercerent suas: ueluti si ago
nitheta quis athletas duos nactus alterum quidem aduersario congre
di paratum omnemq; tolerantiam ostendere coronamq; ex certamine
referre: alterum uō labori illi et erumpne otium delitiasq; preferentē
cōpare atq; aduersario de medio sublato ambos re infecta dimittat. Sic
enim strenuus ille propter alterius ignauiam graui iniuria affectus ui[illegible]
retur. Ignauius autem non fortissimi socii causa malus esset uerum ob [illegible]
cordiam suam. Sed enim hec istorum questio cum de diabolo agitari
uideatur si suo ordine procedat: plurimis in rebus dei prouidentiam in
simulat cunctamq; simul creaturam perimit. Accusat enim oris atque
oculorum fictionem quippe cum per istas queq; illicita concupiscant
atq; in adulterium corruant plurimi. Per hoc autem blasfemant et per
nitiosa dogmata proferant alii. Num ergo sine oculis et lingua debue
runt homines fieri? Pedes quoq; abscidere et amputare manus necesse
erit: cum iste plene sanguine: illi uō prompti ad malum currant. Ne ipse
quidem aures immanitatem rationis huius effugere poterunt. Nam

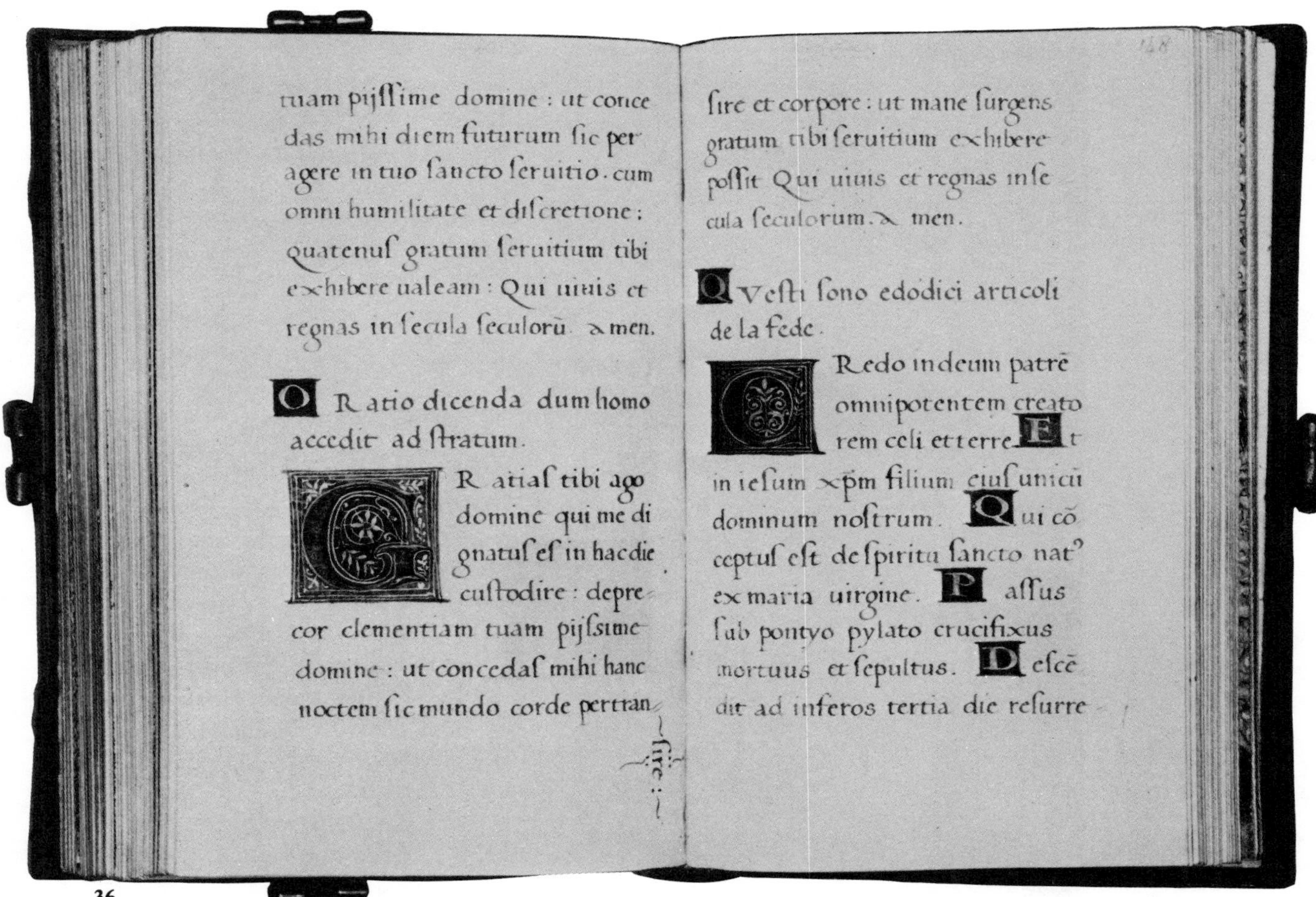

tuam piiſſime domine : ut conce
das mihi diem futurum ſic per
agere in tuo ſancto ſeruitio . cum
omni humilitate et diſcretione :
quatenuſ gratum ſeruitium tibi
exhibere ualeam : Qui uiuis et
regnas in ſecula ſeculorũ . amen.

O Ratio dicenda dum homo
accedit ad ſtratum.

G Ratiaſ tibi ago
domine qui me di
gnatuſ eſ in hac die
cuſtodire : depre
cor clementiam tuam piiſsime
domine : ut concedaſ mihi hanc
noctem ſic mundo corde pertran
ſire :

ſire et corpore : ut mane ſurgens
gratum tibi ſeruitium exhibere
poſſit Qui uiuis et regnas in ſe
cula ſeculorum . Amen .

Q Veſti ſono edodici articoli
de la fede .

C Redo in deum patrẽ
omnipotentem creato
rem celi et terre . E t
in ieſum xp̃m filium eiuſ unicũ
dominum noſtrum . Q ui cõ
ceptuſ eſt de ſpiritu ſancto nat⁹
ex maria uirgine . P aſſus
ſub pontyo pylato crucifixus
mortuus et ſepultus . D eſcẽ
dit ad inferos tertia die reſurre

36

FIGURE 35: Thesaurus adversos hereticos, by St. Cyril, Patriarch of Alexandria [and other works] Florentine 1460–70

This is a good example of the early hand of the Renaissance, which clearly shows its affinities with the Carolingian hand of the ninth and tenth centuries. It continues to exhibit the rotund qualities of the Italian scripts, which had never been superseded by the textura hands as in the north of Europe. The writing is very clear and even.

VICTORIA & ALBERT MUSEUM REID MS.78 30×22

FIGURE 36: Book of Hours (Use of Rome) Florentine c. 1522

This is the style of humanist script that went on being used for liturgical works like this, long after it had been discontinued in secular texts. By now printing was well-established in Europe, and the letters here show a certain affinity with their printed forms. The scribe has made considerable use of colored inks as well as illumination to decorate the manuscript. The catchword written at right-angles to the text at the bottom of the left page was to ensure that the binder assembled the book correctly. The same word appears at the top of the next page, the first of the new gathering, to confirm this.

VICTORIA & ALBERT MUSEUM SALTING MS.1223 f.147/148 14×9

S e de le mie ricchezze care et tante
Et si guardate; ond'io buon tempo uissi
Di mia sorte contento, et meco dissi
Nessun uiue di me piu lieto amante;
I o stesso mi disarmo: et queste piante
A uezze a gir pur la: dou'io scoprissi
Quegliocchi uaghi, et lharmonia sentissi
De le parole si soaui et sante;
L ungi da lei di mio uoler sen'uanno:
L asso chi mi dara Bernardo aita?
O chi m'acquetera, quand'io m'affanno?
M orrommi: et tu dirai mia fine udita;
Questi, per non ueder il suo gran danno,
L asciata la sua donna uscio di uita.

S ignor, che parti et tempri gli elementi,
E'l sole et laltre stelle ел mondo reggi.
Et hor col freno tuo santo correggi
Il lungo error de le mie uoglie ardenti;
N on lasciar la mia guardia, et non s'allenti
La tua pieta; perchio tolto a le leggi
M'habbia d'amor, et disturbato i seggi,
In ch'ei di me regnaua alti et lucenti.
C he come audace lupo suol de gli agni
Stretti nel chiuso lor; cosi costui
R itenta far di me lusata preda.
A ccio pur dunque in danno i miei guadagni
Non torni, el lume tuo spegner si creda;
Con fermo pie dipartimi da lui.

37

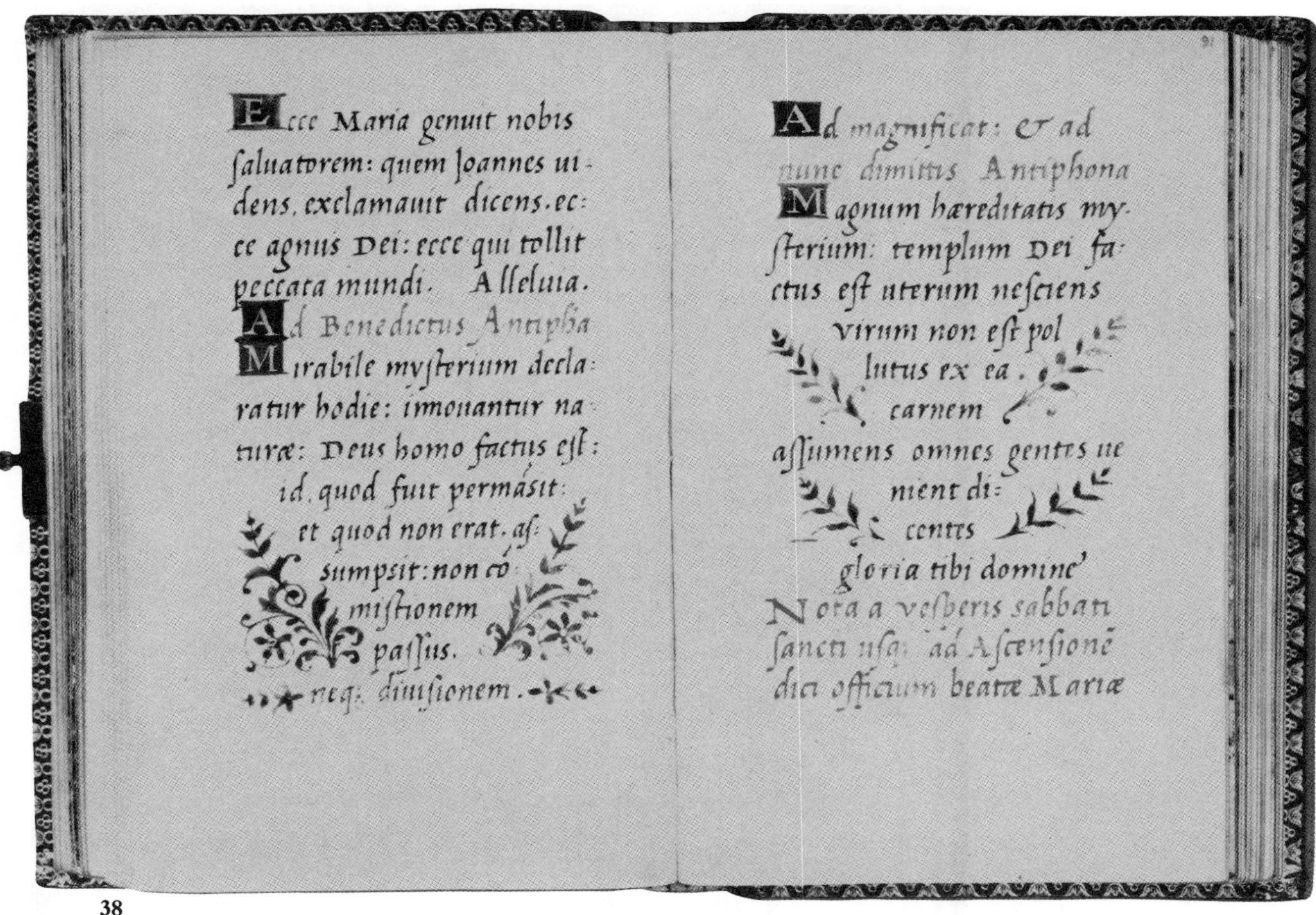

Ecce Maria genuit nobis
saluatorem: quem Joannes ui-
dens, exclamauit dicens. ecce agnus Dei: ecce qui tollit
peccata mundi. Alleluia.
Ad Benedictus Antipha
Mirabile mysterium decla-
ratur hodie: innouantur na-
turæ: Deus homo factus est:
id, quod fuit permansit:
et quod non erat, as-
sumpsit: non cō-
mistionem
passus.
neq; diuisionem.

91

Ad magnificat: & ad
nunc dimittis Antiphona
Magnum hæreditatis my-
sterium: templum Dei fa-
ctus est uterum nesciens
virum non est pol
lutus ex ea.
carnem
assumens omnes gentes ue
nient di-
centes
gloria tibi domine
Nota a vesperis sabbati
sancti usq; ad Ascensionē
dici officium beatæ Mariæ

38

FIGURE 37: Pietro Bembo: Rime [etc.] Italian 1543?

This is a very beautiful small italic script; it is completely undecorated, thus allowing text and script alike to make an impact. It is always difficult to integrate capital letters with italic letters, a problem accentuated where verse is concerned. Nevertheless the scribe has managed to make his capitals look as though they belong here; in some scripts they merely seem to hang on the end of the line!

VICTORIA & ALBERT MUSEUM MS.L.1347–1957 21.5 × 14

FIGURE 38: Book of Hours (Use of Rome), known as the Hours of Eleanora of Toledo Florentine signed and dated 10 February 1540

Notice the date of this little manuscript. Printing was nearly one hundred years old, but the handwritten book still made its appearance in court circles in sixteenth-century Italy. The work is actually signed "Aloysius scribebat *Floren," but the scribe's actual identity remains unknown. Of his work the late James Wardrop wrote "the script is a good example of* cancellaresca formata, *brought to perfection in Italy in the second quarter of the sixteenth century."*

VICTORIA & ALBERT MUSEUM MS.L.1729–1953 13 × 8.5

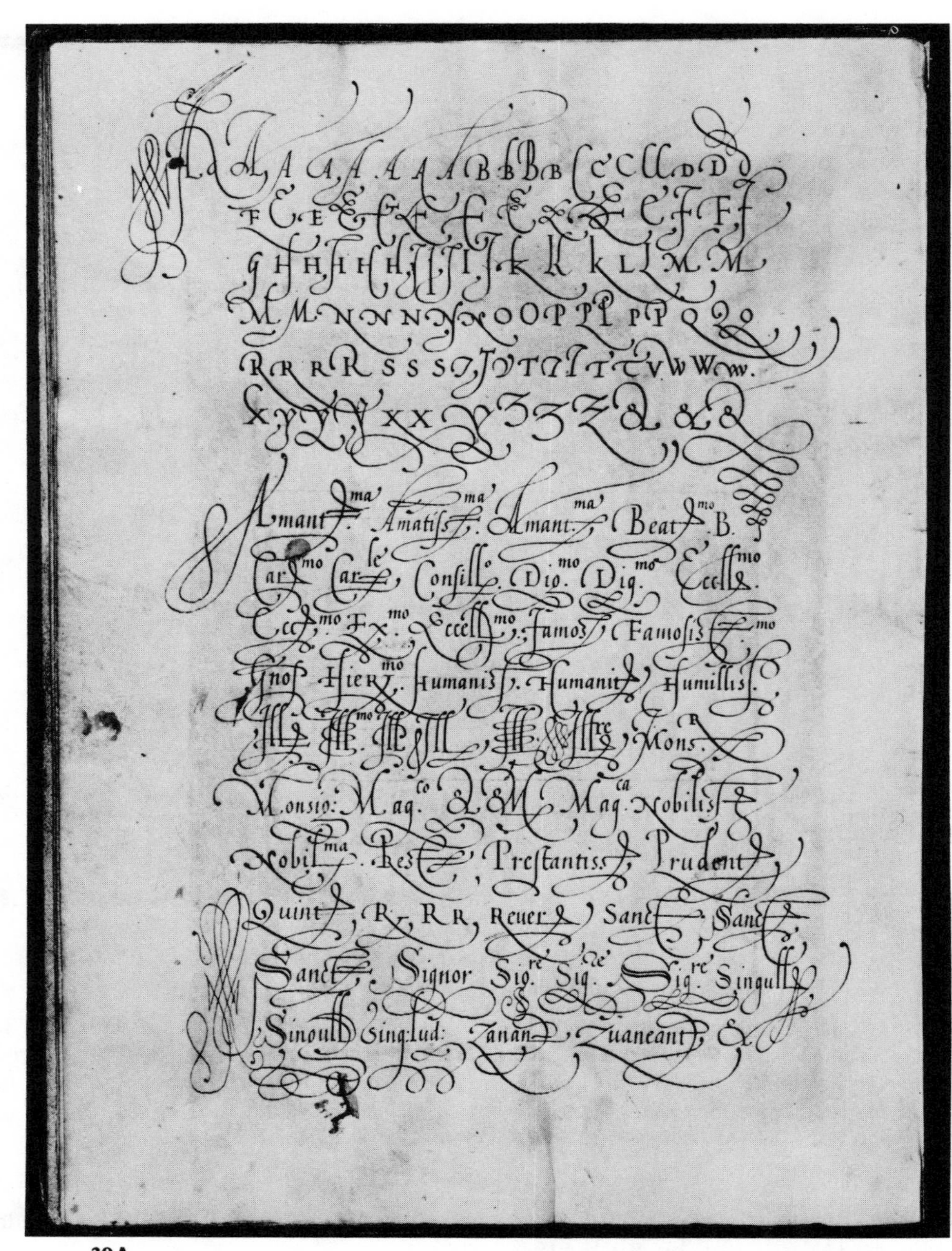

39A

FIGURES 39A & 39B: Francesco Moro, of Pozzoveggiano: Arte della strozaria e farsi perfetto stroziero   Italian   c.1560–70

Only the first fifteen pages of this manuscript actually refer to the treatise on hawking (in spite of the title). The rest of the book consists of a variety of calligraphic examples, two pages of which are illustrated here. The left-hand page not only shows an alphabet (with various forms of the individual letters) but then places it in context, especially in the elaborate forms of address so beloved of the sixteenth-century Italian.

How much more difficult it is for us to read the Gothic script at the bottom of the right-hand page, compared with the Roman forms used elsewhere!

VICTORIA & ALBERT MUSEUM   MS.L.1485–1946   23 × 15.5

IGLIA RAVET VIDELICET REOBARBARO
mumia uidelicet rubba tintorum et rubet In tutto
onze una tanto di luno quanto di laltro et fa
raj pasta et sel sparauiero fusse quasi mor
to gli darraj dj questa una pirola auolta
nel bambaso et, a, sacchetto et gorga uodda
In questo gela darraj et subito che la haue
ra gettata la matina guarira perche, e, me
dicina eccellentissima et e cosa approbata

Rimedio al Mal della testa quando
e sgonfia con gliocchi piccoli et mesti

IGLIA PEVERE GRANI TRE GAROFOLI
grani tre semencina quanto basta et farai pestar tutte
queste cose Insieme In poluere et per tre giorni con
tinui nelle narre et palato del sparauiero à degiuno
gli ponerai de detta poluere et quando hauera cessati
gli stranuti uno terzo di hora dapoi: di bon et cal
do pasto lo passerai et di subito guarira perfettamete.

Al male della testa quando dalle Nare
gli venga mazza puzolente

Hystri tela manu iacientes sollicitabant. Hinc Virgilius eum
dem locum de incluso Turno gratia elegantiore composuit.

Ergo nec clypeo iuuenis subsistere tantum
Nec dextra ualet: obiectis sic undique telis
Obruitur: strepit assiduo caua tempora circum
Tinnitu galea: & saxis solida era fatiscunt.
Discussaeque iube capiti: nec sufficit umbo
Ictibus: ingeminant hastis & troes: & ipse
Fulmineus Menestheus: Tum toto corpore sudor
Liquitur: & piceum (Nec respirare potestas)
Flumen agit: fessos quatit eger anhelitus artus. Homerus ait.

FVRIVS IN QVARTO ANNALI.

Pressatur pede pes: mucro mucrone: uiro uir. Hinc Virgilius ait:
Heret pede pes: densusque uiro uir. Homeri est. Hunc secutus ho-
stius poeta in libro secundo belli hystrici ait. Non nisi mihi lingue centum: atque ora sit etiam totidem uocesque liquate. Hinc
Virgilius ait. Non mihi si lingue centum sint oraque centum. Ho-
merica descriptio est equi fugientis: in hec uerba.

Ennius hinc traxit.

Et tum sicut equus qui de presepibus actus
Vincla suis magnis animis abrupit: & inde

FIGURE 40: Ambrosius Theodosius Macrobius: Saturnalia Italian (Rome)
Completed 14th August 1465

This is a very fine example of the cursive italic script—it looks as though it could be written speedily without losing legibility. Notice how the scribe has placed the text on the page.

VICTORIA & ALBERT MUSEUM MS.L.1769–1952 f.113r 30×20

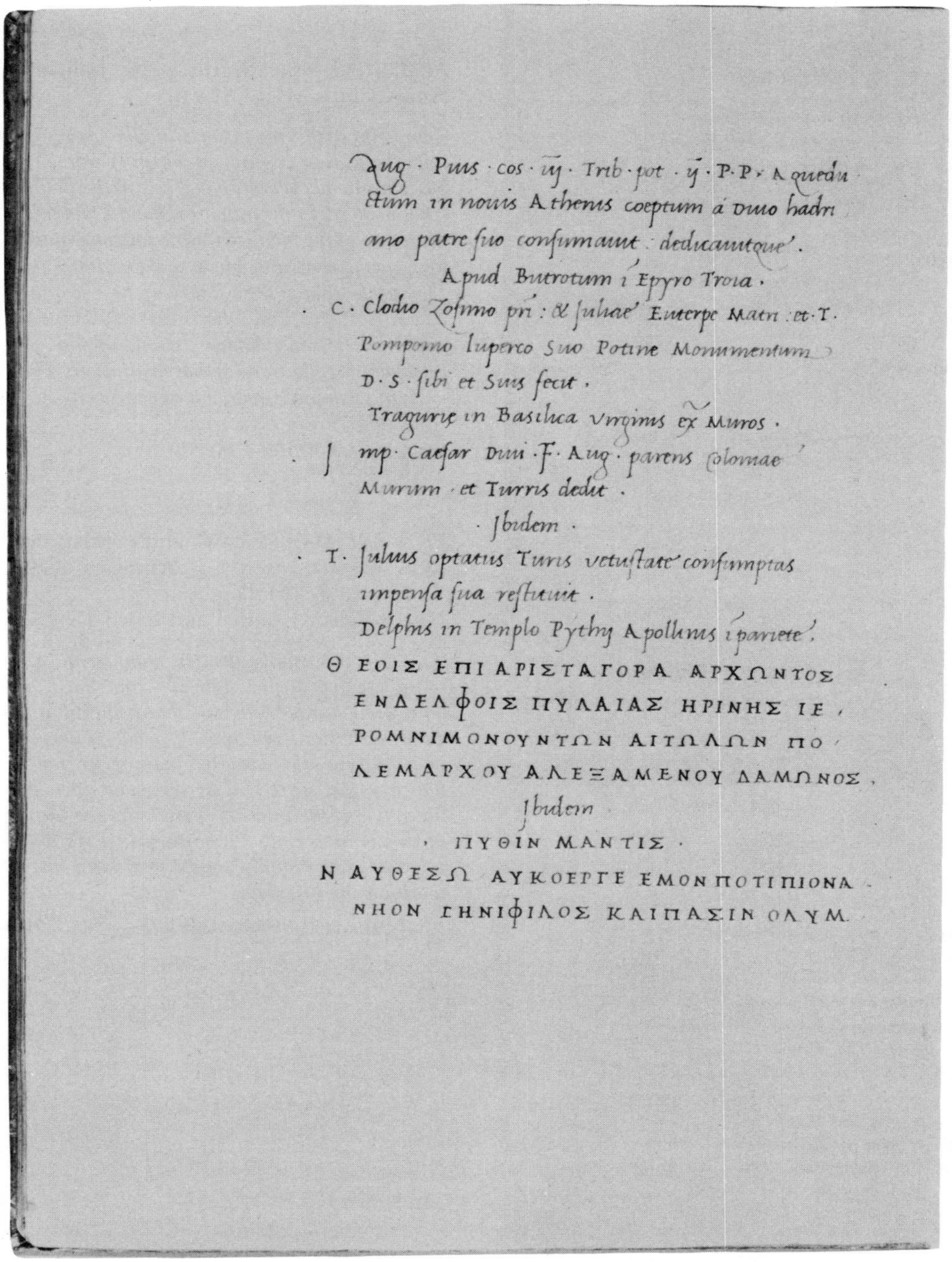
Aug · Pius · cos · iiij · Trib · pot · v · P · P · Aquedu
ctum in nouis Athenis coeptum a Diuo hadri
ano patre suo consummauit · dedicauitque ·
Apud Butrotum i Epyro Troia ·
· C · Clodio Zosimo pri : & Iuliae Euterpe Matri · et · T ·
Pomponio luperco Suo Potine Monumentum
D · S · sibi et Suis fecit ·
Traguriç in Basilica Virginis ex Muros ·
· Imp · Caesar Diui · F · Aug · parens Coloniae
Murum · et Turris dedit ·
· Ibidem ·
· T · Iulius optatus Turris vetustate consumptas
impensa sua restituit ·
Delphis in Templo Pythij Apollinis i pariete ·
Θ ΕΟΙΣ ΕΠΙ ΑΡΙΣΤΑΓΟΡΑ ΑΡΧΩΝΤΟΣ
ΕΝ ΔΕΛΦΟΙΣ ΠΥΛΑΙΑΣ ΗΡΙΝΗΣ ΙΕ
ΡΟΜΝΙΜΟΝΟΥΝΤΩΝ ΑΙΤΩΛΩΝ ΠΟ
ΛΕΜΑΡΧΟΥ ΑΛΕΞΑΜΕΝΟΥ ΔΑΜΩΝΟΣ
Ibidem
· ΠΥΘΙΝ ΜΑΝΤΙΣ ·
Ν ΑΥΘΕΣΩ ΛΥΚΟΕΡΓΕ ΕΜΟΝ ΠΟΤΙ ΠΙΟΝΑ
ΝΗΟΝ ΖΗΝΙ ΦΙΛΟΣ ΚΑΙ ΠΑΣΙΝ ΟΛΥΜ

FIGURE 41: Publius Victor: P. Victoria De Notis Antiquis [collection of classical inscriptions]
Italian c.1500

This manuscript has several claims to our attention, quite apart from the historical nature of its text. Early in this century it was owned by the English calligrapher Edward Johnston, who greatly admired the beauty of the script. He reproduced a page from it in his important book, Writing & Illuminating, & Lettering, *1906. A copy of the book came into the hands of the young James Wardrop, who modelled his own handwriting on the same script. On Johnston's death Wardrop acquired the manuscript, and it is now in the Library of the Victoria and Albert Museum, London, which also possesses many examples of Johnston's own calligraphy.*

VICTORIA & ALBERT MUSEUM MS.L.5161–1977 28×20

Vat. Lat. 3595.

Statius. Vellum. (21 x 12) cm. No foliation. Typical decoration – spolia opima; Emperor on horseback. Shield blank. f. 1v (3v if blanks are counted), leaf of rose-stained vellum with coarsely executed design: inset, poem in gold "AD LIBRVM" evidently by B.S. Initials, headings and caps. also in his style. Miniature of Orpheus at 6th leaf from end. (no. 56 in Vatican Exhibition, 1950. "Written in Rome by Partenio Minuzio Paolino, the friend of Pomponio Leto." See Cat. p. 43) — B. S.

Vat. Borg. Lat. 336.

Fra Giocondo. On paper, without decorations (21 x 14) cm. Written in brown and red inks. An early work of il nostro.* In dedication, f. 26 reference to Alessandro Cortesio (see supra, Vat. Lat. 10228). — B. S. See Campana's letter 4·IX·48 / A. Cortesius

*I am now disposed to give most of this MS. to Questenberg, for several reasons; but particularly for the peculiar Et ligature. B.S. perhaps wrote the Calendar.

Vat. Lat. 13679.

A. Cortesius, but not, apparently, autograph. (See Vat. schedario) — A. Cortesius

Ottob. Lat. 2989.

Augustino Mafeo. (Questenberg). Writing resembles that of B.S. marginal notes in red, reminiscent of his style. — Questenberg

Ottob. Lat. 1732.

On paper. (Questenberg) Capitals, but not as accomplished as with B.S. For Questenberg see G. Mercati, "Questenbergiana". (Opere Minori, IV, pp. 437-461) — Questenberg

Vat. Lat. 3366.

Xandra. Vellum (18·5 x 11) cm. Christoforo Landino's autograph copy presented to Bernardo Bembo. The script is interesting, & seems to be related to* MS. Bodl. Canon. Class. Lat. 85; N. York Public Lib. MS. 28; and Modena Cod. Est. Lat. K. 6. 15. Sepia & blue inks. At f. 3 fine initial of Leda & the swan. [See for this MS. Nolhac p. 240] — C. Landino / B. Bembo

* but not identical with

42

·80·

oßerua al presente. sua Ser.^ta non s'habbia à impedir, ma li Procuratori di eßa Chiesa habbino il carico di gouernar et amministrar dette entrade, come li parerà per ballottation, et termination della maggior parte di loro. Et se il Ser.^mo Principe si resentiße d'alcuna cosa, che faceßero li detti Procuratori circa le dette entrate, sua Ser.^tà poßa dedurre tal materia trà li sopranominati, ouero etiam al Consiglio di pregati, come meglio li parerà. Restando etiam ogn'altra giurisdittione, et authorità, ch' ha sua Ser.^ta nella ditta Chiesa, alla presente parte non repugnante, et sempre sia, et eßer s'intenda riseruata l'authorità, ch' ha il Zudegà nostro di Procurator quanto alle cose al suo officio pertinenti :–

IL FINE.

Presbyter Joannes de Vitalibus Brixiae scripsit, et literis aureis celestinisqз ornauit hunc librum Anno Domini. M. D. L VIII.

43

FIGURE 42: James Wardrop: Iter Italicum Anno Salutis MCMXLVIII

The script of this manuscript should be compared with the Italian original on which Wardrop based his hand. Wardrop was one of the first scholars to study the humanist hands, and this is his record of the manuscripts he saw on a study tour in Italy in 1948. He was at that time Deputy Keeper of the Library of the Victoria and Albert Museum, where this manuscript now reposes, and did much to build up the calligraphic collections of that institution. The modern example is every bit as good as its sixteenth-century counterpart!

VICTORIA & ALBERT MUSEUM
MS.L.4287-1964 25 × 20.5

FIGURES 43 & 44: Laws and regulations to be observed by the Procurators of the Basilica of St. Mark's, Venice
North Italian signed and dated 1558

This is a beautifully written manuscript, and so perfect that at first sight it seems that it must have been printed—except that printing at that date would not have been so good! It was just the type of "one-off" manuscript for which scribes were still needed even after the invention of the printing press. And the writer of this manuscript, "Johannes de Vitalibus Brixiae" has proudly signed and dated his work on the last page.

VICTORIA & ALBERT MUSEUM MS.L.2158–1947
25.5 × 19

Quod Iudices Procuratorum non se impediant de domibus. Statijs, et affictibus ad Ecclesiam Sancti Marci pertinentibus. Capitulū. C x viij:–

L.1490. Die. 5. Martij. Inter Dominos Consiliarios:–
A nostra Ill.ma Signoria cōmanda à uoi Signori Zudesi de Procurator, che non debbiate impedirue in alcuna cosa delle Case. Botteghe. Statij, et affitti pertinenti alla Chiesa nostra di San Marco. Saluo tanto, quanto. i. Signori Procuratori de ditta Chiesa richiederà. Però che à loro cōmesse sono, et voleno, che comesse siano tutte le cose pertinente alle affittation, et exattion d'affitti delle dette Case, et Statij, si come hanno la libertà i Signori del Sal delli affitti pertinenti ad esso suo officio et si come sempre è stato osseruato per. i. detti Signori Procuratori.

Consiliarij

S Ioannes Mauro. S Dominicus Marino.
S Hieronym.⁹ de Cada Pesaro. S Philippus Trono.

Procuratores Sancti Marci non possunt esse Sapientes Consilij, et de additione, nisi vnus tantum pro Procuratia. Capitulum. C xix:–

C 1495. Die 7 Februarij. In maiori Consilio.
Aptum opportunè fuit in maiori Consilio, quòd pro

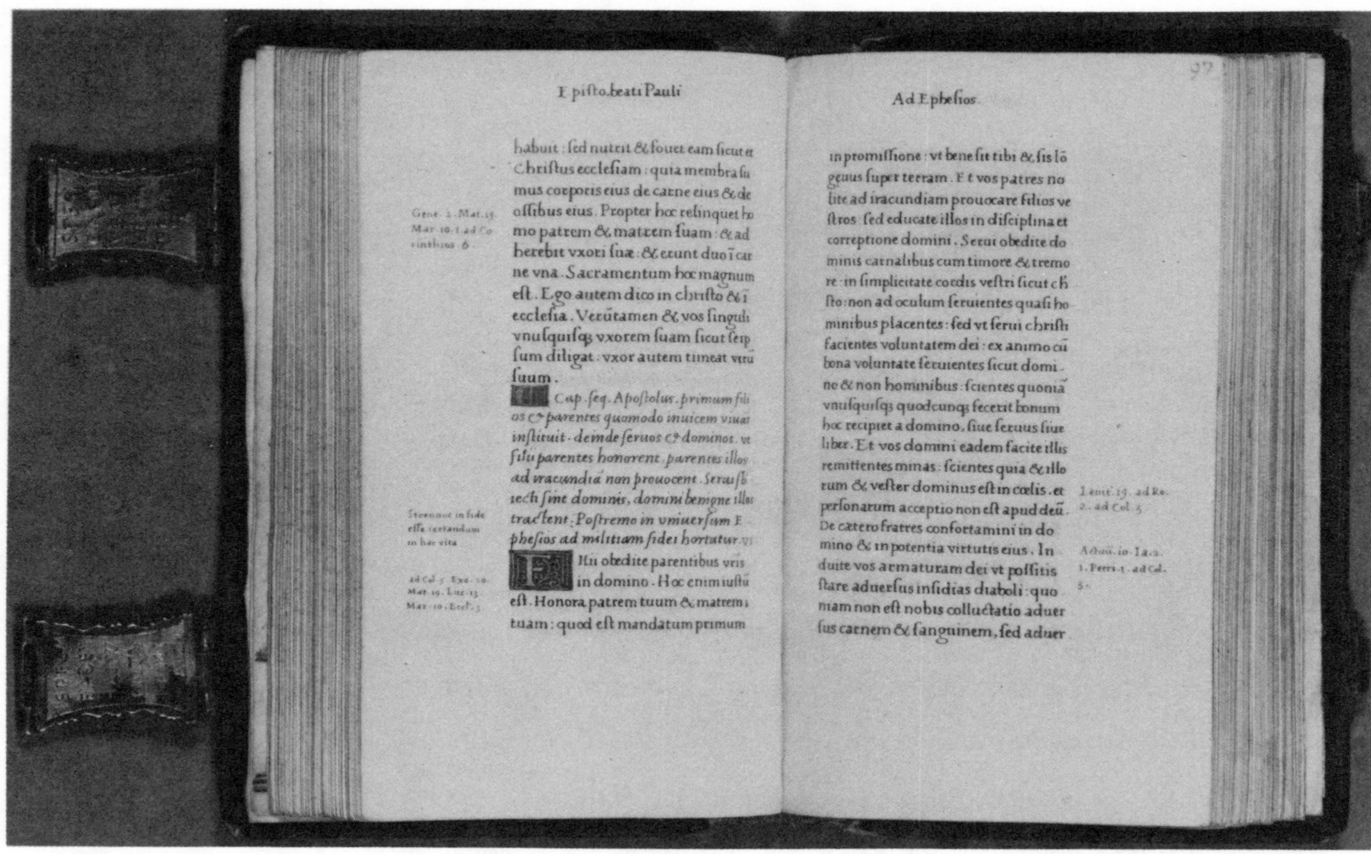

45

FIGURE 45 Epistles French c. 1500

This little manuscript is interesting because it shows the two Renaissance scripts being used together. The right-hand page is entirely written in the antiqua script, while the left-hand page shows both antiqua and italic. The manuscript is made of fine white vellum, very smooth, on which the scribe has been able to write his letters very small, but very clearly. Even the tiny annotations in the margins are easily read.

VICTORIA & ALBERT MUSEUM MS.L.1721–1921 f.96/97 11 × 6.5

FIGURE 46: Victor Brodeau: Traicté à la louenge de Dieu French "escrit a Rome l'an Iubile du 1550"

Although written by a Frenchman for a Frenchman ("pour Monsieur Claude d'Urfé") the manuscript was produced at Rome and shows the influence of contemporary Roman scripts. Already we can see some of the exaggerations that were to plague most scripts over the next hundred years, in particular the rather heavy ends to the ascenders and descenders.

VICTORIA & ALBERT MUSEUM MS.L. 1964–1957 f.30r 19.5 × 13.5

Alors seront tous nous liubres ouuers,
Et de noz cœurs les secretz decouuers,
De noz desirs, & nostre fantasie,
Las ne seront aulcuns masques diuers,
Habitz entiers, ou barres de trauers,
Aultant vauldront les noirs comme les vers,
Pour deguiser la faulçe hypocrisie.

Soubz beau parler, et doulce contenance,
Soubz frans propoz et modeste semblãce
Apparestra mainte orde punaisie,
Mainte luxure en guyse d'attemprence;
Pour charite, vne occulte vengence,
Pour humble port, vne estreme arrogance,
Et pour amour, sans amour ialousie.

LITERA DA BREVI

Aabcdeeéfggghiklmnopqrsſtuxyz

~: Marcus Antonius Casanoua :~

Pierij vates, laudem si opera ista merentur,
Praxiteli nostro carmina pauca date.
Non placet hoc; nostri pietas laudanda Coryti est;
Qui dicat haec; nisi vos forsan uterq; mouet;
Debetis saltem Dijs carmina, ni quoq; et istis
Illa datis. iam nos mollia saxa sumus.

A A B B C C D D E E F F G G H H I I
K L L M M M N N O P P Q Q R R S
S T T U V V X X Y Z & & Et & Et

Ludouicus Vicentinus scribebat Romae anno
salutis MDXXIII

Dilecto filio Ludouico de Henricis laico
Vicencio familiari nostro.

The Spread of Printing and The Rise of The Writing Masters

It is impossible to overestimate the importance of the invention of printing in the fifteenth century. Only then was it possible for the first time to produce quickly a number of identical copies of the same book. With quantity came a lowering of costs, and an increase in the number of people who could afford to buy books for themselves. This encouraged yet more people to learn to read and write, and so further increased the demand for books. The first books to be printed were produced at Mainz in Germany. The handwriting in use there at that time was, of course, the Gothic or "textura" script, which was in general use throughout most of northern Europe in that period. So naturally the first printers used the style of letters with which they were most familiar. In Germany this type of Gothic lettering remained in use until the Second World War, and even today we can often see these "black letter" types employed whenever there is a desire to indicate antiquity—the word "antiques" is a frequent candidate for such treatment!

In Italy, the first printing press was set up at Subiaco in 1464, and here again the printers used the local form of letters, which in this case was not the textura script of the north, but, as we have seen, a quite different, rounder, style of writing: rotunda. As the new Renaissance learning spread throughout Europe, it did so in books printed in this Roman type, and its clarity and elegance gradually overcame the old-fashioned black letter in

FIGURE 47: Ludovico degli Arrighi, surnamed Vicentino: Regola da imparare scrivere varii caratteri de littere con li suoi compassi et misure. Et il modo di temperare le penne secondo la sorte de littere che vorrai scrivere [etc.] 1533

This is a reprint of a work published the previous year, which was itself printed from the blocks of Arrighi's La Operina, *the first copybook to be published, in 1522. This plate shows the form of script used in writing Papal briefs.*

VICTORIA & ALBERT MUSEUM L.960–1901 19×13

most countries. The text of the present book is printed in a Roman type that derives directly from the form of letters originally used in Italy in the fifteenth century. When Aldus Manutius of Venice set out to print cheap copies of classical texts, he did so in the italic type based on the humanist script of the period, which enabled him to compress lengthy texts into a comparatively small volume, and this type is still in use today, too.

The advantages of the printed book were soon obvious, but to one group of people the disadvantages were equally clear. This group was made up of the scribes and copyists whose livelihood was gradually taken from them as the printing press spread its activities throughout Europe. Since printing was only commercially viable where large numbers of copies were concerned, a certain amount of handwritten work still remained for the scribes, of course. When what we today call "one-off" items were required—diplomas, grants, addresses, and similar special documents, for example—the scribe continued to be needed, as he or she is right down to our own day. The multiplicity of books was in itself only one factor in the increased demand for literacy among people in general. There were other forces at work, such as the growth of national states and their attendant bureaucracies, the voyages of discovery leading to an increase in world trade, and the religious controversies of the period with all the pamphlets and other writings produced by the various sects. All this meant that by the beginning of the sixteenth century more and more people wanted to learn to write, while at the same time there was more work for those who could produce a good, clear, clerkly hand.

If there is a demand for a commodity, someone will soon supply it, and so we see the old-style scribe and copyist becoming the new type of writing master, ready to supply copies of suitable handwriting to eager pupils. At first, the proponents of fine writing were often the scholars themselves, and anyone with pretensions to participate in the new learning would endeavor to write a good humanist script; Queen Elizabeth I of England, a good scholar, was among those who wrote a fine Italian hand. But as the sixteenth century progressed, the teachers of writing became more professional, and the increasing demands of commerce meant that mercantile hands began to take precedence over more artistic scripts.

However, as competition grew among the writing masters, they had to consider new ways of selling their wares—their writing skills. At first, of course, they would personally teach a group of pupils, and perhaps circulate manuscript copies of their own handwriting for other pupils to copy. But gradually they realized that the printing press could be used to distribute their work to a far wider audience than they could otherwise hope to reach, and so the copybook was born. The first published writing book (or copybook) was *La Operina* by Ludovico degli Arrighi, issued in 1522. The next master to publish his work was Giovanni Antonio Tagliente, who in 1524 issued a work *Lo presente libro . . .*, in which he had some of the text set in italic type to match the scripts taught in the book. However, it was not until as late as 1571, with the publication of *Essemplare utile* by Giuliantonio Hercolani, that copperplate engraving was used for the illustration of the various scripts. This was an important innovation that was to affect the form of handwriting very considerably in the next century.

So far only Italian writing masters have been mentioned, since they were the first in the field, and maintained their supremacy for most of the sixteenth century. But of course scribes in other countries followed their example, and the present book includes a selection of illustrations from the works of all the great European writing masters. But as styles of handwriting changed (there are fashions in calligraphy as in dress or furniture), the lead passed to the French and Dutch masters, until, with ever-increasing emphasis on mercantile hands, by the eighteenth century it was the English who reigned supreme.

On the whole, however, it must be said that writing masters were not so much a group as a collection of individuals, and fairly contumacious ones at that! The prefaces to their copybooks fairly bubble with arguments—over scripts, over their rivals, over their engravers—and each one is sure that he is right and all others are wrong! But their position in society was always an anomalous one, and this may in part account for their tetchiness. Scholars and teachers had their place in society, but writing masters? Where did they fit in? If we look carefully at seventeenth-century copybooks (and some later ones too) we notice an attempt at scholarship in the number of Latin—and even Greek—passages set for their pupils to copy. Nor were the masters really artists, though they claimed writing to be an art, which they proved by the ever-increasing dexterity with which they decorated and elaborated their writing. And this was where the use of copperplate engraving proved such a snare. Certainly the good engraver of calligraphy contributed in no small way to the success of the master's work; but engravers were a proud race too, and there was a tendency for the engraver to outdo the writing master, if he could. As we can see from many of the seventeenth-century examples in this book, there was an inclination for the pen to follow the graver, rather than the graver to follow the pen, performing convolutions that have nothing to do with legible handwriting. Eventually we actually have the elaboration known as "copperplate" writing, which owes more to the way the steel needle behaves on a copperplate, than it does to the action of the pen on paper.

The seventeenth century was perhaps the most exciting period for the writing masters, and a varied selection of their works is illustrated in the present book. There was still something of the exuberance of a new art form, still a need to prove their value and importance. Look at the titles the writing masters gave to their published works, especially such prolific exponents as Edward Cocker. Look too at all the figures and embellishments known as "strikings" or "command of hand"—what fun they must have had, devising yet more subtleties! That others accepted this state of affairs can be proved by the fact that such a noted connoisseur as the diarist Samuel Pepys formed a collection of calligraphy, with many examples taken directly from "surviving maister pen-men" of his own and other countries. When he retired from his post at the Admiralty in London, he set about arranging his collection, having it mounted and annotated. It can still be seen today, with the rest of his library, in his old college, Magdalene College, Cambridge, to which it was bequeathed. Each country, as can be seen from the examples in the present book, brought something different to the art, or craft, of writing. But, perhaps sadly, this variety was soon to be subdued to the needs of commerce, and writing was to remain in the doldrums until the present century.

FIGURE 48: Ludovico degli Arrighi, surnamed Vicentino: Regola da imparare scrivere [etc.] 1533

Another page from Arrighi's influential manual, showing how to make the ligatures which were so characteristic of this style, as well as the various joining strokes of other letters.

VICTORIA & ALBERT MUSEUM L.960–1901 19 × 13

Seguita lo essempio delle lre che pono
ligarsi con tutte le sue sequenti, in tal mo=
do Cioe

aa ab ac ad ae af ag ah ai ak al am an
ao ap aq ar as aſ at au ax ay az

Il medesmo farai con d i k l m n u.
Le ligature poi de c f s ſ t sonno
le infra=
scritte

ct, fa ff fi fm fn fo fr fu fy,
st st

ſt ſſ ß ſt, ta te ti tm tn to tq tr tt tu
tx ty

Con le restanti littere de lo Alphabeto, che
sono, b e g h o p q r x y z z
non si deue ligar mai lra
alcuna sequente

16

See below an example of the letters that can be joined with any that follow to Wit

aa ab ac ad ae af gg ah ai ak al am an ao ap ag ar as aſ at au ax ay az,

The same can be done with d i k l m n u.

The ligatures for c f s ſ t are written below

ct, fa ff fi fm fn fo fr fu fy, st st

ſt ſſ ß ſt, ta te ti tm tn to tg tr tt tu tx ty

Concerning the other letters of the Alphabet, which are b e g h o p q r x y z ʒ one ought not to tie any to the letter following.

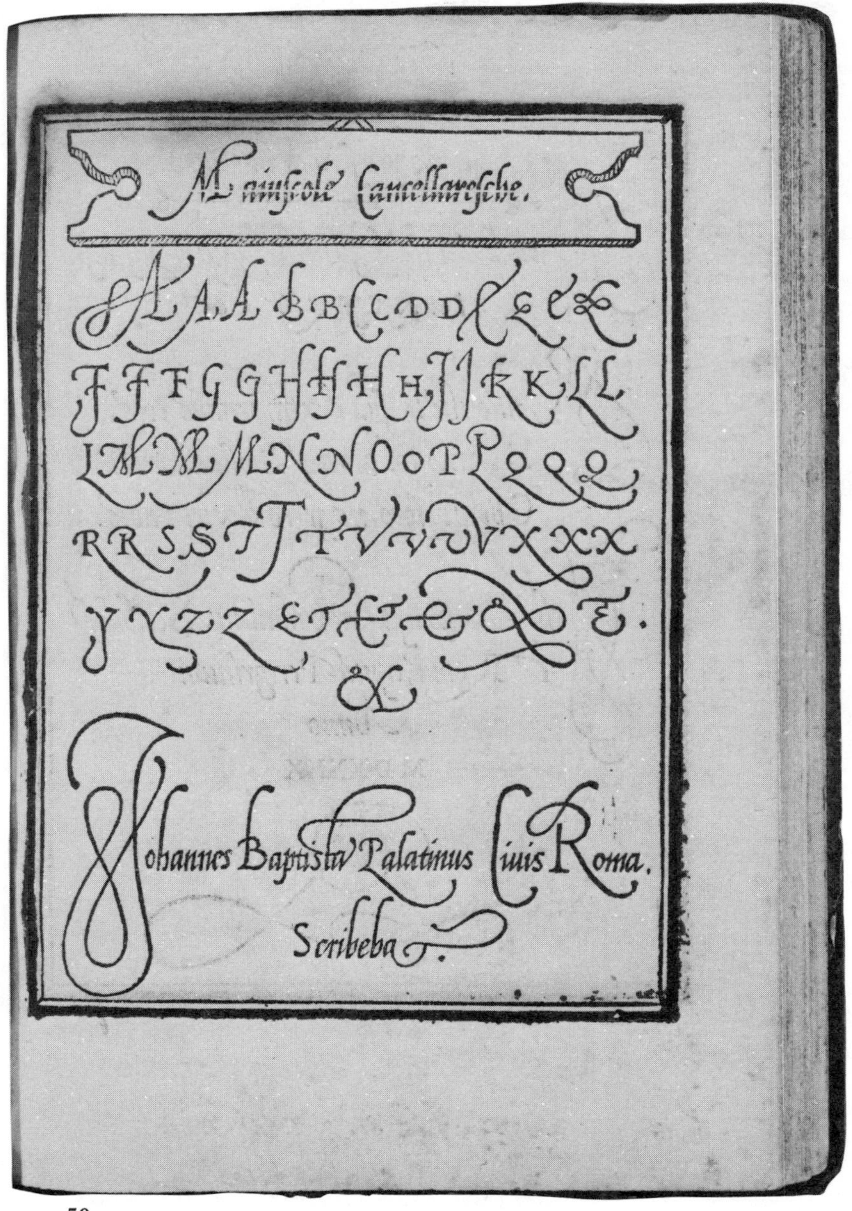

50

FIGURE 49: John Howard Benson: The first writing book: an English translation & facsimilé text of Arrighi's *Operina,* the first manual of the Chancery hand, with introduction and notes by J. H. Benson 1955

This interesting tour-de-force shows what can be done with the calligraphic models included in this section of the present book. Not only has Benson translated the Arrighi text, but he has planned it as a counterpart to the Italian original—with what success can be seen.

VICTORIA & ALBERT MUSEUM L.873–1955 21.5 × 14.5

FIGURE 50: Giovanni Battista Palatino: Libro nel quale s'insegna a scrivere ogne sorte lettere 1548

*This is a reissue of a work first published in 1545. Notice the various forms of the capital letters (*maiuscole = *majuscules) which he offers, some very distorted. Little is known about Palatino's life, but he was obviously very proud of his Roman citizenship, which he frequently included with his signature, as at the bottom of this plate.*

VICTORIA & ALBERT MUSEUM L.2138–1952

A A B C D E F G J K L M N O P Q R S T V.

Se dal mondo sempre non fussero state in somma ueneratione le sacrosante lettre humanissimo lettore non haurebbono gli antichi cosi longamente conteso à cui douesse donar la palma della inuentione di esse Imperoche alcuni attribuiuano q̃ gloria al Magnanimo Hercule, alt. a Nicostrata od'à Carmenta, altri a Palamede nella guerra Troiana, molti a Numa Pompilio à cui erano diuine cose reuelate dalla Nimp. Egeria, & pure erano quelle dal suo principio roze, et mal formate, Pensa tu adunque di che laude siano degni quelli che ornate et terse anoi le dimostrano &

A a a b b c d d e f f g Giouan Batt. Car.mo b h i k l m n o p q r.mo

51

De profundis clamaui ad te dñe: dñe exaudi uocem meam. Fiant aures tuæ intendentes in uocem deprecationis meæ

Herculanus scribebat 1574.

Questa lr̃a cancellaresca commune, & l'altre lettere tutte uuole pendere uerso mano destra, essere uguale, diritta, netta; il spacio fra le righe sia equale, fra le parole et fra le lr̃e ancora.

A a a b b b c c d d e e d e f f g g h h h i i l m n o p p petrus p p q q r r s s t t t u u v v i x y z r r e e w p p s t Vigilantibus acquiritur. &c.

Herculanus scribebat 1574

Si iniquitates obseruaueris dñe domine quis sustinebit? Quia apud te propitiatio est: & propter legem tuam sustinui te domine Deus.

1574

Beneficentia è una virtù, la quale solamente in se contiene il fare beneficio ad altri senza aspettatione alcuna d'esserne rimunerato, et è propio dell'huomo grande et magnanimo qual debbe seguitar nõ il frutto ma il beneficiare. 1574.

cancellaresca circonflessa

Sappia ciascuno che li spacij che sono fra lr̃a et lr̃a uogliono essere equali et non più grandi che si sia il bianco che è dentro il spacio dei corpi delle lr̃e, fra le parole li spacij capiscano una i.

Herculanus Sbat. 1574

Maiuscole cancel. che piu facili

A A A A B B C C C C D D E E
E J F G G H J J L M M N O P P Q
R R R S S T T T V V X Y Z &

1574

Questa cancellaresca formasi sciolta e tondeggiante per tutto doue in essa intrauiene il tratto taglio à differenza della cancellaresca acuta. et il taglio intrauiene in queste lr̃e a b c d e g h i l m n o p q r s u x y a

52

53

FIGURE 51: Vespasiano Amphiareo: Un novo modo d'insegnar a scrivere et formar lettere di piu sorti 1548

Apart from the fact that he was a Franciscan friar, little is known about Amphiareo, although his only printed work is of some significance in the history of the copybook. His development of the chancery script involved the employment of loops and joins more common in the mercantile hands, but the result enabled it to be written at greater speed.

VICTORIA & ALBERT MUSEUM L.2037–1931 15×21.5

FIGURE 52: Giuliantonio Hercolani: Lo scrittor' utile 1574

Hercolani's works were the first copybooks to be produced by copperplate engraving. In this example we can see both the freedom conferred on the scribe by the new method and also the restraint with which it was used—compare the use made of it by writing masters in the next century! Certainly the graver (or burin) was much better at reproducing pen strokes than wood engraving had been.

VICTORIA & ALBERT MUSEUM L.1061–1901

FIGURE 53: Tomaso Ruinetti: Idea del buon scrittore 1619

Ruinetti was the first of the writing masters to use copperplate engraving to reproduce not only a variety of scripts (as Hercolani had been the first to do in 1574) but also the very elaborate borders. This fashion, which threatened to almost overwhelm the scripts themselves, was known as "striking" or "command of hand." The later masters, as we shall see, took up the idea with great enthusiasm and virtuosity.

VICTORIA & ALBERT MUSEUM L.2323–1952 23×32

18

Al molto Ill.re S.r mio e Prone oss.mo Il Sig.re Horatio Felici Scr.e Eccellent.mo

S'io publicassi la presente mia opera di scriuere senza fregiarla del nome di V.S.
mostrerei di non conoscere il pregio ch'ella può dar ad essa, ch'à quell'eccellenza di
questa nobil professione si è auuanzata, alla quale l'altrui penne in vano di giun
ger s'affaticano. Piacciale, ch'io mi prenda da lei quest'honore, e che faccia palese ad
vn'hora à gli altri, quanto io riuerisca in V.S. quella virtù, che non posso aggua:
gliare, che sarà pur vn'accrescere à se stessa lode, et à me nuouo obligo di seruir:
la, benche ne tenga già mille cagioni della singolar humanità sua.

Oblig.mo Ser.re
Leopardo Antonozzi
Osimano

54

FIGURE 54: Leopardo Antonozzi: De caratteri, libro primo 1638

Antonozzi was one of the scriptors to the Pope. His chancery script, shown here, is pleasant to look at but already contains some distortions such as the curious raised bowl of the h. *His book also contains a wide variety of border decorations.*

VICTORIA & ALBERT MUSEUM L.123–1903 20 × 29

FIGURE 55: Giovanni Battista and Francesco Pisani: Engraved copybook

Both the Pisani published copybooks in the 1640's, and this work contains examples by both of them, though it lacks a title page. The two engraved figures exactly match those in the manuscript also shown here (Figure 56). Both books probably go back to an earlier source, and show the widespread influence of the published copybook.

VICTORIA & ALBERT MUSEUM L.3076–1960 18 × 25

FIGURE 56: Liber Collectarum iuxta ritum Sac. Ordinis Cartusiensis . . . 1620

The Victoria and Albert Museum purchased this manuscript as an example of contemporary Italian calligraphy; one of the pages (shown here) is, however, given up entirely to this illustration, done by "striking" or "command of hand"; it helps to prove the source of the style, since it relates very closely to the illustration in the copybook by the Pisani, also shown here (Figure 55).

VICTORIA & ALBERT MUSEUM MS.L.6630–1978 32 × 22

55

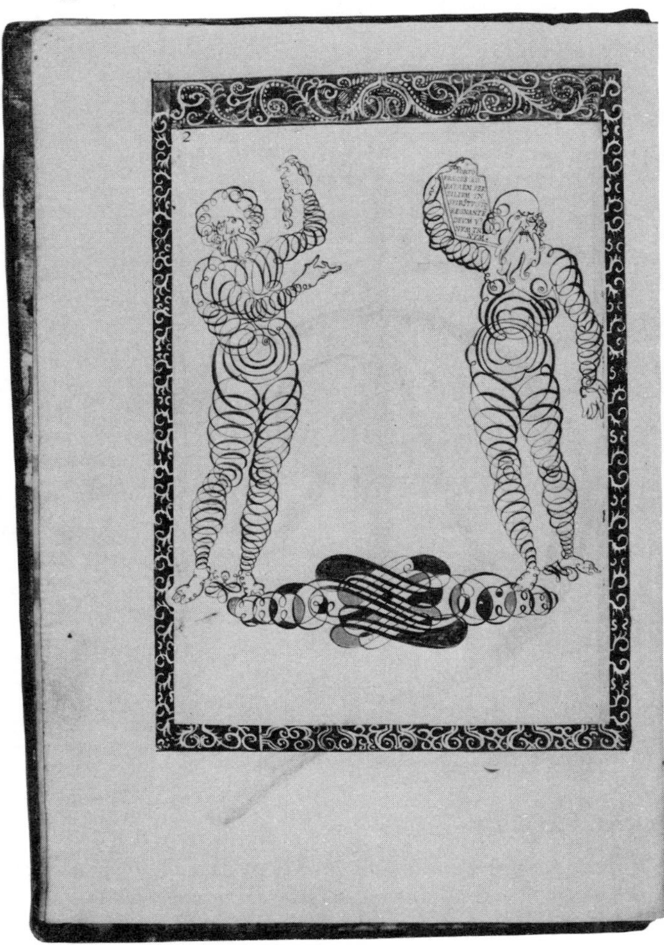

56

Lectorum dicti celeberrimi Studij Pataui=
ni Mag.cum et admodū Reuerendū D.ñum
FRANCISCVM Mag.ci Domini,
ALEXANDRI RIATI Patauini,
Filium {qui poſt multa, et longa ſtudia, ac
meditationes, variaq. eius probitatis, et eru=
ditionis documenta, fidem Catholicam ver=
bis iuxta Bullæ bonæ memoriæ Pij Papæ
IV. tenorem conceptis palam et ſolemniter
coram nobis profeſſus eſt} a Promotoribus
ſuis adductum, et nobis oblatū ad ſubeun=
dum ſuum rigoroſum examen, punctiſq.
ei {vt moris eſt} in ſacra Theologia præaſ=
ſignatis, fecimus coram Nobis, et admo=
dum R.do Decano, ac alijs prædicti ſacri
Collegij Doctoribus, et Magiſtris ibidem
exiſtentibus diligenter, & rigoroſe exami=
nari, qui autem in huiuſmodi examine, ſua
Puncta aſſignata magiſtraliter recitando,
argumenta quæcunq., et dubia omnia, et
quaſſi=

57

FIGURES 57 & 58: Two diplomas   seventeenth century

These two illustrations show the type of manuscript for which demand remained even after the invention of printing. They are both diplomas, made for individuals. It was by this means that calligraphy was kept alive and the variety of scripts continued, at a time when the printed copybooks concentrated more and more

re soluendis, in omni deniq; periclitatione sui tam
egregie, prudenter, docte, honorifice, laudabiliter,
excellenter, magistraliter, & Doctoreo more se
gessit, talemque, ac tantam ingenij, memoriæ, do:
ctrinæ, cæterarumque rerum, quæ in consumma:
tissimo Iuris Vtriusque Doctore desiderari
solent vim ostendit, vt magnam sui expectatio:
nem, quam apud omnes concitauerat, non so:
lum sustinuerit, sed etiam longe superauerit: &
ob eam rem ab omnibus Excellentissimis dicti
Sacri Collegij Doctoribus ibidem continuo
existentibus, VNANIMITER, ET CON:
CORDITER, CVNCTISQVE SVF:
FRAGIIS, AC EORVM NEMINE
PENITVS, ATQVE PENITVS DIS:
CREPANTE, AVT DISSENTIEN:
TE, NEC HÆSITANTE QVIDEM,
idoneus, & sufficientissimus in Vtroque Iure
fuerit iudicatus, & merito quidem approbatus;
sicut ex eorum votis secreto in scrutinio No:
bis

58

on business hands. The earliest illustration, of 1614, confers a doctorate in Theology on Franciscus Riatus, and the script shows the influence of contemporary printing. The later one conferred a doctorate in Law on Quintilio Carbò in 1627; the more important passages are written in gold.

VICTORIA & ALBERT MUSEUM MS.L.2494 and 2493–1886 23.5 × 16.5

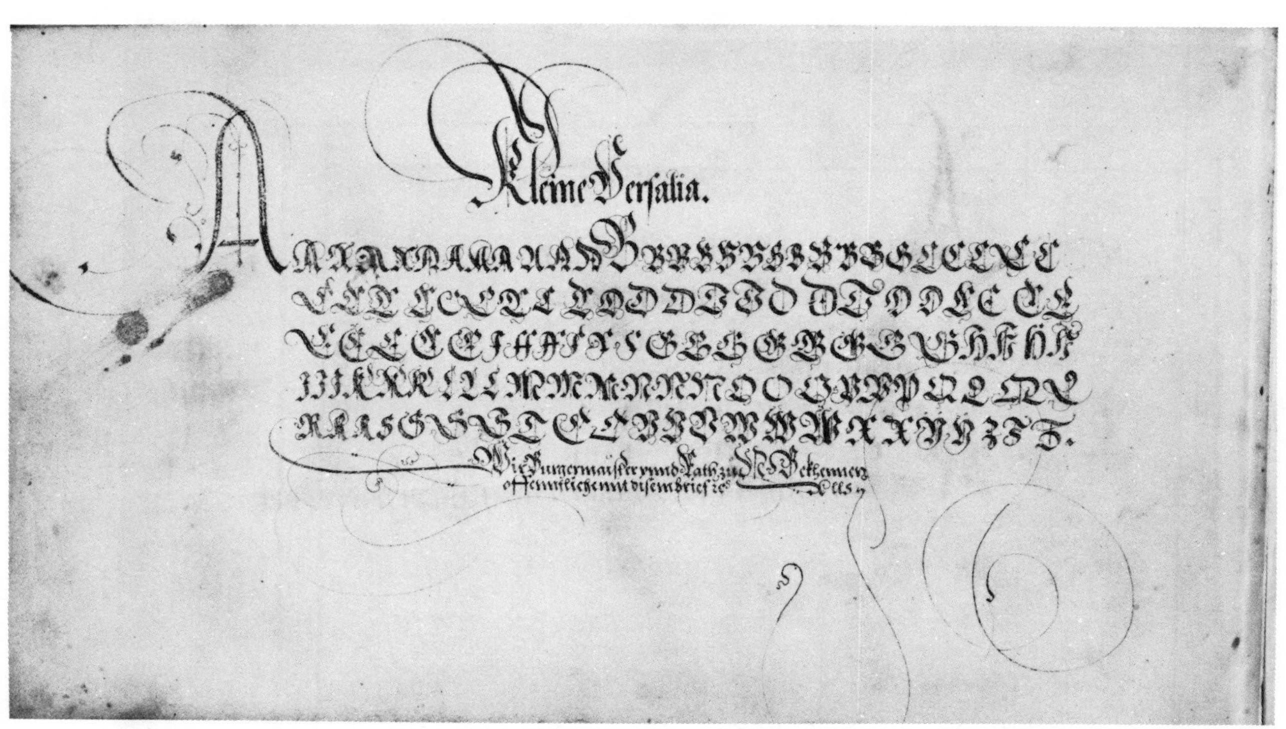

FIGURE 59: Johann Neudörffer the Younger: Ein gutte Ordnung [etc.]   1561

This manuscript was probably written out by Neudörffer himself, or at least one of his pupils. The original work was published in 1538 and was an important landmark in the development of German "Fraktur" script. Notice how many different forms he gives of the individual letters—from the simple to the almost unrecognizable!

VICTORIA & ALBERT MUSEUM   MS.L.2067–1936   17 × 29

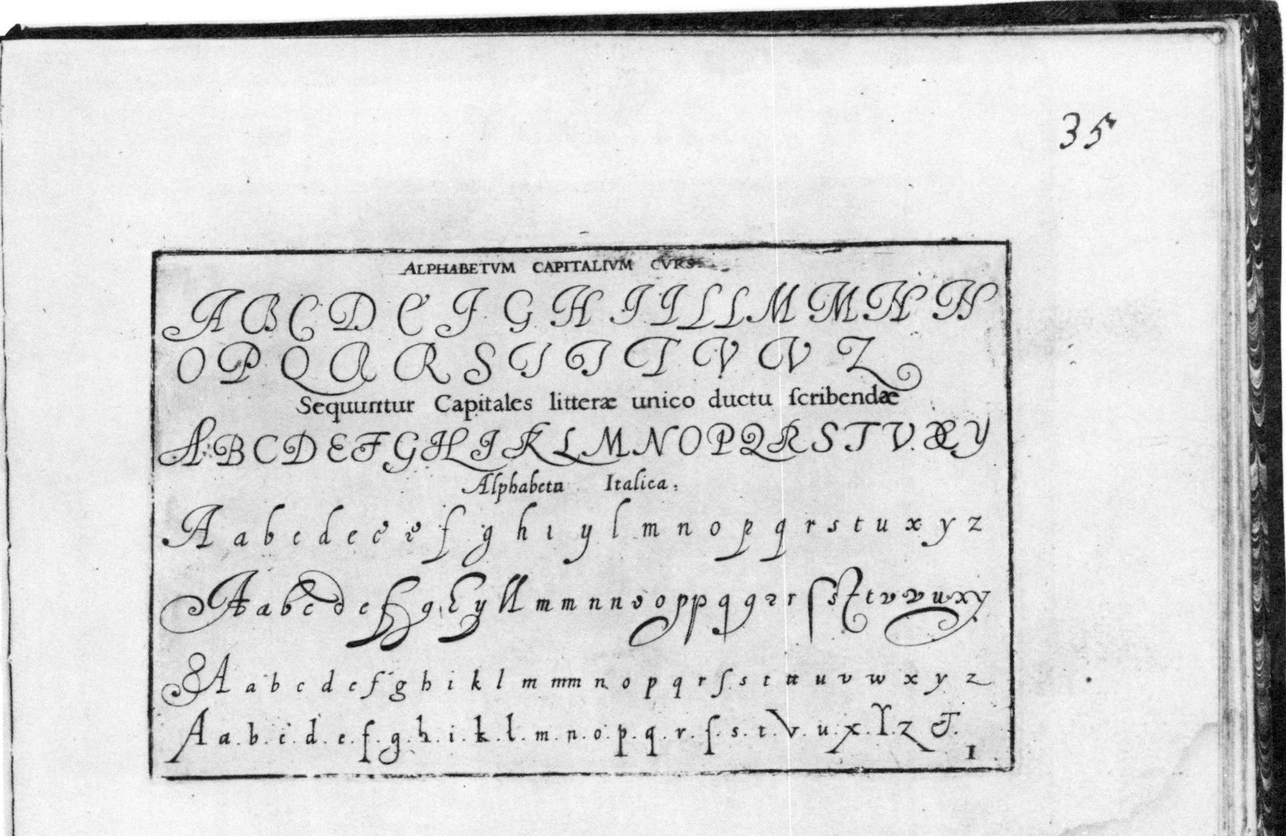

60

FIGURE 60: Johann Theodor and Johann Israel de Bry: Alphabeten und aller art Characteren 1596

This work, which was published in Frankfurt, was an anthology of various scripts in different languages, of the kind that was to become increasingly popular in the next century.

VICTORIA & ALBERT MUSEUM 10.x.1871 14×20

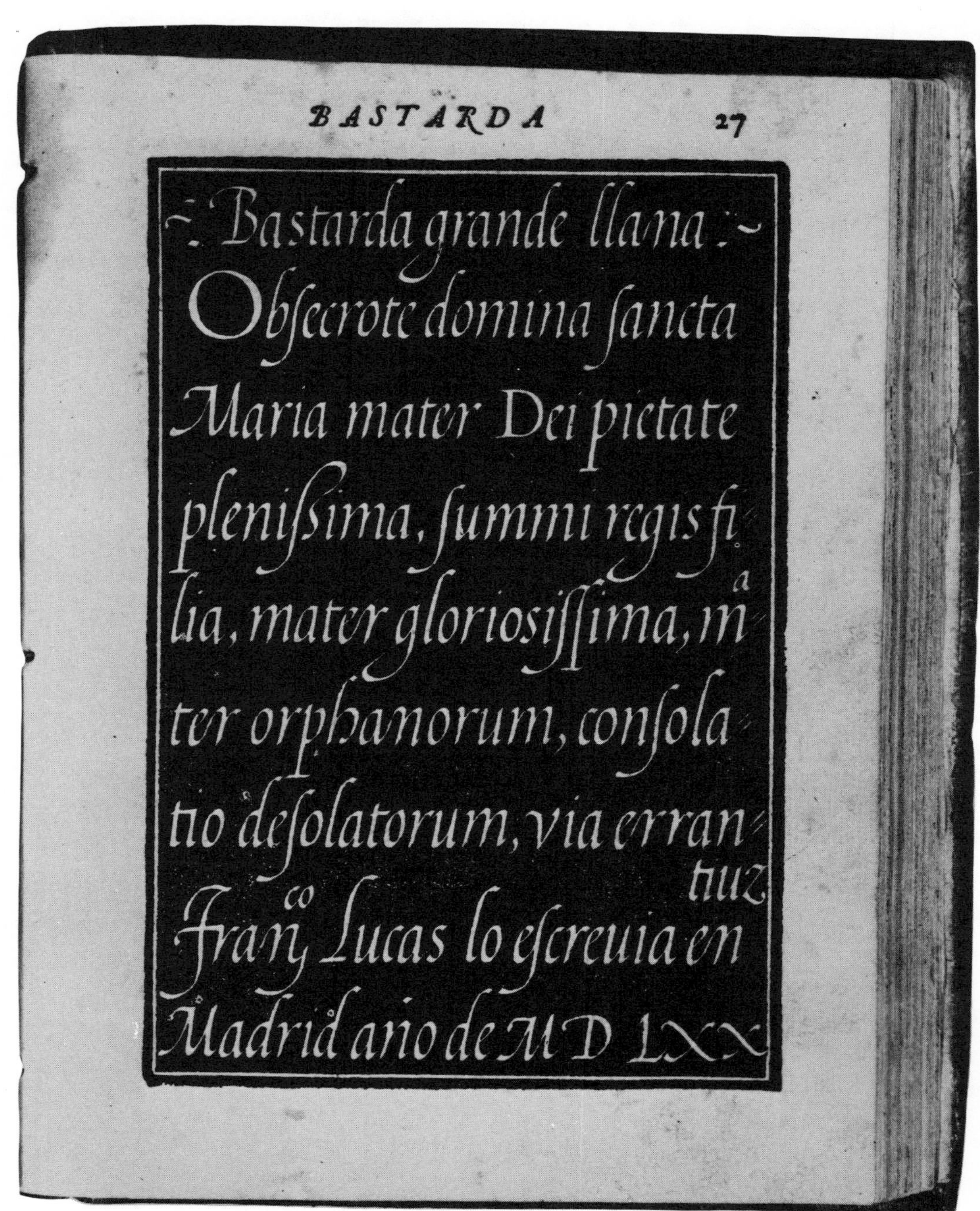

BASTARDA 27

Bastarda grande llana
Obsecrote domina sancta
Maria mater Dei pietate
plenissima, summi regis fi
lia, mater gloriosissima, m^a^
ter orphanorum, consola
tio desolatorum, via erran
tiuz
Fran^co^ Lucas lo escreuia en
Madrid año de MD LXX

FIGURE 61: Francisco Lucas: Arte de escrevir 1577

Lucas's book was particularly significant for Spanish calligraphy since the forms he introduced retained their importance for nearly two centuries. He was one of a number of writing masters who provided examples of white-on-black writing and we shall see that this has also been taken up again by contemporary scribes in the twentieth century.

VICTORIA & ALBERT MUSEUM 19×14

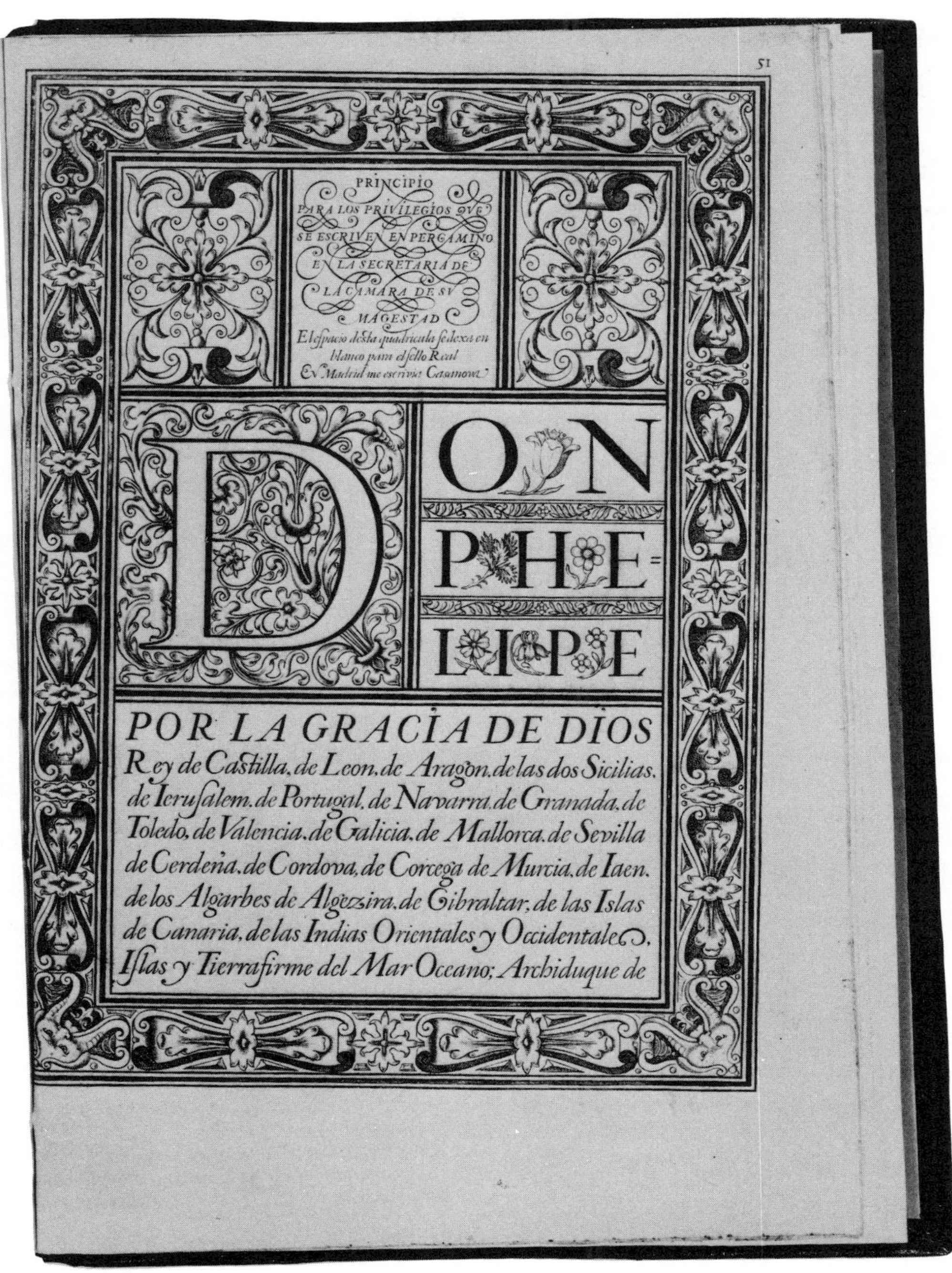

51

PRINCIPIO PARA LOS PRIVILEGIOS QVE SE ESCRIVEN EN PERGAMINO EN LA SECRETARIA DE LA CAMARA DE SV MAGESTAD

El espacio desta quadricula se dexa en blanco para el sello Real

En Madrid me escrivia Casanova

DON PHELIPE

POR LA GRACIA DE DIOS

Rey de Castilla. de Leon. de Aragon. de las dos Sicilias. de Ierusalem. de Portugal. de Navarra. de Granada. de Toledo. de Valencia. de Galicia. de Mallorca. de Sevilla de Cerdeña. de Cordova. de Corcega de Murcia. de Iaen. de los Algarbes de Algezira. de Gibraltar. de las Islas de Canaria. de las Indias Orientales y Occidentales. Islas y Tierrafirme del Mar Oceano: Archiduque de

FIGURE 62: José de Casanova: Primera parte del arte de escrevir todas formas de letras 1650

Casanova displays a great variety of hands in his book, but the most important was the lettera bastarda, *which he did much to introduce into Spain. This example, however, is typical of the script and decoration of Spanish official documents, which continued until the nineteenth century. In common with many writing masters, Casanova was not satisfied with the skill of the engravers available to him, so he learnt the art himself in order to engrave his own work.*

VICTORIA & ALBERT MUSEUM 16.x.1871 30×21

63

FIGURE 63: Maurice Jausserandy: Le miroir d'escriture ou sont representées plusieurs sortes de lettres & charactères 1600

Jausserandy came from Avignon in the south of France, a city that offered a meeting place for French and Italian influences—it had once been the home of the Popes. In common with a number of writing masters, Jausserandy offered a special hand for ladies (shown here), chosen for its supposed simplicity!

VICTORIA & ALBERT MUSEUM L.2899–1950 26 × 18.5

FIGURE 64: Heures Nouvelles dediée a Madame la Dauphine. Ecrites et gravées par L. Senault

This work by Senault is undated but probably comes from the last quarter of the seventeenth century. If you could not afford to commission a handwritten prayer book, then this engraved one was the next best thing, as it looked very much like a manuscript. Louis Senault also published a number of important copybooks, and his daughter was also a fine calligrapher.

VICTORIA & ALBERT MUSEUM L.1690–1888 37.5 × 25.5

A PRIME

E vous saluë Marie pleine de grace &c. O Dieu venez a mō secours. Gloire soit au Pere &c.

HYMNE

Christe Redemptor omniū.

Christ Redempteur de tout le mōde,
Du Principe éternel diuin écoulement
Dieu qui né sans commencement
Viens naître dans le temps d'vne
Vierge feconde.
Toy qui du Pere des lumières

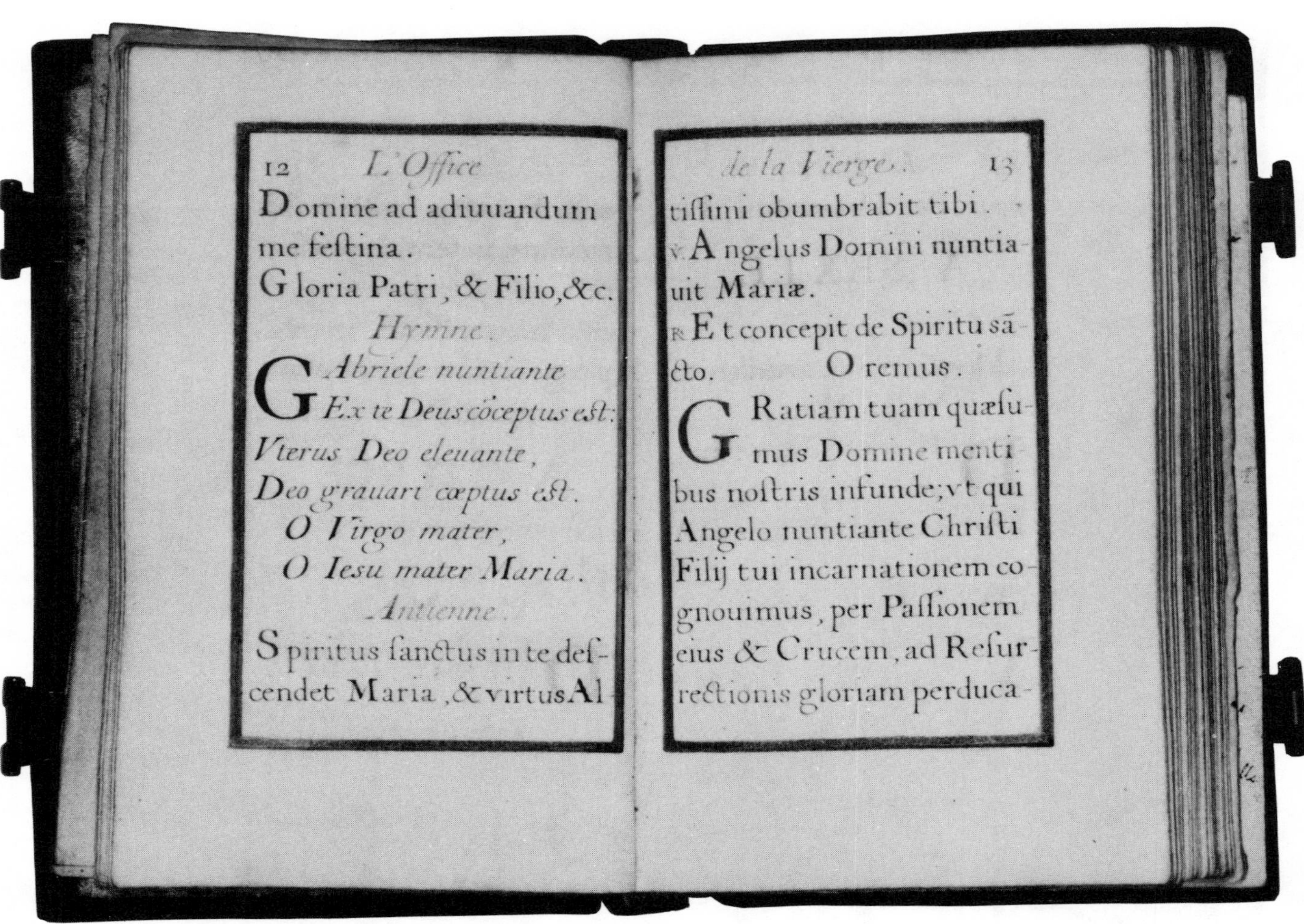

12 *L'Office*

Domine ad adiuuandum
me feſtina.
Gloria Patri, & Filio, &c.

Hymne.

Gabriele nuntiante
Ex te Deus cōceptus eſt:
Vterus Deo eleuante,
Deo grauari cœptus eſt.
O Virgo mater,
O Iesu mater Maria.

Antienne.

Spiritus ſanctus in te deſ-
cendet Maria, & virtus Al-

de la Vierge. 13

tiſſimi obumbrabit tibi.
℣. Angelus Domini nuntia-
uit Mariæ.
℟. Et concepit de Spiritu sā-
cto. Oremus.
Gratiam tuam quæſu-
mus Domine menti-
bus noſtris infunde; vt qui
Angelo nuntiante Chriſti
Filij tui incarnationem co-
gnouimus, per Paſſionem
eius & Crucem, ad Reſur-
rectionis gloriam perduca-

FIGURE 65: L'Office de la Vièrge (Prières de St. Augustin) Paris 1661

This tiny manuscript is signed and dated on one of the pages by Nicolas Jarry, one of the most famous exponents of the court school of calligraphy which flourished during the reign of Louis XIV. At a time when the handwritten book was almost extinct elsewhere in Europe, it enjoyed a renewed vogue in France, where many such exquisite works were produced for court ladies and their circle.

VICTORIA & ALBERT MUSEUM MS.L.1171–1949 9×6

verdadero de la passion de
mi Señor Iesu Christo para
sentir y reformar el desor-
den de mi vida Amen.

63

MYSTERIOS
GLORIOSOS
Se han de rezar Miercoles
y Domingo.

Mysterio I.
Conſideracion de la Re-
ſurection.
Marci 16. Luce. 14. Ioan. 20.

Oracion y ofrecimiento

O Muy dulce amorosa y
siempre virgen Maria, yo te
ofrezco humilmente estas
diez Aue Marias, y un Pa-
ter noster, al inefable gozo
que tuviste en la gloriosa
Resurrection de tu Hijo muy
amado que segun la mu-

66

FIGURE 66: Memoria espirituel de devotas y contemplatives oraciones y otras Christianas devociones. En Brusselas escrito por G. H. Wilmart año 1673

Surviving manuscripts show Wilmart to have been a competent calligrapher and this little manuscript is a good example of his work. It makes use of various scripts, though the italic hand predominates. The penwork decorations, in black and gold, are especially charming.

VICTORIA & ALBERT MUSEUM MS.L.1760–1894
10.5×7

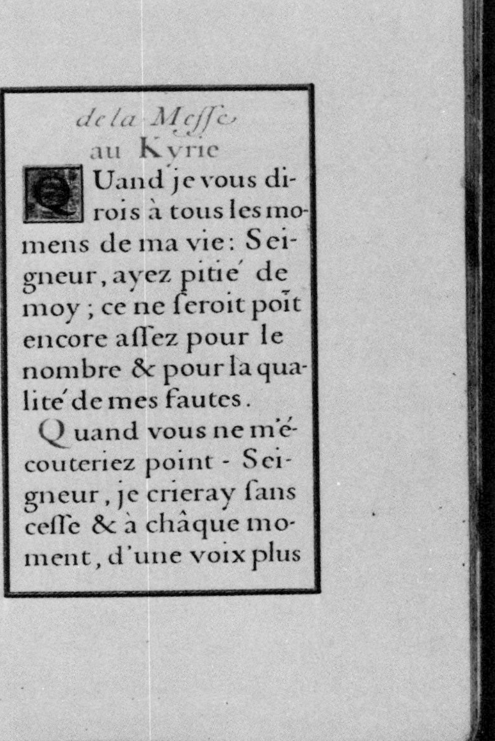
de la Meſſe
au Kyrie

QUand je vous di-
rois à tous les mo-
mens de ma vie: Sei-
gneur, ayez pitié de
moy; ce ne ſeroit poĩt
encore aſſez pour le
nombre & pour la qua-
lité de mes fautes.

Quand vous ne m'é-
couteriez point - Sei-
gneur, je crieray ſans
ceſſe & à châque mo-
ment, d'une voix plus

67

FIGURE 67: Prières de la Messe écrites par J. F. Rousselet Paris c. 1710

The illustration does not reveal whether this is a manuscript or a printed book. In fact, the letters look more like printing than writing. However, it is one of the manuscripts produced during the resurgence of the handwritten book in France, though its debt to the printed letter is obvious. In the original work the decorations are in red and gold.

VICTORIA & ALBERT MUSEUM MS.L.1430–1950
16×10

68

FIGURES 68 & 69: A book of alphabets, with examples of calligraphy c. 1540–c. 1567

Little is known about the manuscript from which these two examples are taken: it may have been a scribe's sample book, to show potential patrons what he could do for them. Certainly the pictures are well-drawn in sepia ink on the vellum, and there are a variety of different scripts, too. The two major alphabets have

69

been identified: the elaborate letters at the top of these two pages are taken from a grotesque alphabet by Nöel Garnier (1470/75–c. 1544), while among the scripts are the italic and the secretary. The manuscript was probably made in England, although the scribe was apparently familiar with continental engraved alphabets.

VICTORIA & ALBERT MUSEUM MS.L.2090–1937 29.5 × 21

32

May it please your Lo: &c.

I was vppon my way to haue waited vppon yor Lo: too Mr Hackars
but when I was about stocke I had certen word yor L. came
not before night, and went a longe iorny to morrowe
so as to haue visited yor L. theare to night had ben to
haue incurred Mr Hackar (thoughe he very courteously inuited
me) and to haue importund yor Lo: Therfore I humblie pray yor
L. to take the affect for the efect, and to vouchsafe to accept
the humble remembrance of my saruice. I humblie thanke yor
L. for yor noble fauour in sendinge me these inclosed the
Collections of one I haue seene here like to proue very
saruisable. this Chappell is cum to this parfection since I
was at Florence yet then in doinge. Yo^r L. knows those
parts better then I though I haue beene there twise this not
withstandinge is my opinion y^t the Ruins of the Ancient
Romans both at Roome and of Prouince ar fairer
then the greatest buildings in all Europe y^t ar not
ancient; If yor L. desier to increase yor magnificence
then my Lo: let me haue the honnor to persuade you to
imploy Mr Cooke to prouide you of the works of Benedict
Palma at Venise, who exceeds in doinge large pictures
as mutche as the hole side of a greate chamber vppon
cloth as in the subject History. for Pictors of Counterfet let him send you
of the workes of Sipion Gastano in Roome who is longe
in finishinge but dun most excellent. for Statua most
esteemed amongst the Italians there is a litle auld
man called John Bollognia the Dukes saruant and at Florence who is not inferiour mutch
to Michell Angello. 2 of these I sawe and for John Bollognia
I count him the rarest man y^t I sawe of any profession
for his profession. pardon my L. this my presumtion
vanities and make full account if yor L. thinke me
worthy of so mutch honnor y^t I am yor Lo:

Most humble saruant

W. Langley

W^th your L. permission I
humblie desier likewise to be
remembered as a most humble
saruant to my most honorable Lady
to whome I wishe a prosperous iorny
and all other happines whatsoeuer.

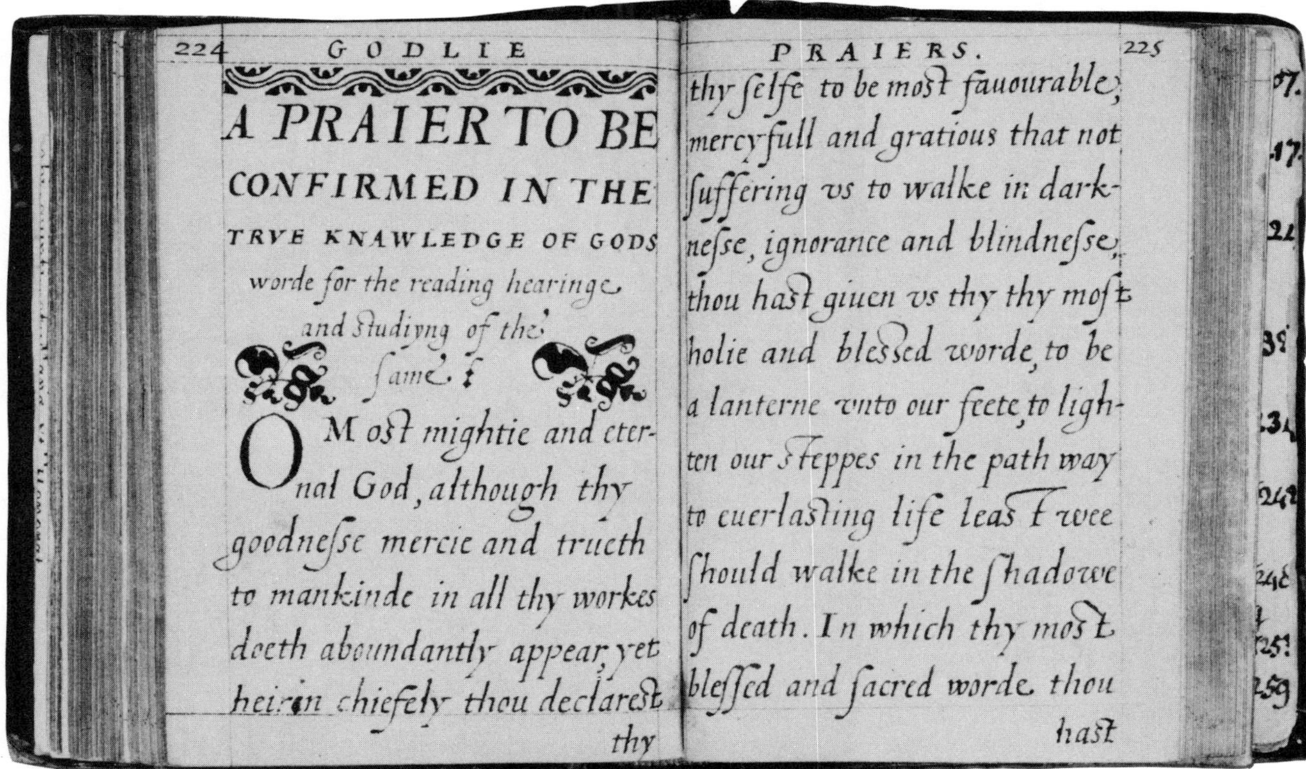

224 GODLIE

PRAIERS. 225

A PRAIER TO BE CONFIRMED IN THE TRVE KNAWLEDGE OF GODS worde for the reading hearinge and studiyng of the same.

O Most mightie and eter-nal God, although thy goodnesse mercie and trueth to mankinde in all thy workes doeth aboundantly appear, yet heirin chiefely thou declarest thy

thy selfe to be most fauourable, mercyfull and gratious that not suffering vs to walke in dark-nesse, ignorance and blindnesse, thou hast giuen vs thy thy most holie and blessed worde, to be a lanterne vnto our feete, to ligh-ten our steppes in the path way to euerlasting life least wee should walke in the shadowe of death. In which thy most blessed and sacred worde thou hast

71

FIGURE 70: Letter from Lord Burghley to the Earl of Shrewsbury 23 July 1609

This letter is the equivalent of the modern telephone call. It was not written by a professional scribe, though by a man well-used to writing. It shows a mixture of current hands, though based on the italic. After looking at so many writing masters' examples, it is as well to see the hand of an ordinary educated man in a hurry! Can you read it?

VICTORIA & ALBERT MUSEUM FORSTER MS.66 31 × 20

FIGURE 71: Esther Inglis: Summarie expositions upon sundrie notable sentences of the Olde Testament made in form of praiers last quarter of sixteenth century

Esther Inglis is one of the few known women calligraphers of the early period. Her family were Huguenot refugees who settled in Edinburgh, Scotland, where much of her work was done. In this tiny volume she has written her texts in a great variety of contemporary hands. She was of course working during the same period as William Shakespeare.

VICTORIA & ALBERT MUSEUM MS.L.3087–1960 8.5 × 6

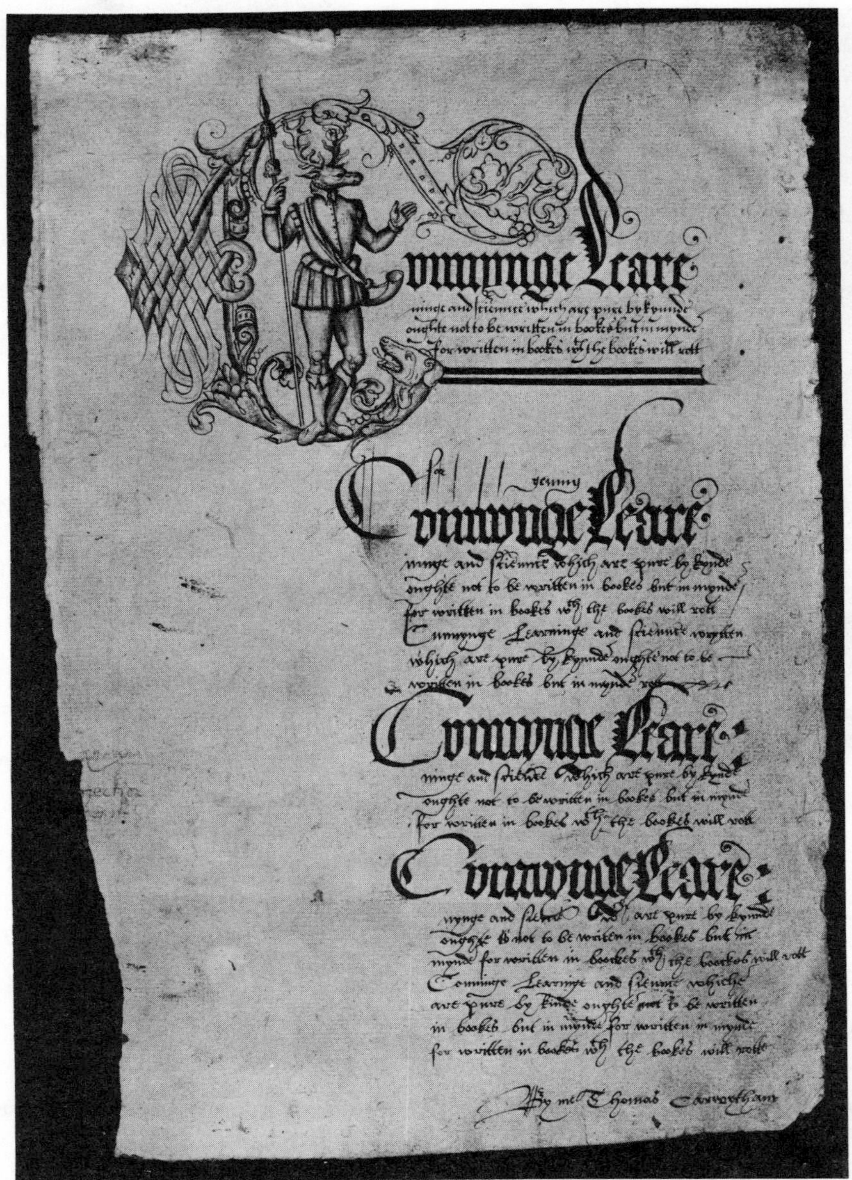

72

FIGURE 72: A writing master's copysheet c. 1600

The copysheet was to have a long life: in later days it was often something that the schoolchild took home to show off his or her progress. In this example, the master has written out the first section, and then the pupil has repeated it three times below—getting worse on each occasion! He has wisely not attempted to copy the beautifully drawn letter C, but he was obviously sufficiently proud of his efforts to sign his name at the bottom of the sheet "By me Thomas Carwytham."

VICTORIA & ALBERT MUSEUM MS.L.1482–1945 31 × 11.5

FIGURE 73: Richard Jackman: From a book of copies, mostly in legal hands 1620

There is no reason for including this example except the same one that gave rise to it in the first place—the sheer fun of it! It is found in a manuscript that probably belonged to a tutor or writing master in a private family, and it does provide an elegant example of an English italic hand at the beginning of the seventeenth century. Nothing is known about the manuscript except that it was found in one of the beams of Tangley Manor, in Surrey, England. How ever did it get there—and why?

VICTORIA & ALBERT MUSEUM MS.L.3051–1960 15 × 27

to write and name please is much. to please and not to write is paine then rather write and serve thy god then spende thie tyme in vaine. october 16. Anno Domini 1620.
tenn precepts coucht in this globes rounde fraime
all the worlde well to obserue the same

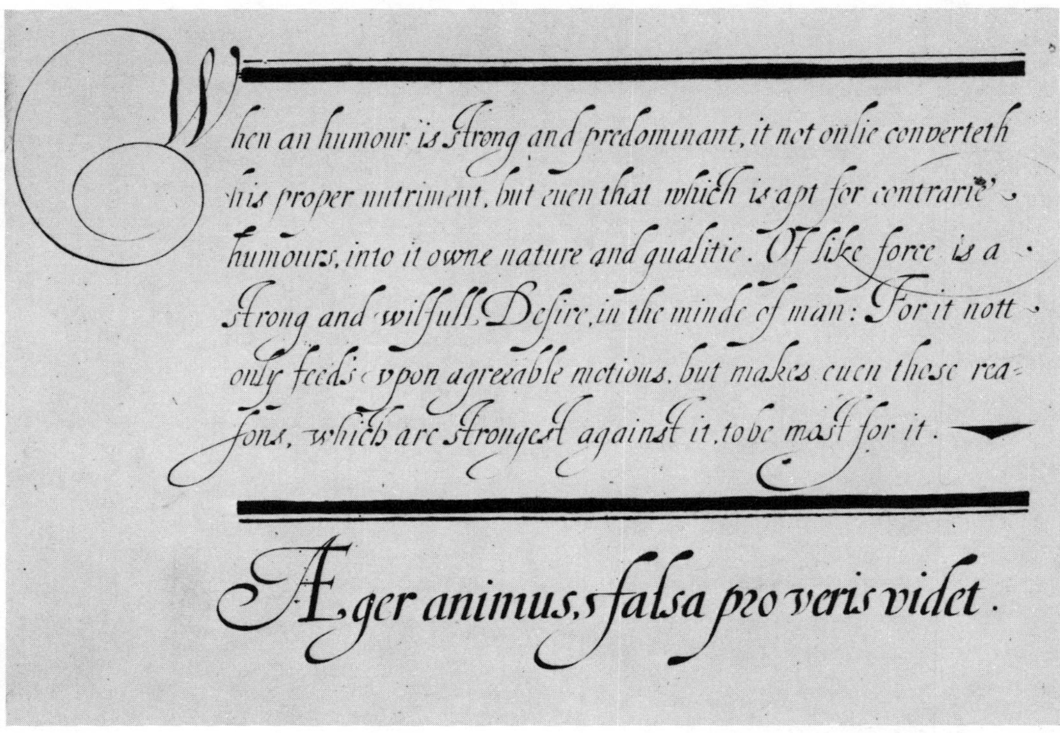

When an humour is strong and predominant, it not onlie converteth his proper nutriment, but euen that which is apt for contrarie humours, into it owne nature and qualitie. Of like force is a strong and wilfull Desire, in the minde of man: For it nott onlie feeds vpon agreeable motions, but makes euen those reasons, which are strongest against it, tobe most for it.

Æger animus, falsa pro veris videt.

FIGURE 74: Martin Billingsley: The pens excellencie; or, the secretaries delighte 1618

Martin Billingsley was noted for his Italian hand, of which this is an example. Sir Ambrose Heal considered his work to be the first English copybook of any pretension, and it contained a variety of styles besides the one shown here.

VICTORIA & ALBERT MUSEUM L.3061–1960 13×18

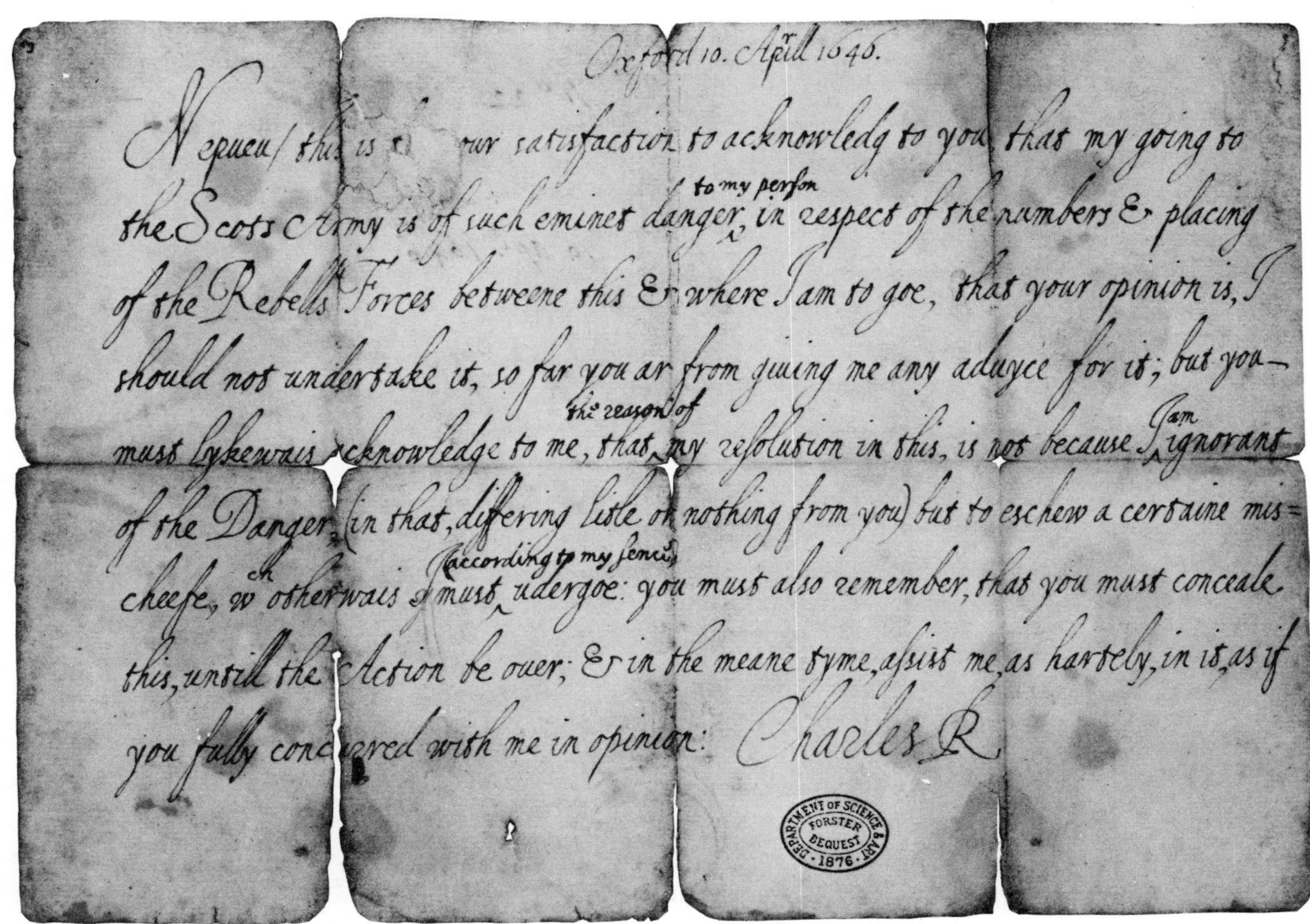

Oxford 10. April 1646.

Nepueu / this is to your satisfaction to acknowledg to you that my going to the Scots Army is of such eminet danger to my person, in respect of the numbers & placing of the Rebells Forces betweene this & where I am to goe, that your opinion is, I should not undertake it, so far you ar from giuing me any aduyce for it; but you must lykewais acknowledge to me, that the reason of my resolution in this, is not because I am ignorant of the Danger, (in that, differing litle or nothing from you) but to eschew a certaine mis=cheese, wch otherwais I must according to my sence undergoe: you must also remember, that you must conceale this, untill the Action be over; & in the meane tyme, asist me as hartely, in it, as if you fully concurred with me in opinion: Charles R.

FIGURE 75: King Charles I: Letter to his nephew Prince Rupert 1646

Although this is a letter from a royal hand, it is not in the least formal, being more in the nature of a hasty note. Charles I was taught writing when Prince of Wales by Martin Billingsley (Figure 74) whose copybook was dedicated to him. The writing is much easier to read than that of Lord Burghley (Figure 70) written thirty years earlier, and by an older man.

VICTORIA & ALBERT MUSEUM FORSTER MS.101

76

FIGURE 76: Edward Cocker: The pen's transcendencie; or faire writings labyrinth 1667

This is an example of exuberant virtuosity carried to extremes. Cocker was very proud of his ability, but it has little to do with writing, although he himself suggested that "Some may be drawn, as I was, by delight/ In apish fancies, and so learn to write." We note from this title page that Cocker was his own engraver, which was probably just as well!

VICTORIA & ALBERT MUSEUM L.3064–1960 18.5 × 26

FIGURE 77: Edward Cocker: Penna volans; or the young man's accomplishment 1661

Cocker could on occasions produce a quite simple style of writing, suitable for commercial use; but even here he felt the need for decoration. This over-elaborateness is very typical of the post-Restoration style in England, in furniture and costume just as in calligraphy.

VICTORIA & ALBERT MUSEUM L.3071–1960 18 × 25.5

FIGURE 78: Edward Cocker: Magnum in parvo; or, the pen's perfection 1672

This shows us the step-by-step method of producing those "curious knotts and flourishes" that were so characteristic of the late seventeenth-century writing masters. Try the letter for yourself!

VICTORIA & ALBERT MUSEUM L.114–1889 15 × 20

Barter is a Rule amongst Merchants wch
informes them in the Exchanging of one
Commoditie for another so to proportion
their Rates, as yt neither shall sustaine loss.
Aabbcddeæfgghhiijkklmnopp
qrzfsettt&c.
Edward Cocker
7

77

Since your ambition prompts you to Excellency in
the making of curious Knotts & Flourishes, I here
present you with a Method for the exact performing
of those belonging to Text Capitals.
1
2
3
4
5
6
7
1
2
3
Cocker

78

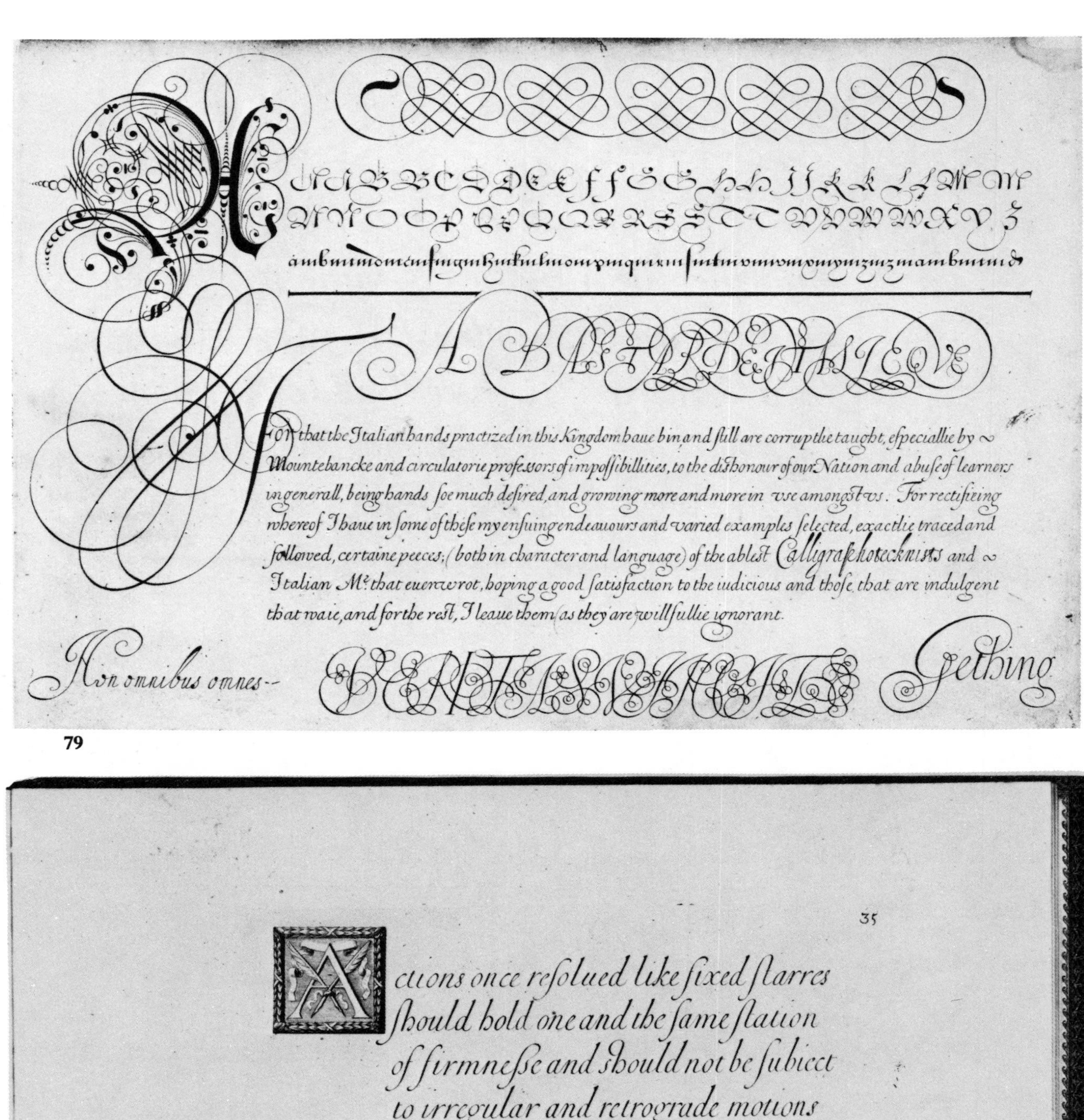

For that the Italian hands practized in this Kingdom haue bin, and still are corruptlie taught, especiallie by ~ Mountebancke and circulatorie professors of impossibillities, to the dishonour of our Nation and abuse of learners in generall, being hands soe much desired, and growing more and more in vse amongst vs. For rectifieing whereof I haue in some of these my ensuing endeauours and varied examples selected, exactlie traced and followed, certaine peeces; (both in character and language) of the ablest Calligraphotecknists and ~ Italian Mr. that euer wrot, hoping a good satisfaction to the iudicious and those that are indulgent that waie, and for the rest, I leaue them (as they are) willfullie ignorant.

Non omnibus omnes -- Gething

79

35

Actions once resolued like fixed starres should hold one and the same station of firmnesse and should not be subiect to irregular and retrograde motions

80

81

FIGURE 79: Richard Gething: Chiro-graphia; or, a book of copies containing sundrie examples 1645

Richard Gething was a somewhat austere practitioner in an age of baroque endeavor, and his examples are usually comparatively plain with few concessions to decoration. This example shows his "bastarde italique," *in which he makes a scathing attack on his rivals or less able "Calligraphotecknists" as he calls them!*

VICTORIA & ALBERT MUSEUM L.1898 19×29

FIGURE 80: Peter Gery: Gerii viri in arte scriptoria quondam celeberrimi opera c. 1667

Peter Gery's only known copybook was probably produced after his death, since he was apparently not satisfied with engraved results of his work. His style forms an austere contrast to that of his contemporaries, although even he felt the need for some attempt at decoration, albeit of a rather chaste kind.

VICTORIA & ALBERT MUSEUM L.3082–1960 21×32.5

FIGURE 81: John Stonestreet: Copybook 1688

This example is taken from a manuscript copybook, possibly the work of a pupil rather than a master. It is interesting because it shows the persistence of older styles of writing, since both the decorative initial and the "letter frisée" can be found in published copybooks of a century earlier.

VICTORIA & ALBERT MUSEUM MS.L.3052–1960 13×19.5

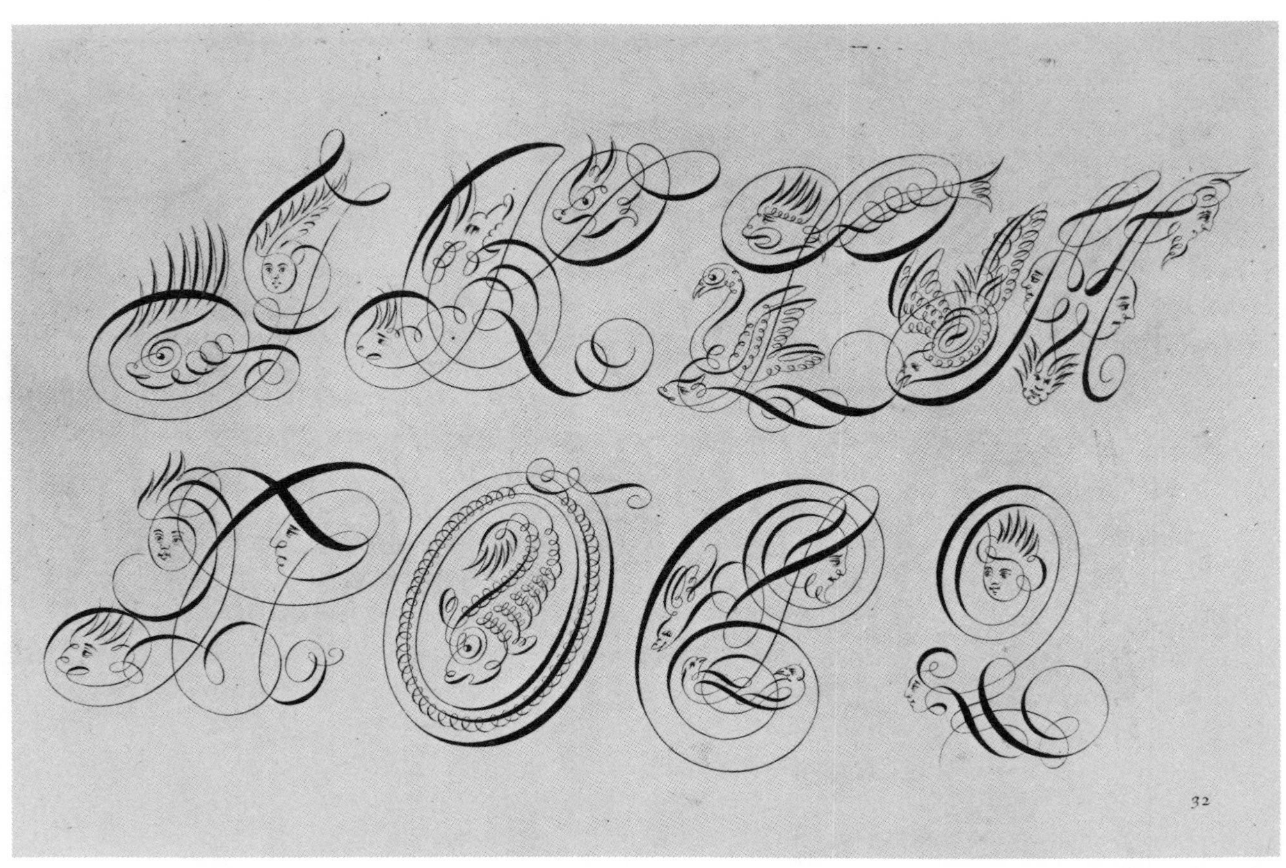

FIGURE 82: John Seddon: The pen-man's paradis, both pleasant & profitable 1695

This example of Seddon's work must surely come in the "pleasant" part of his title, because it can scarcely have been very "profitable" for the aspiring clerk! It comes at the end of the century, and although Seddon was highly regarded by his contemporaries, the future development of writing lay along quite different lines.

VICTORIA & ALBERT MUSEUM 11.iv.1872 34 × 22

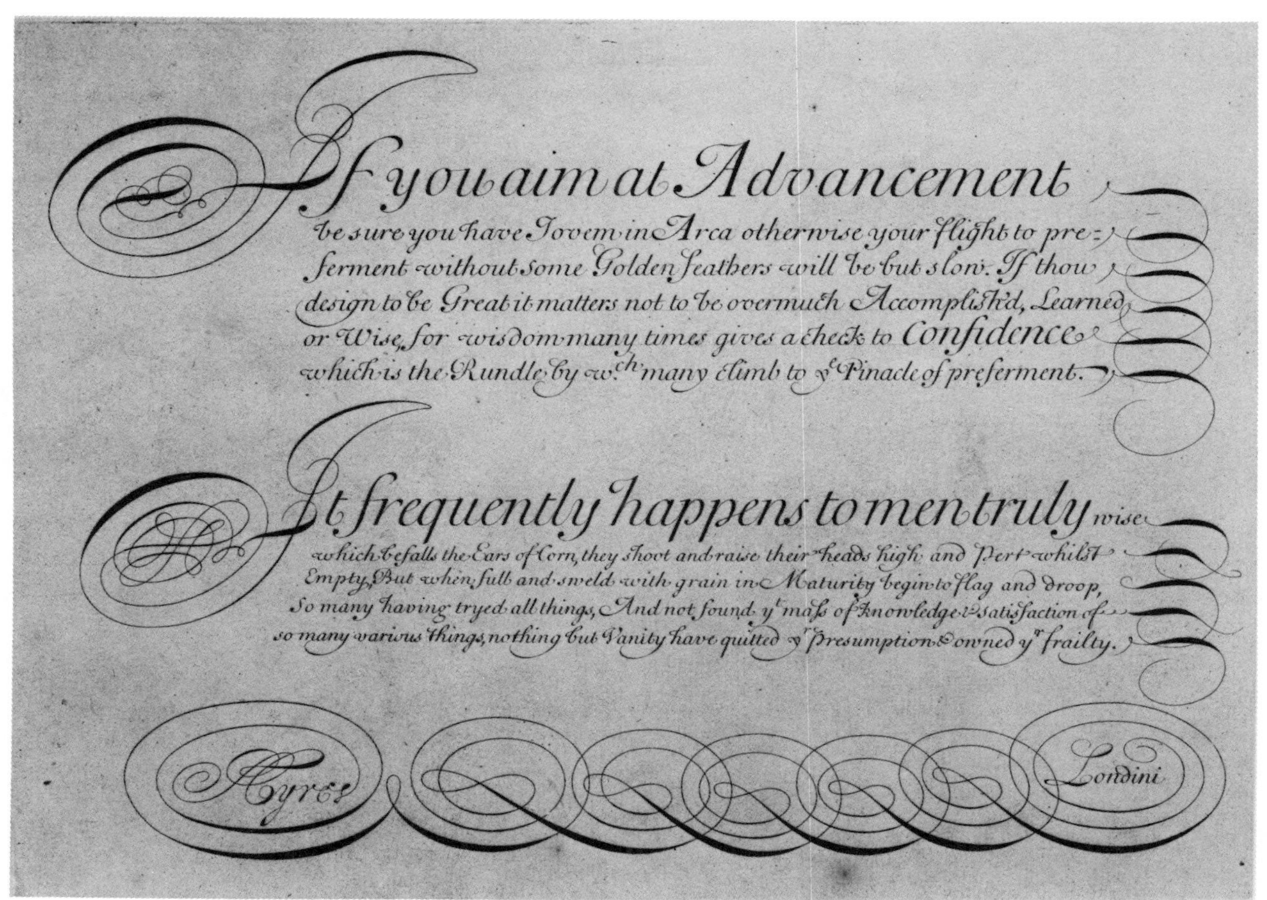

FIGURE 83: John Ayres: A tutor to penmanship; or, the writing master   1698

Samuel Pepys, the great diarist, was an admirer of the work of John Ayres and included a number of examples of his work in his own collection of calligraphy, the first such to be made in England. Ayres offers a much more businesslike hand, but he too still feels the need to embellish the form of his letters.

VICTORIA & ALBERT MUSEUM   L.1581–1880   25.5 × 41

Non belle faciam sed Juvat hoc facere
The happy Quills
Laureats write
Hinder y Birds but
raise y Poets
flight
To all kind Judges my Endeavors bow,
I'm not conceited but must faults allow:
Pray ben't too nice my Art is very young,
Then blast it not by a too rigid tongue.
Joseph Nutting
Sculp.t 1705

London printed for Rob.t Sayer at N.o 53 in Fleet Street. price 6.d

THE EIGHTEENTH AND NINETEENTH CENTURIES

THE eighteenth and nineteenth centuries in both Europe and America portray an end and a beginning. At the commencement of the eighteenth century there still survived something of the old exuberance and an insistence on the decorative aspect of handwriting. But by the end of the century, the demands of commerce had reduced most copybooks to the purveyors of three basic styles of round-hand writing, and one, a much simpler style, considered suitable for women. The nineteenth century saw the beginning of an antiquarian interest in the handwritten book among certain sections of the public, which was eventually to affect people like William Morris and lead, at the end of the century, to a revived interest in the art of fine writing, the results of which are happily very apparent today. The nineteenth century also witnessed the end of the supremacy of handwriting, a supremacy that it had enjoyed since the beginning of the Christian era. Now the invention of the typewriter and the telephone made possible other, less laborious, means of communication.

In the eighteenth century, writing had a very positive place in the school curriculum, and together with reading and arithmetic was firmly placed as one of the "three R's" at the head of every qualification required by employers. But the form of writing had become tediously regularized; a clear, quick hand was all that was required, and to obtain it the pupil spent wearisome hours practicing copies of monotonous uniformity. The various nations continued to produce handwriting that had certain idiosyncracies, but the

FIGURE 84: Calligraphy by John Dundas 1705

This extraordinary tour-de-force was written by John Dundas, Junior, and engraved by Joseph Nutting in 1705. Within the two roundels held by the angels are examples of microscopic writing; that on the left begins "Our Father. . . ." Can you make out the one on the right?

VICTORIA & ALBERT MUSEUM

English round-hand was the predominating model. The reason for this was the spread of British commerce throughout the globe, for with trade went the accounts and the bills of lading, all produced according to the English copybook method. Even in far away Russia, the English merchants brought their style of writing with them, and a copybook was produced for their clients in a country that would normally only use the Cyrillic alphabet. Copybooks had always included certain exotic alphabets, mainly to show off the masters' abilities, but now the inclusion of Arabic and Far Eastern alphabets had more point, as trade spread in ever-widening circles.

So for the most part writing was merely a matter of preparation for later life. But one charming result of this was the copysheet. This was produced in school as proof of progress, and taken home in triumph at the end of term; such sheets have survived in quite large numbers. They could be bought at stationers' shops, often with decorative borders within which the child wrote his copy. Frequently the pupil was expected to produce a great variety of scripts—a legacy from earlier centuries—even though he or she would never need to use such alphabets after leaving school. Today such writing sheets are desirable collectors' items. While in Britain there was an overall sameness about eighteenth- and nineteenth-century scripts, a greater variety existed in the United States because of the various countries from which the immigrants came, bringing with them their national styles. One of the most interesting expressions of this is to be found (and not only in writing of course) in the style known as "Pennsylvania Dutch" (Deutsch). The importation into America by German immigrants of the style of their homeland added a welcome variety to the monotonous level of competence elsewhere. For, as we have seen earlier, German-speaking lands tended to preserve "Fraktur" or "black letter" script long after it was abandoned in other countries in favor of Roman letters. It was this older style which the immigrants used for their documents, even as they used traditional motifs in the various artifacts produced in their new homeland. Good examples of this indigenous work are to be found in the Philadelphia Museum of Art, and are well-illustrated in several books on the subject.

In the British Isles, any variation from the standard copybooks tended to take an antiquarian form. In the late eighteenth century, under the influence of Horace Walpole (of Strawberry Hill fame) such interest inclined to the dilettante, but in the next century the interest in early manuscripts—and therefore early handwriting—became much more informed, and scholarly works on the subject were produced from the mid-century onwards. With the introduction about that time of commercially viable color printing, the general public could see for the first time what a medieval manuscript really looked like, and immediately desired to emulate the work of the old scribes and illuminators. As with the production of the early copybooks, when there was a demand it was soon supplied. So there appeared a series of manuals on how to imitate medieval manuscripts, both in decoration and script. But since it was recognized that not everyone was equally gifted, outline copies could be purchased by the less enterprising, who had only to fill in and color the existing pictures and text—rather like painting by numbers! There was a general interest in all things medieval during the middle decades of the nineteenth century, which resulted in (among other manifestations) such unlikely things as Gothic railway stations. But in spite of some of its absurdities, this interest did help to pave the way for a genuine interest in fine handwriting at the end of the century.

That interest emerged at the right time, since the introduction of universal primary school education in both Britain and America had meant that every child was now expected to be able to read and write. But inevitably the books provided for such schools took account of the fact that not every child was going to be able to write well, and so the copybooks were kept fairly basic—and dull. For many immigrants to the United States it was a question of first learning English, and then learning the American way of doing things. As a result, the business school was a great feature of the later nineteenth-century American scene. It taught all the skills the adult clerk was likely to need in his new land, and of course among such skills a good handwriting style was important. Handwriting has always been more stylized in the United States than in Britain, and is much more easily recognizable as a national style. In Britain, although at different periods certain styles have been popular with the majority of instructors, a considerable amount of latitude has been permitted to the individual teachers. This has led to greater variety in writing among English children (and adults) and was one reason for the ready spread of italic writing in more recent decades.

But perhaps the most remarkable influence on nineteenth-century writing on both sides of the Atlantic was the development of the steel pen. The metal pen was not a new invention; the Romans had had one, a gold or silver pen had been the reward for winners of writing competitions in the sixteenth century, and portable writing sets had sometimes included a metal pen. But the important fact about the nineteenth-century version was that it could be mass-produced to a regular standard of reliability. The quill pen had been in use for centuries. It was easily and cheaply obtained, and it could be cut to the shape desired by the individual user. In fact, it had to be repeatedly shaped, which was one of its great disadvantages. For the "neb," or writing point of the quill, quickly wore with use, and a pen knife for re-cutting the point was part of everyone's equipment. What was needed was a point that would not wear so easily, and metal was the obvious answer. But metal was quickly corroded by the type of ink then in use, and it was not until the invention of the aniline-based inks of the nineteenth century that this problem was overcome. The great step forward came when a method of mass-producing nibs from flat metal was first devised, and from then on the steel nib for use with the dip-pen rapidly superseded the old-fashioned quill, which had more or less disappeared by the middle of the century.

The new steel pen proved much more flexible than the old quill, and as a result the style of writing began to change. It was essentially, because of its cheapness, the pen provided for use in schools, so that it is in the school copybooks that we see the best examples of the new style. This showed itself especially in the emphasis given to the thick and thin strokes, particularly the looped ascenders and descenders, which were such a feature of "copperplate" writing. When carried to extremes, which it often was, the result was that the writing became difficult to read, as the thin strokes became so fine that they disappeared altogether! This was the style of writing that was widely taught in schools, and was therefore the commonest form of handwriting among most people until well into the twentieth century. The steel pen, was however, a great improvement for the writer, who no longer had to keep stopping to "mend" his pen, and there was an increasing variety of different-shaped nibs to suit most users. But the very ease with which it could be used, and the style of writing then current, all tended to make handwriting dull and often ill-formed. People began to feel that some kind of reform was needed. Urgent business matters could now be dealt with by the telephone or typewriter, so that it was to some extent personal hands that began to come under scrutiny. The time was ripe for a completely new approach to handwriting, and this was just what the twentieth century set out to provide.

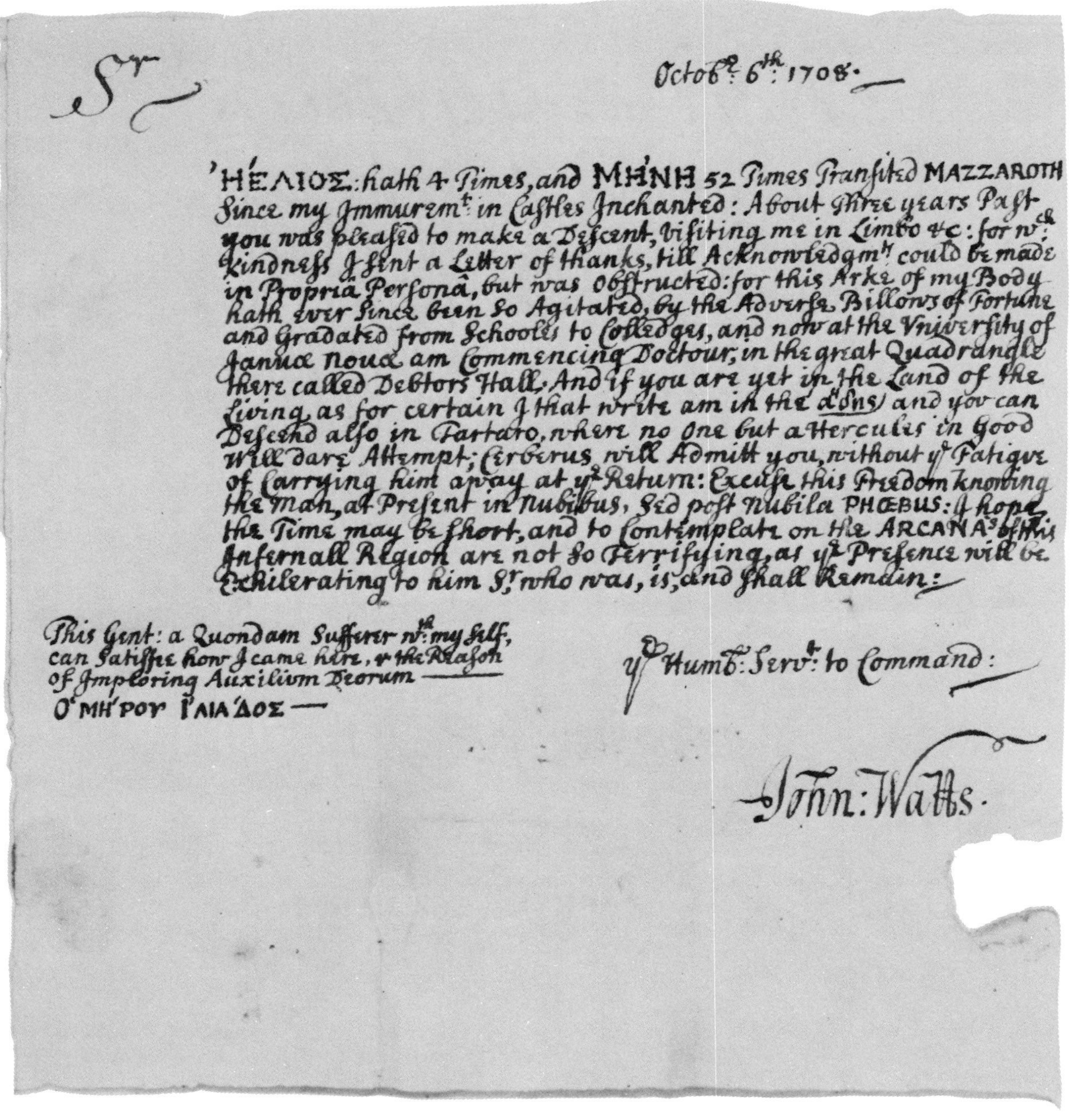

Sr

Octob.r 6th: 1708.

'ΗΈΛΙΟΣ: hath 4 Times, and ΜΗ'ΝΗ 52 Times Transited MAZZAROTH
Since my Immuremt. in Castles Inchanted: About Three years Past
you was pleased to make a Descent, visiting me in Limbo &c: for wch.
kindness I sent a Letter of thanks, till Acknowledgmt. could be made
in Propriâ Personâ, but was Obstructed: for this Arke of my Body
hath ever since been so Agitated, by the Adverse Billows of Fortune
and Gradated from Schooles to Colledges, and now at the University of
Januæ Nouæ am Commencing Doctour, in the great Quadrangle
there called Debtors Hall. And if you are yet in the Land of the
Living, as for certain I that write am in the ___ and you can
Descend also in Tartaro, where no One but a Herculis in Good
Will dare Attempt; Cerberus will Admitt you, without ye Fatigue
of Carrying him away at yr. Return: Excuse this Freedom knowing
the Man, at Present in Nubibus, Sed post Nubila PHŒBUS: I hope
the Time may be short, and to Contemplate on the ARCANA's of this
Infernall Region are not so Terrifying, as yr. Presence will be
Exhilerating to him Sr. who was, is, and shall Remain:

This Gent: a Quondam Sufferer wth. my Self,
can Satisfie how I came here, & the Reason
of Imploring Auxilium Deorum ———
Ο'ΜΗ'ΡΟΥ ΙΛΙΑ'ΔΟΣ ——

Yr Humb: Servt. to Command:

John: Watts.

FIGURE 85: Letter from John Watts to James Sotheby 6th October 1708

Watts was in Newgate Prison, London, and in this facetiously learned letter he is asking Sotheby (perhaps his patron) to come and bail him out! The letter is carefully written, and well set out on the page, and it makes an interesting comment on the formal teaching of handwriting to be found in contemporary copybooks.

VICTORIA & ALBERT MUSEUM MS.L.1768–1966 20 × 15

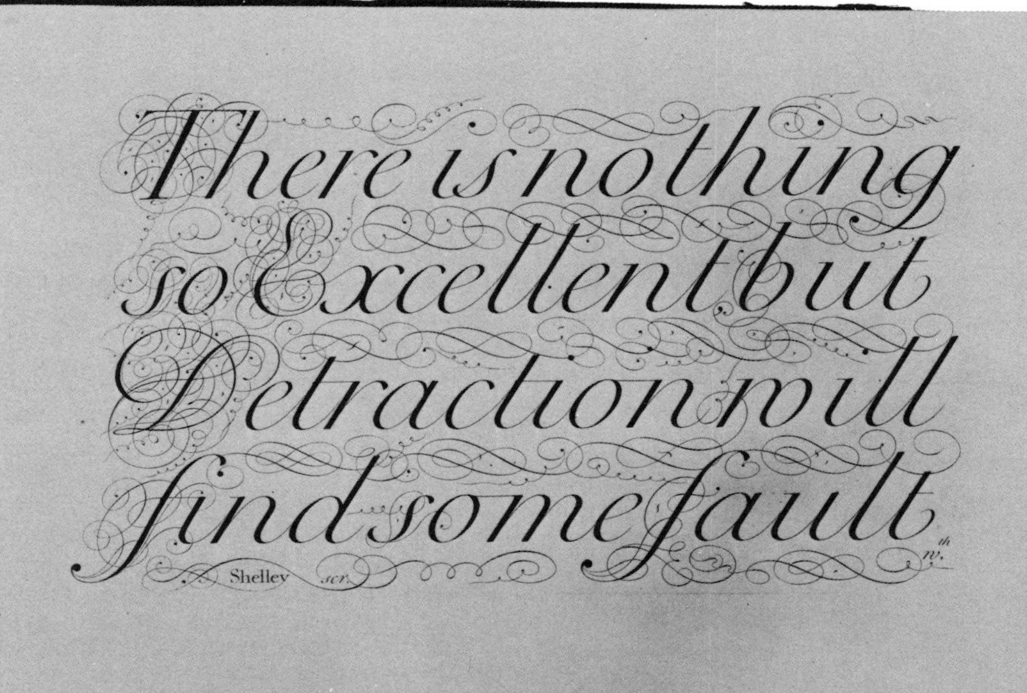

There is nothing
so Excellent but
Detraction will
find some fault
Shelley

86

TO
Mr Peter Monger
and
Mr John Cartlitch Senr.

Gentlemen,

Tho I hazard the Loss of Yor Favour by making Your Names Public, yet
I cannot Omit ye Opportunity of letting You know, that I shall ever
Retain a Grateful Remembrance of the Extraordinary Generosity, and
Genteel Treatment I met wth in my Teaching Yor Sons.
They're such Gentlemen as yor Selves yt Invigorate a Master's Endeavors &
to whome ye Worlds oblig'd for all ye Advances made in Penmanship

Sr
Yor most Obliged & Obedient Servt
G Shelley.

87

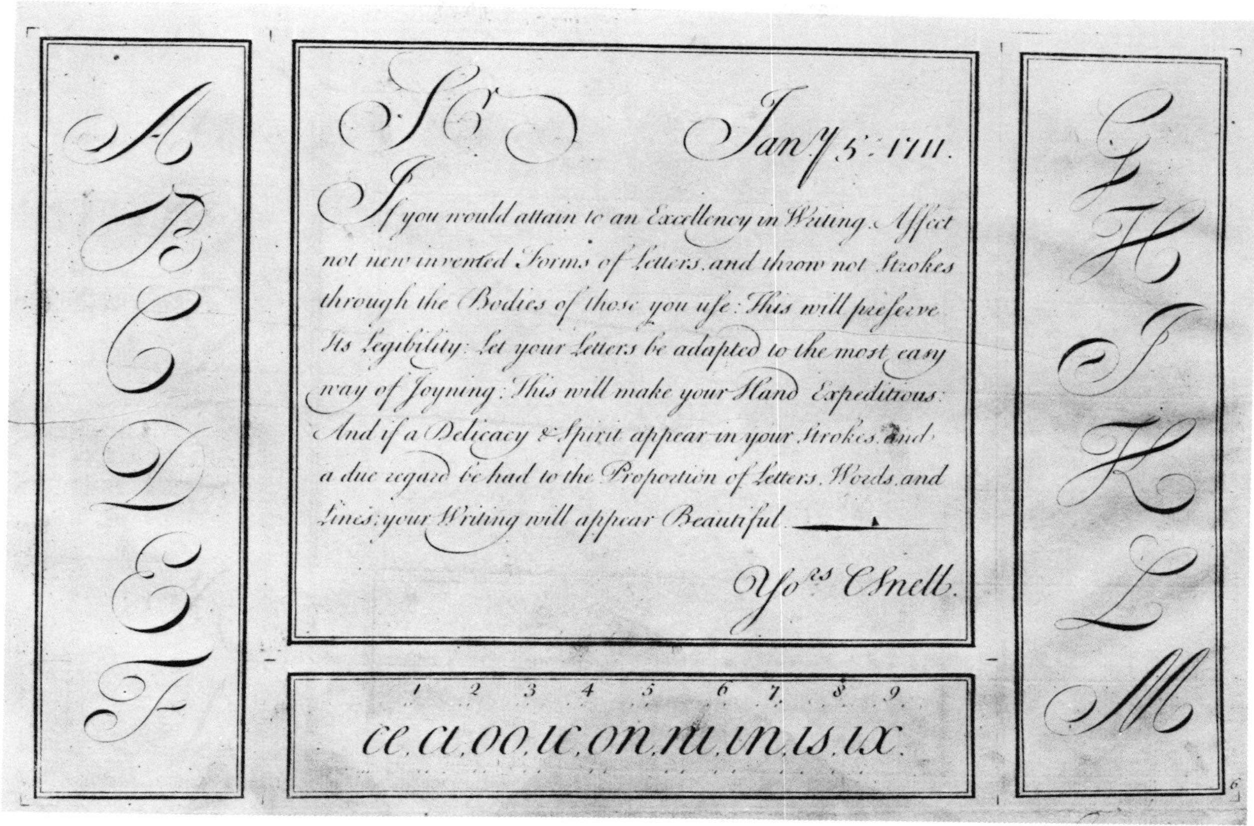

88

FIGURE 86: George Shelley: Natural writing in all the hands, with variety of ornament 1709

If we remove the underlying decoration on this page we are left with a good example of the plain round-hand, for which Shelley was famous. It was this simplified form of writing that was eventually to supplant all other hands in the course of the eighteenth century.

VICTORIA & ALBERT MUSEUM L.2035–1884 23 × 36

FIGURE 87: George Shelley: Penna volans, after ye English, French & Dutch way c. 1710

This example not only shows the student how to set out and word a formal letter, but it also manages to include a little self-advertisement, something to which most writing masters were especially prone. The title of the work indicates those countries whose scripts were considered especially important at this period.

VICTORIA & ALBERT MUSEUM L.537–1939 19.5 × 27.5

FIGURE 88: Charles Snell: The art of writing in its theory and practice 1712

The text of this letter should be read, since it shows the style of writing which Snell advocated in his copybook. He endeavored to formulate "standard rules" for making letters, and emphasized the importance of speed and legibility. But even he cannot avoid decorating his capital letters with a certain amount of flourishing, perhaps because it was suggested that those who opposed flourished letters did so because they were not competent to make them!

VICTORIA & ALBERT MUSEUM L.599–1879 23.5 × 34

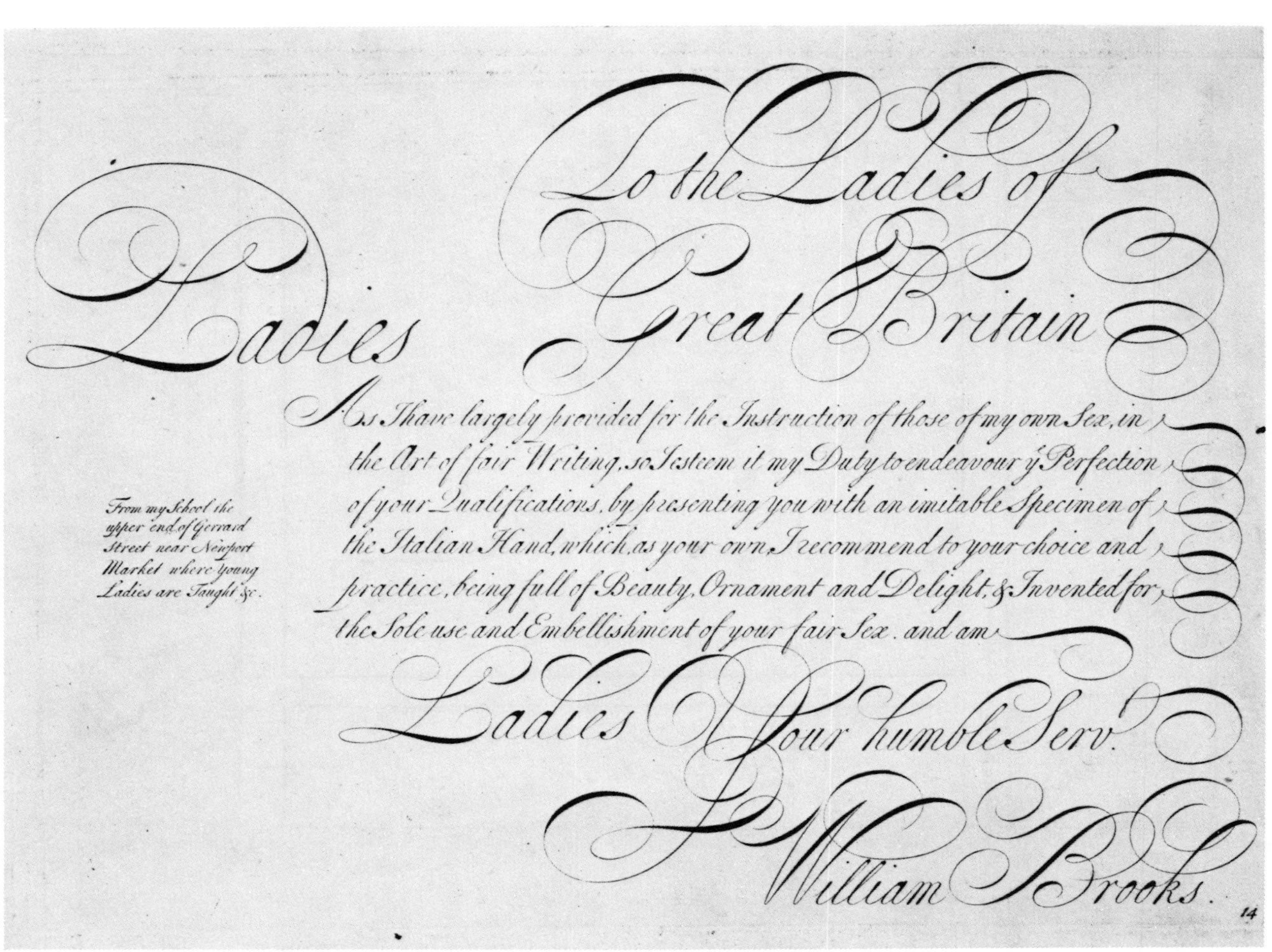

FIGURE 89: William Brooks: A delightful recreation for the industrious 1717

Throughout the seventeenth and eighteenth centuries, writing masters constantly advocated the Italian hand as being most suitable for ladies, because it was the easiest! At the beginning of the seventeenth century Martin Billingsley had written "they (having not the patience to take any great paines, besides fantastical and humorsome) must be taught that which they may easily learne . . . because their minds are (upon light occasion) easily drawn from the first resolution"!

VICTORIA & ALBERT MUSEUM L.1744–1922 23×36.5

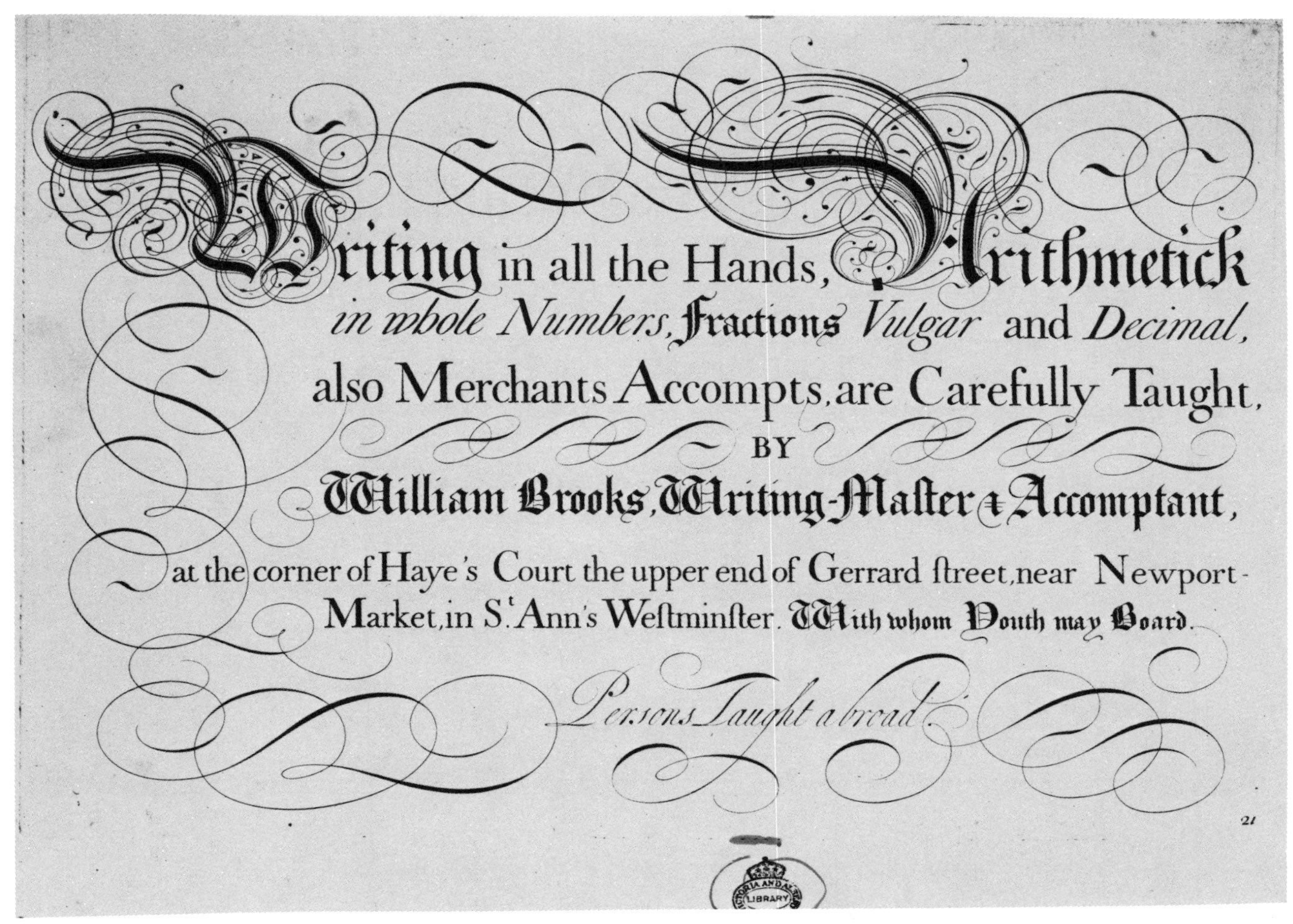

FIGURE 90: William Brooks: A delightful recreation for the industrious 1717

How many different scripts can you see in this advertisement which appeared in William Brooks's copybook? It is similar to many of the title pages of contemporary works, in that it acted as a form of self-advertisement for the master's skill. Many of these hands were unlikely to be of much use to his pupils by this date.

VICTORIA & ALBERT MUSEUM L.1744–1922 25 × 37

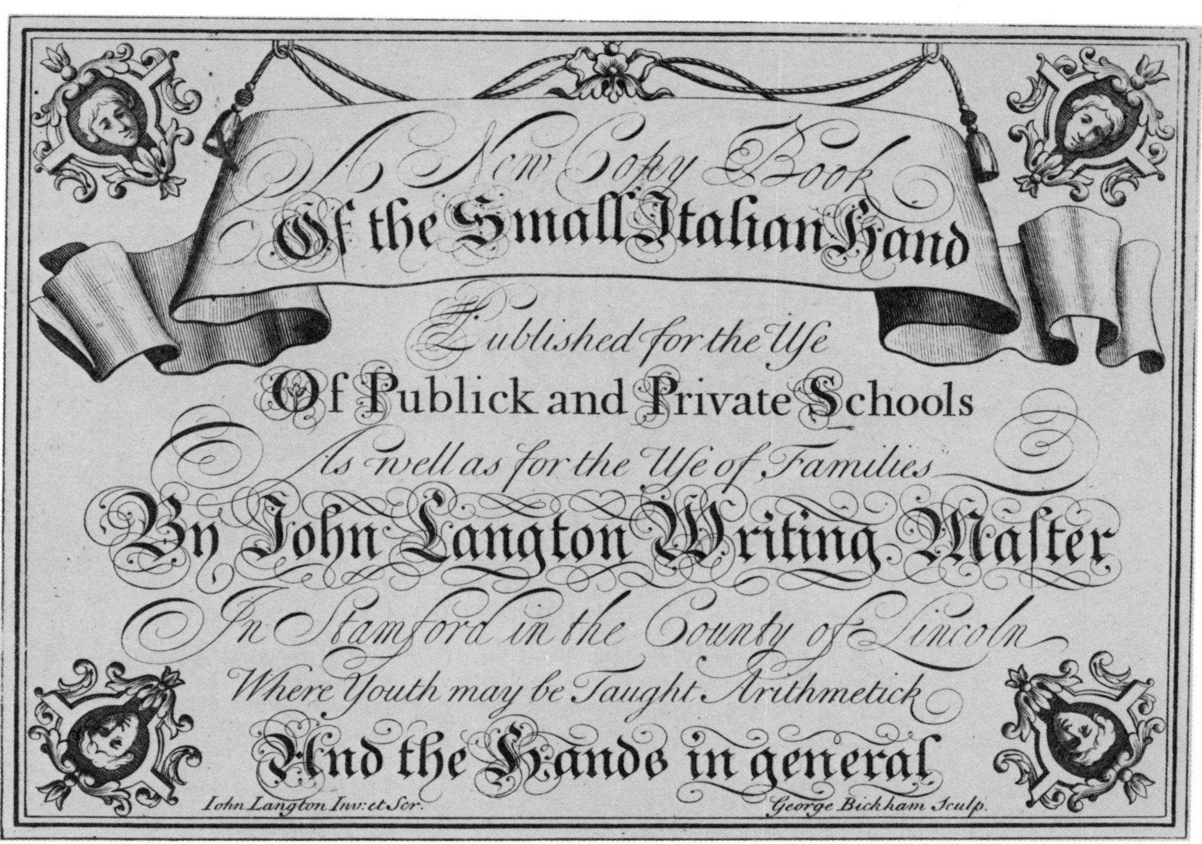

A New Copy Book
Of the Small Italian Hand
Published for the Use
Of Publick and Private Schools
As well as for the Use of Families
By John Langton Writing Master
In Stamford in the County of Lincoln
Where Youth may be Taught Arithmetick
And the Hands in general
John Langton Inv: et Scr.
George Bickham Sculp.

91

FIGURE 91: John Langton: A new copy book of the small Italian hand 1727

This title page should be compared with the advertisement of William Brooks; it serves exactly the same purpose, indicating to prospective pupils the scope of the work to be found within. Only legal clerks were likely to really need to write "Gothic" or "black letter" script at this date.

VICTORIA & ALBERT MUSEUM L.1397–1922 19×31

FIGURES 92, 93, & 94: George Bickham: The universal penman 1743

This work, which appeared almost in the middle of the eighteenth century, was one of the most important copybooks to be issued, and one of the largest. It was a folio volume with 212 plates, written and engraved by some of the best writing masters and engravers of the day. A great variety of scripts were included, but business hands predominated. Bickham engraved many of the plates himself, but he was also a good calligrapher. In addition to the variety of the calligraphy, the volume is also adorned with genre scenes and a wealth of rococo decoration, which combine to make it a magnificent and attractive book. The first example, shown here, is both written and engraved by the compiler, George Bickham.

VICTORIA & ALBERT MUSEUM 39×26

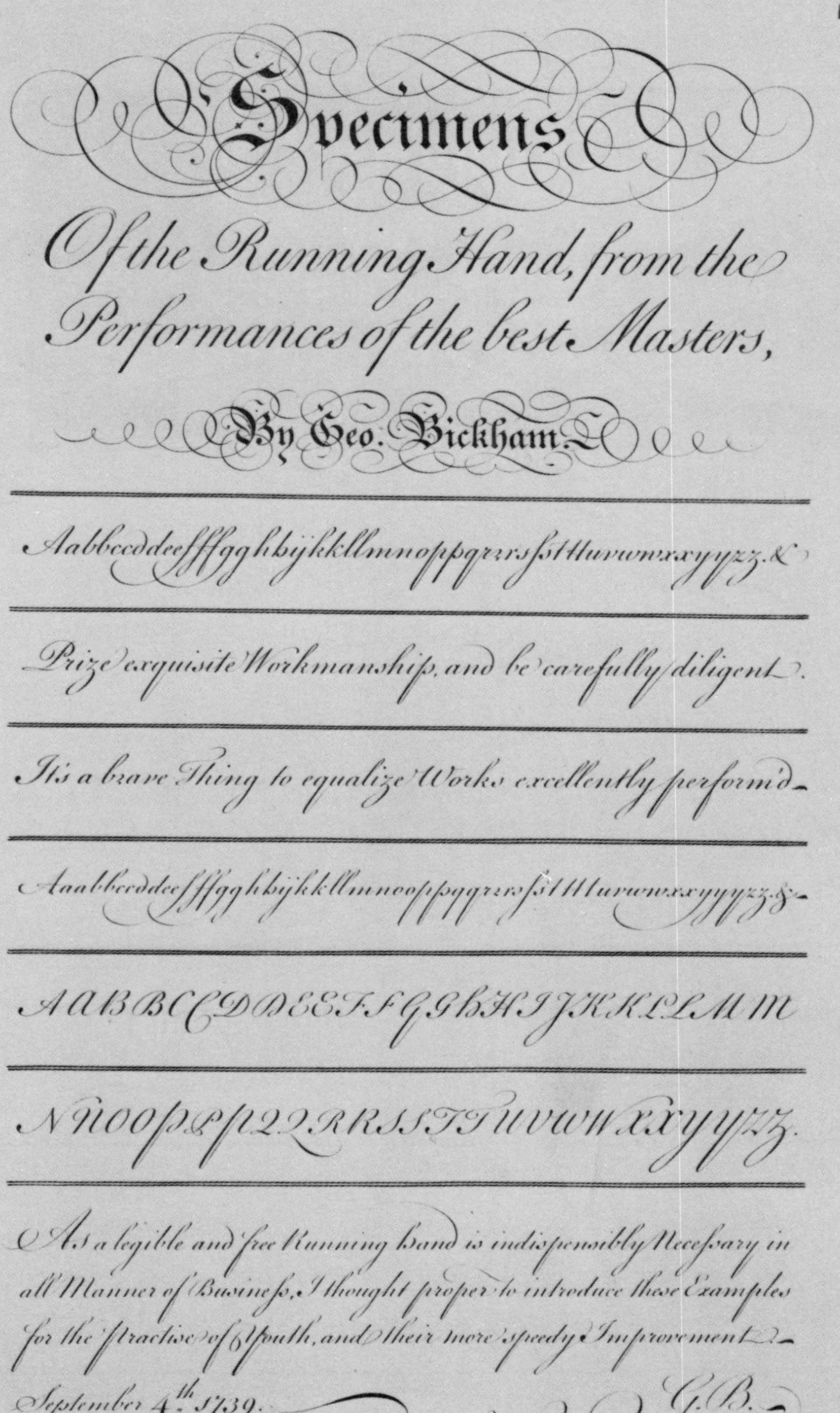
163

Specimens

Of the Running Hand, from the Performances of the best Masters,

By Geo. Bickham.

Aabbccddeefffgghhbijkkllmnoppqrrsſsttuvwxxyyzz.&

Prize exquisite Workmanship, and be carefully diligent.

It's a brave Thing to equalize Works excellently perform'd.

Aaabbccddeefffgghhbijkkllmnooppqqrrsſsttuvwxxyyzz.&

A A B B C C D D E E F F G G H H I J K K L L M M

N N O O P P Q Q R R S S T T U V W W X X Y Y Z Z.

As a legible and free Running hand is indispensibly Necessary in all Manner of Business, I thought proper to introduce these Examples for the Practise of Youth, and their more speedy Improvement.

September 4th 1739. G.B.

The Good Samaritan. 40

Good-Nature is the Foundation of all Virtues, either Religious or Civil; Good-Nature, which is Friendship between Man and Man, good Breeding in Courts, Charity in Religion and the true Spring of all Beneficence in General.

Good-Nature and good Sense must ever join;
To err is Human, to Forgive, Divine.

Good Sense and Good-Nature are never separated, tho' the ignorant World has thought otherwise; Good-Nature, by which I mean Beneficence and Candor, is the Product of right Reason, which of necessity will give allowance to the Failings of others, by considering that there is nothing perfect in Mankind.

93

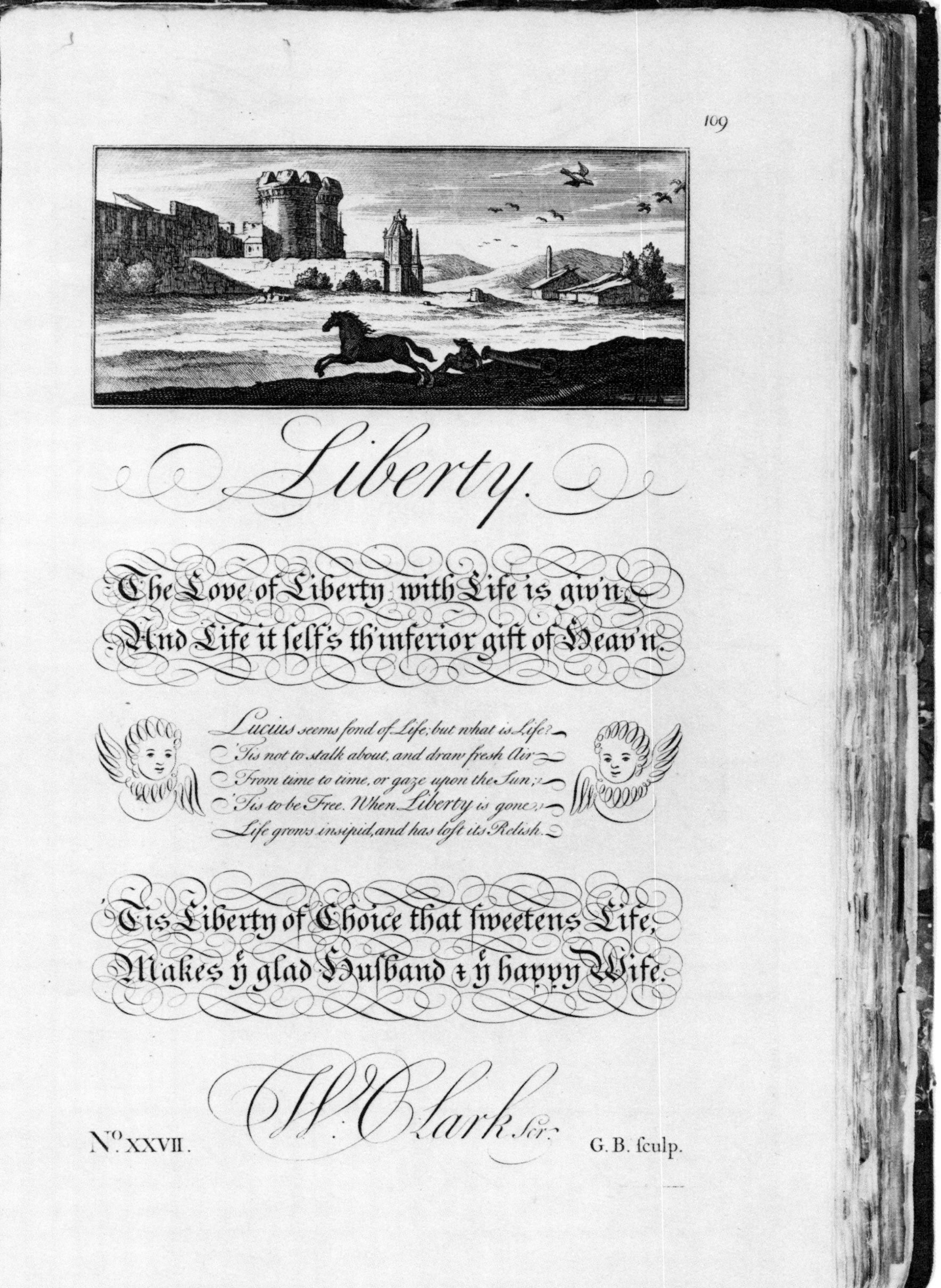
109
Liberty.
The Love of Liberty with Life is giv'n,
And Life it self's th'inferior gift of Heav'n.
Lucius seems fond of Life; but what is Life?
'Tis not to stalk about, and draw fresh Air
From time to time, or gaze upon the Sun;
'Tis to be Free. When Liberty is gone
Life grows insipid, and has lost its Relish.
'Tis Liberty of Choice that sweetens Life,
Makes y^{e} glad Husband & y^{e} happy Wife.
W. Clark Scr.
N°. XXVII.
G. B. sculp.

94

152

THE

RECEIPT.

TO

Mrs. Biddy Floyd.

When Cupid did his Grandsire Jove entreat
To form some Beauty by a New Receipt;
Jove sent and found, Far in a Country Scene,
Truth, Innocence, Good-Nature, Look serene:
From which Ingredients, first the dextrous Boy
Pick'd the Demure, the Aukward, and the Coy:
The Graces from the Court did next Provide
Breeding, and Wit, and Air, and decent Pride:
These Venus cleans'd from ev'ry spurious Grain
Of Nice, Coquet, Affected, Pert, and Vain.
Jove mix'd up all, and his best Clay employ'd;
Then call'd the happy Composition Floyd.

J. Champion Script. St. Paul's Church-yard, LONDON.

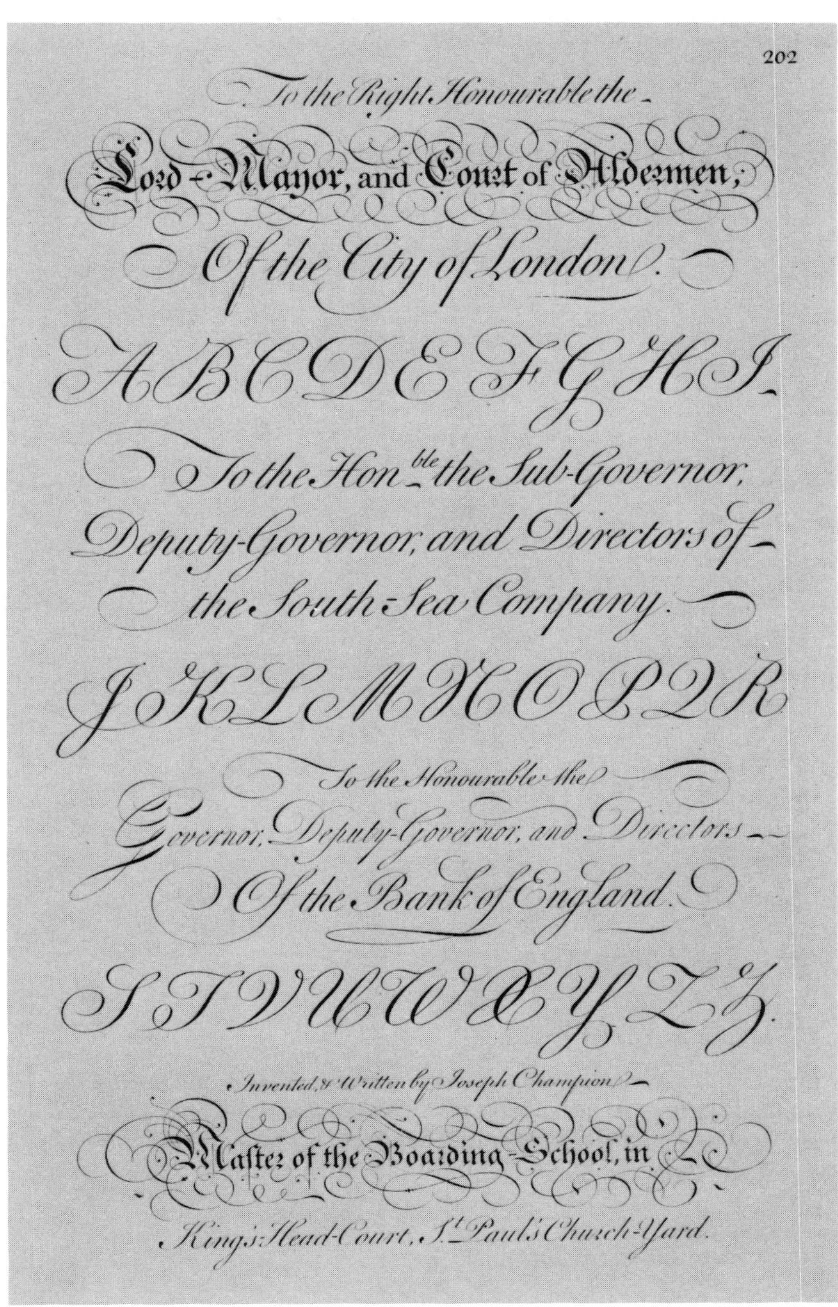

96

FIGURES 95 & 96: George Bickham: The universal penman 1743

These two plates are by Joseph Champion, who was probably the most important contributor to Bickham's work. Between them they show a variety of scripts, most of which are fairly plain, except for the capital letters and headings. They clearly show the future development of handwriting.

VICTORIA & ALBERT MUSEUM 39×26

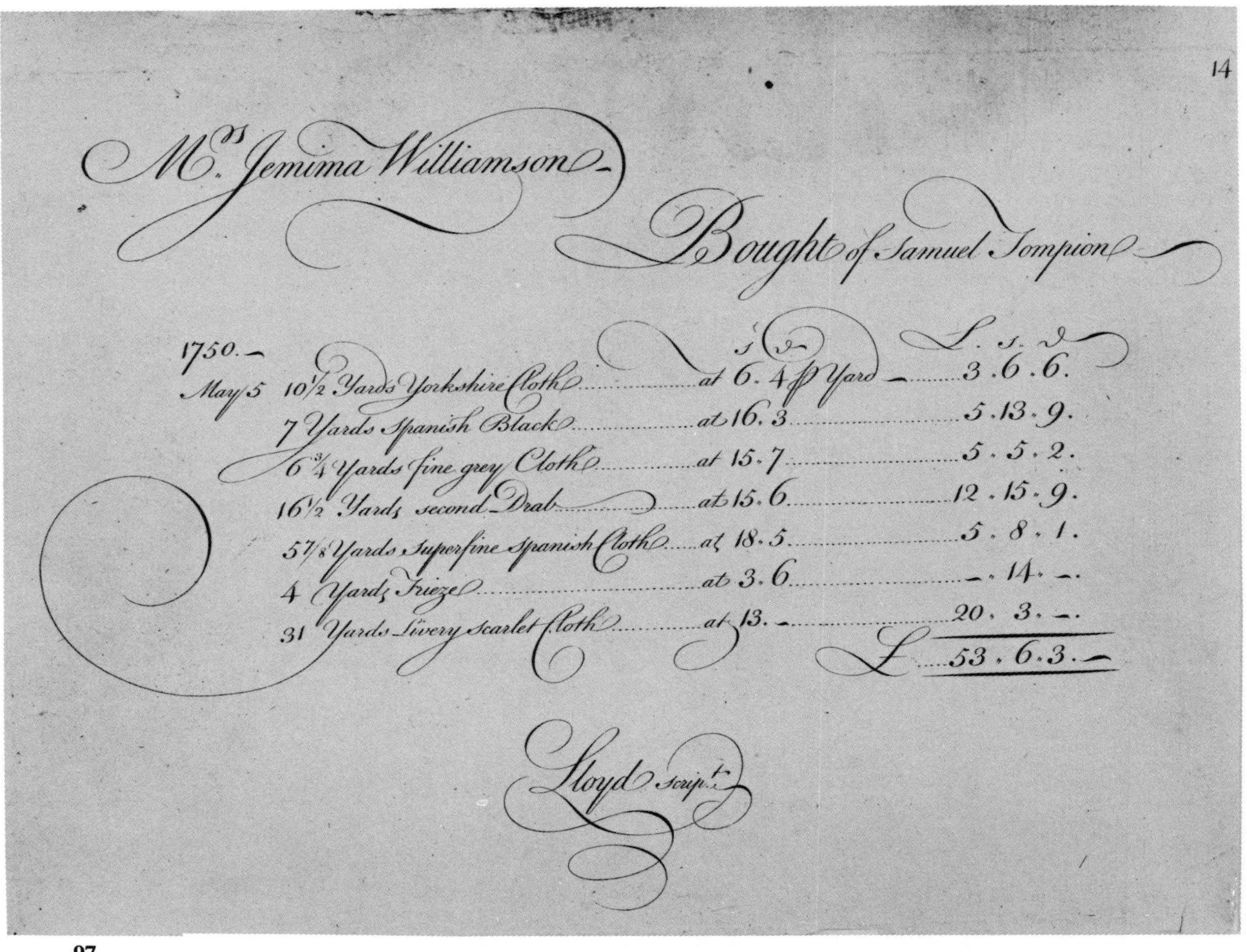

14

Mrs Jemima Williamson

Bought of Samuel Tompion

			£. s. d.
1750.		s. d.	
May 5	10½ Yards Yorkshire Cloth	at 6. 4 ℔ Yard	3 . 6 . 6.
	7 Yards Spanish Black	at 16. 3	5 . 13 . 9.
	6¾ Yards fine grey Cloth	at 15. 7	5 . 5 . 2.
	16½ Yards second Drab	at 15. 6	12 . 15 . 9.
	5⅞ Yards Superfine Spanish Cloth	at 18. 5	5 . 8 . 1.
	4 Yards Frieze	at 3. 6	— . 14 . —
	31 Yards Livery Scarlet Cloth	at 13. —	20 . 3 . —
		£	53 . 6 . 3 . —

Lloyd Script.

97

FIGURE 97: Edward Lloyd: The young merchant's assistant 1751

The title tells us what we may expect in this work, and the example illustrated shows us the English round-hand put to use for business affairs. It was the ubiquity of the English trader that carried such bills throughout the world, and so made familiar the style of handwriting in which they were written.

VICTORIA & ALBERT MUSEUM L.534–1939 23.5 × 37

FIGURE 98: Duncan Smith: The academical instructor 1794

We have come a long way since the flamboyant titles of the seventeenth century, and the writing is equally prosaic, though no doubt much more practical. This illustration shows the weakness inherent in the style, with its emphasis on the contrast between the thick and thin strokes. Carried to excess, the words could become almost illegible.

VICTORIA & ALBERT MUSEUM L.539–1939 23 × 29

Avoid bad companions. d.

Beware of ostentation. w

Confine your paſsions. ma

Deride no infirmities. ak.

Endeavour to improve. m,

Fear attends the guilty. m,

18

Mr. Walter Smith,

Bought of Samuel Fringham 7. Aug. 1774.

12 Yards of Broad Cloth	at 17.9 ℘ Yd.	£10.13.0
9 Yards of Black Cloth	at 15.6	6.19.6
10 Yards of Shalloon	at 1.5	0.14.2
15 Yards of Serge	at 2.4	1.15.0
7 Yards of Frieze	at 5.4	1.17.4
12 Yards of Scarlet	at 19.6	11.14.0
		£ 33.13.0

99

FIGURE 99: Joseph Webb: Useful penmanship 1796

By the end of the eighteenth century we see the type of script which alone had survived from those in use at the beginning of the century. The plain simple hand of business is here used to show the young clerk how he should set out his invoice.

VICTORIA & ALBERT MUSEUM L.542–1939 20×29

FIGURE 100: William Mate: Copysheet 1856

Copysheets were popular in England and in the United States. They enabled pupils to show the progress they had made in their writing, and were no doubt taken home in triumph at the end of term. This example is dated "Christmas AD 1856," and William Mate had every reason to be proud of his virtuosity. But the result is so like an engraving that careful inspection of the original is necessary in order to be sure that it has been written out by hand!

VICTORIA & ALBERT MUSEUM MS.E.847–1951

OUR
FATHER
which art in
HEAVEN,
HALLOWED BE THY
NAME
Thy Kingdom come. THY WILL be done in Earth, as
it is in
HEAVEN.
Give us this
Day our daily
BREAD
And forgive us our
TRESPASSES,
as we forgive them
that trespaſs against us.
And lead us not
into Temptation:
but deliver us
from Evil:
For thine is the Kingdom,
the Power, and the Glory,
FOR
EVER.
AMEN!

THE TEN COMMANDMENTS.

2nd
Thou ſhalt not make to thyſelf any graven IMAGE, nor the likeneſs of any thing that is in Heaven.&c&c.

1st
THOU shalt have no other GODS before ME. EXODUS Ch. XX. Ver 3.

6th
THOU ſhalt do no MURDER.

3rd
Thou ſhalt not take the Name of the LORD thy GOD in vain. &c.&c.

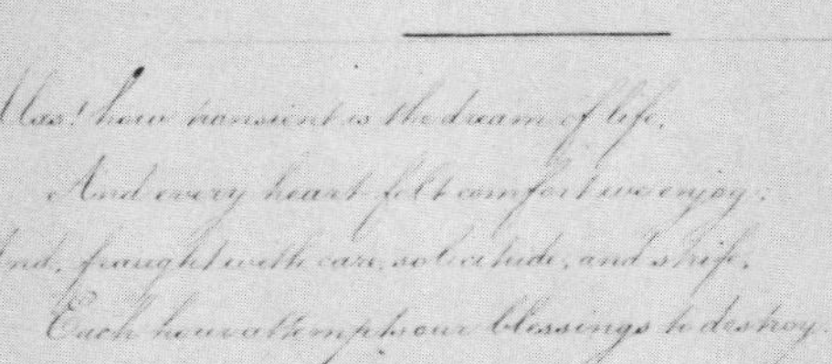

TIME and ETERNITY.

Alas! how transient is the dream of life,
And every heart-felt comfort we enjoy;
And, fraught with care, solicitude, and strife,
Each hour attempts our blessings to destroy.
All human scenes are subject to decay,
And time asserts an all-prevailing power;
Expanding beauties to the morning's ray,
We bloom to wither, as the tender flower.

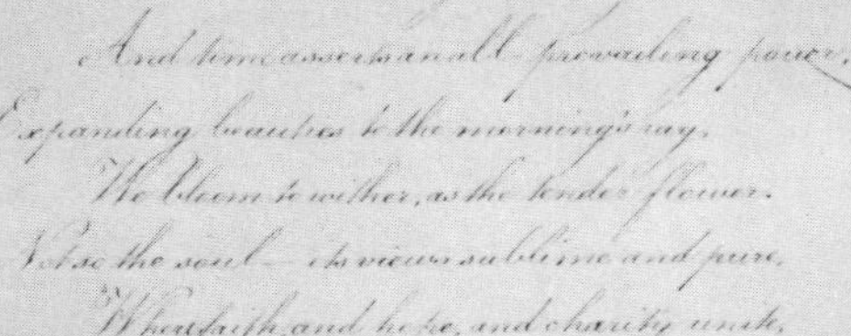

Not so the soul—its views sublime and pure,
Where faith, and hope, and charity unite,
Shall rise, and dwell eternally secure,
In heaven's unfading mansions of delight.

7th
THOU ſhalt not commit ADULTERY.

4th
Remember that thou keep holy the Sabbath-Day. Six days ſhalt thou Labour. &c.&c.

8th
THOU ſhalt not STEAL.

Our best friends are those who tell us of our faults, and teach us how to correct them.

Joseph Crosfield Junior;
11th of 12th month 1812.

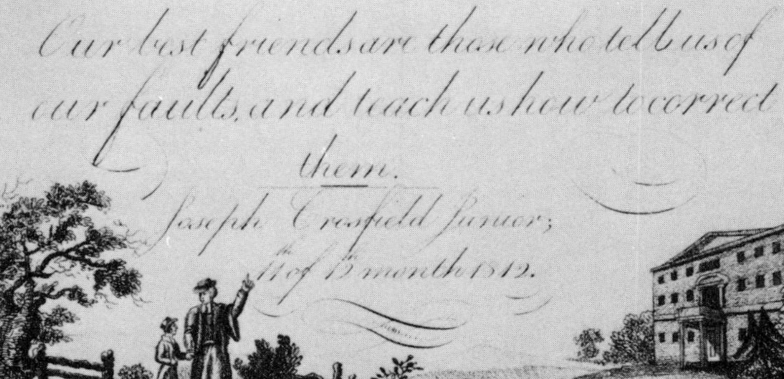

5th
Honour thy FATHER & thy MOTHER, that thy Days may be long in the Land which the LORD thy GOD giveth unto thee.

10th
Thou ſhalt not covet Thy Neighbour's House. &c.

9th
Thou ſhalt not bear falſe witneſs againſt thy NEIGHBOUR.

London. Published by R. Harrild. 20. Great Eastcheap.

FIGURE 101: Joseph Crosfield: Copysheet 1812

Earlier in date than the previous copysheet, this example is more elaborate in one way, since it was obviously bought from a stationer's with the border decoration depicting the Ten Commandments already printed. Joseph Crosfield had only to write out his piece in the middle, which he has done quite elegantly.

VICTORIA & ALBERT MUSEUM
MS.L.2534–1979

FIGURE 102: Cassell's Popular Educator, vol. II 1853

This example is very typical of its period and place, for it appeared in a journal whose aim was to assist those whose education had been inadequate—very much in line with mid-nineteenth century self-help ideas. The three most useful styles of handwriting are offered here.

VICTORIA & ALBERT MUSEUM
27.5×19

FIGURE 103: Moffatt & Paige: Moffatt's copybook 1890

This type of rather soulless copybook was typical of the late nineteenth century and early twentieth century, in both England and America. The repetition of examples does not necessarily lead to improved writing but more likely encourages boredom!

VICTORIA & ALBERT MUSEUM
17×21

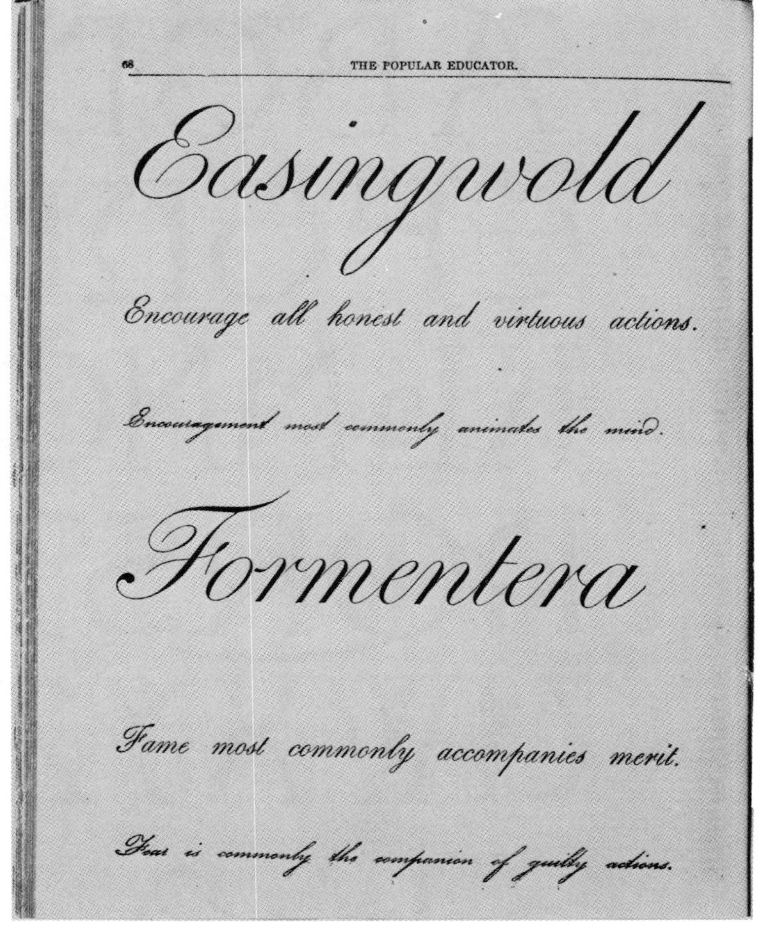

68 THE POPULAR EDUCATOR.

Easingwold

Encourage all honest and virtuous actions.

Encouragement most commonly animates the mind.

Formentera

Fame most commonly accompanies merit.

Fear is commonly the companion of guilty actions.

Ottawa possesses rich pine forests. O

Puma is a native of tropical America

103

ABCD
EFGHIJ
KLMNO
PQRST
UWXYZ

abcde
fghijk
lmnop
qrstuv
wxy
z

104

FIGURE 104: Lewis F. Day: Alphabets old and new [etc.]. 1898

This collection of alphabets included one by the artist and book illustrator Walter Crane, who was greatly influenced by the Art Nouveau style of the period. Recent years have seen a renewed interest in this type of lettering.

VICTORIA & ALBERT MUSEUM
L1195–1899 18.5 × 12.5

FIGURE 105: Owen Jones: The Victoria Psalter 1861

This is one of the original manuscript designs for the Victoria Psalter that was dedicated to Queen Victoria. The middle of the nineteenth century saw a revival of interest in all things medieval, from the design of railway stations and town halls to books like this one. Owen Jones is known to have possessed a medieval Psalter (now in the Victoria and Albert Museum, London), and it is interesting to see how he has transformed the medieval style into an essentially neo-Gothic mid-nineteenth century one.

VICTORIA & ALBERT MUSEUM MS.L.462–1952

108

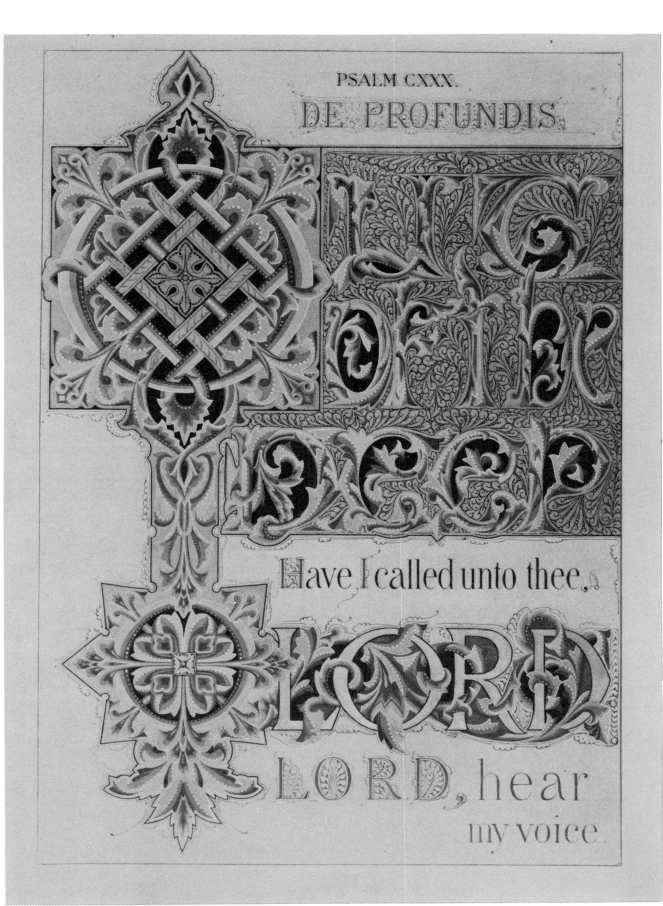

PSALM CXXX.
DE PROFUNDIS
Have I called unto thee,
LORD
LORD, hear
my voice.

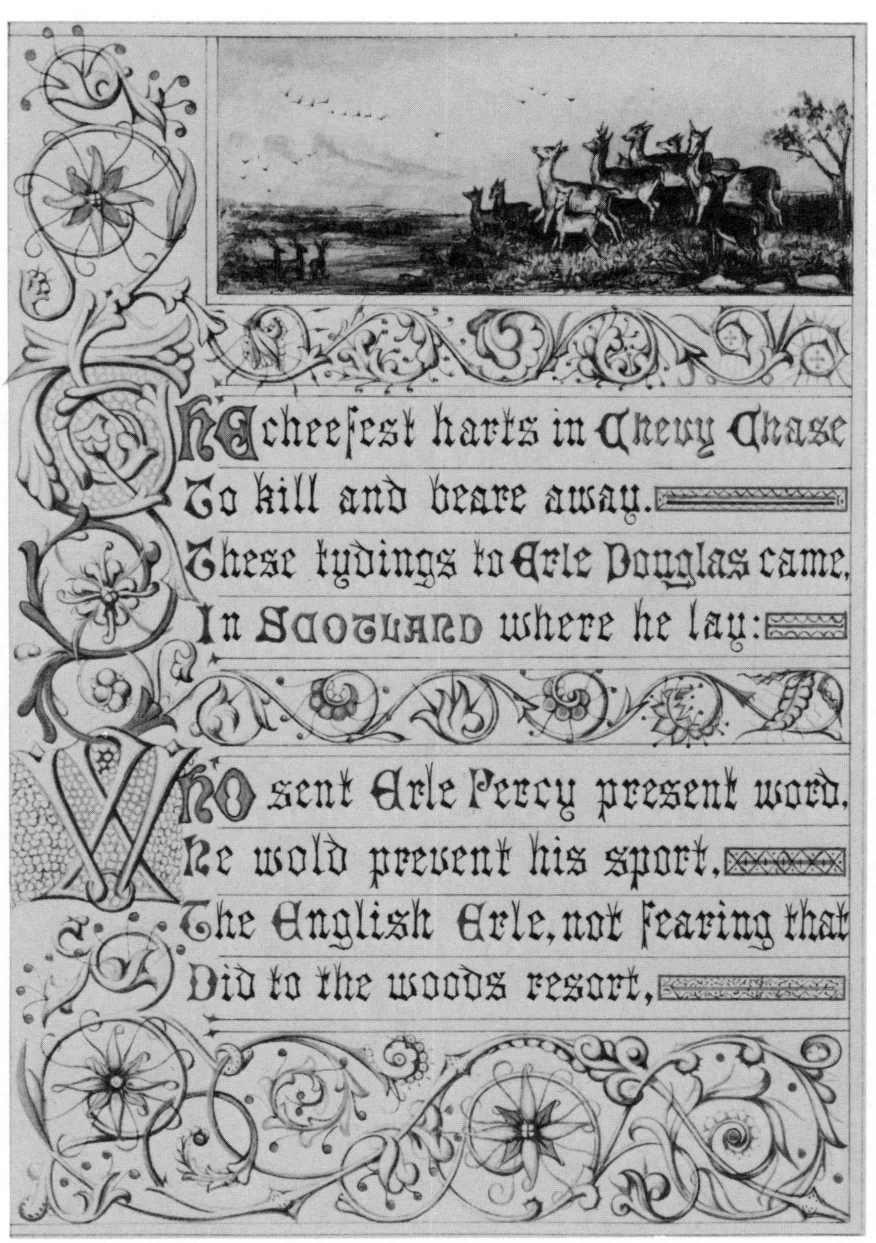

The cheefest harts in Chevy Chase
To kill and beare away.
These tydings to Erle Douglas came,
In Scotland where he lay:
Who sent Erle Percy present word,
He wold prevent his sport.
The English Erle, not fearing that
Did to the woods resort,

106

FIGURE 106: Chevy Chase: a ballad. Illustrated and illuminated by James Douglas 1865

A further example of the revived interest in things medieval, probably done by a gifted amateur using a metal pen rather than a quill, which makes the script look more "Gothic" than medieval writing ever did!

VICTORIA & ALBERT MUSEUM MS.L.4150-1971 25 × 20

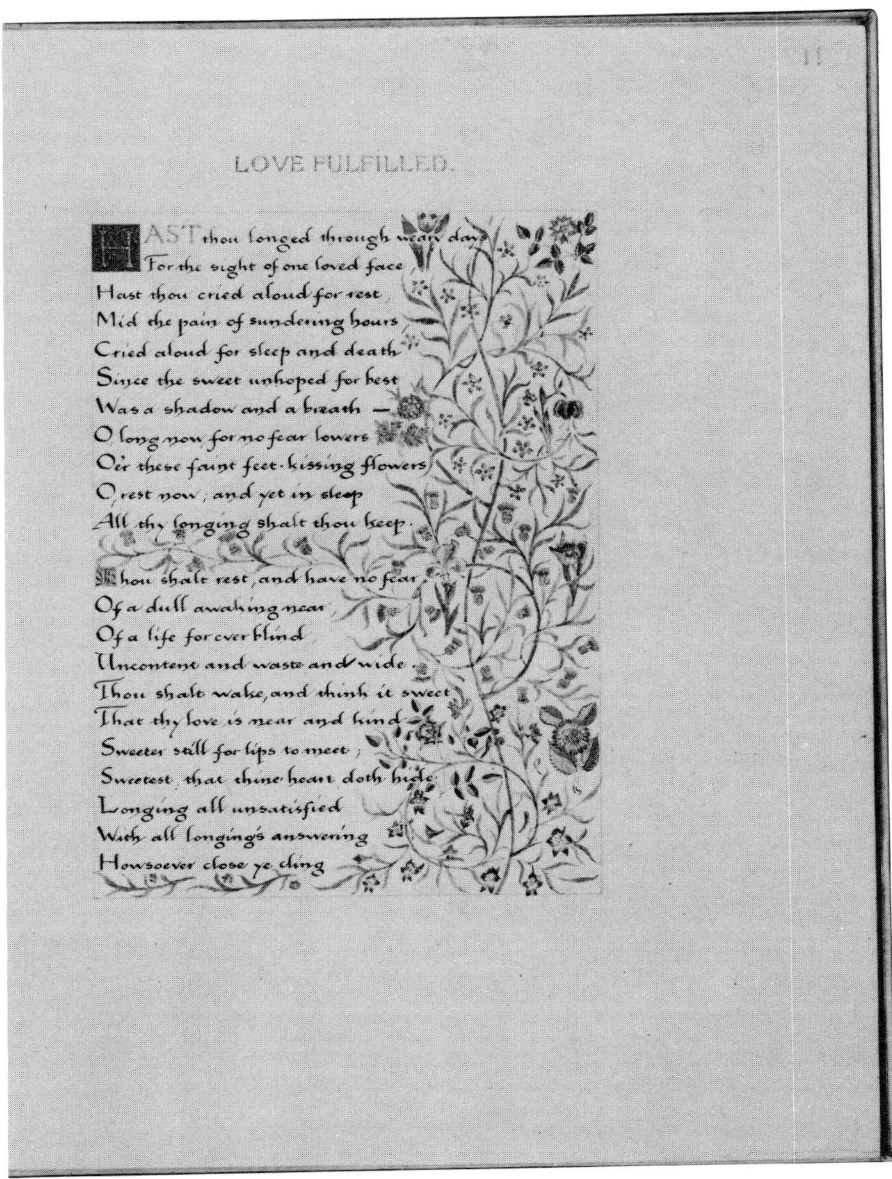

11

LOVE FULFILLED.

HAST thou longed through weary days
For the sight of one loved face
Hast thou cried aloud for rest,
Mid the pain of sundering hours
Cried aloud for sleep and death
Since the sweet unhoped for best
Was a shadow and a breath —
O long now for no fear lowers
O'er these faint feet-kissing flowers
O, rest now; and yet in sleep
All thy longing shalt thou keep.

Thou shalt rest, and have no fear
Of a dull awaking near
Of a life for ever blind
Uncontent and waste and wide.
Thou shalt wake, and think it sweet
That thy love is near and kind
Sweeter still for lips to meet;
Sweetest that thine heart doth hide
Longing all unsatisfied
With all longing's answering
Howsoever close ye cling

107

FIGURE 107: William Morris: A book of verse 1870

This delightful manuscript was made for Lady Burne-Jones; a number of different artists worked on it, but it was William Morris who completed it and wrote out all his own poems for her. Morris was not alone in his desire to reproduce the handmade book of the Middle Ages, as we can see from other illustrations in the present book, but he was no slavish imitator of older styles. Instead he evolved a characteristic style of his own. By his concern for all aspects of the art of the book he was to have a considerable effect on twentieth-century book production and calligraphy.

VICTORIA & ALBERT MUSEUM MS.L.131-1953 27.5 × 21

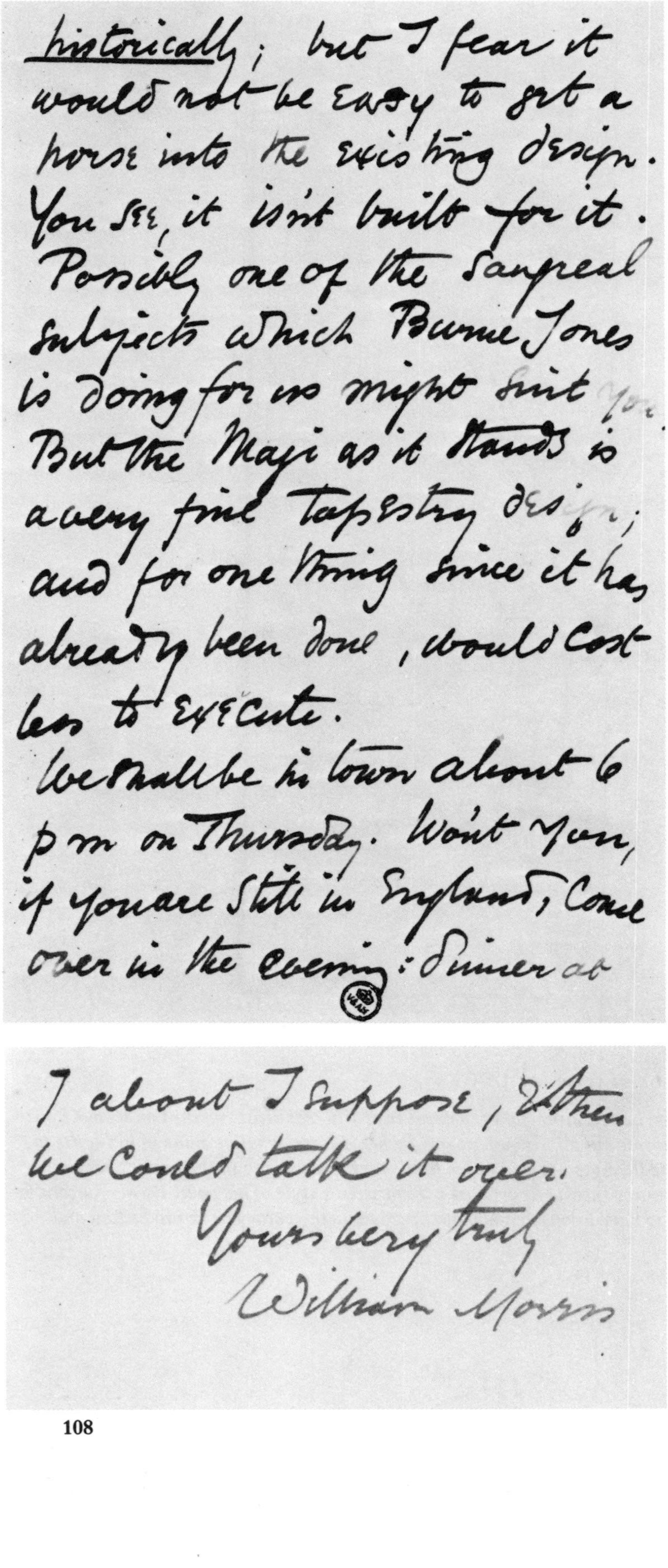

historically; but I fear it would not be easy to get a horse into the existing design. You see, it isn't built for it. Possibly one of the Sangreal subjects which Burne Jones is doing for us might suit you. But the Magi as it stands is a very fine tapestry design; and for one thing since it has already been done, would cost less to execute.

We shall be in town about 6 p m on Thursday. Won't you, if you are still in England, come over in the evening: dinner at 7 about I suppose, & then we could talk it over.

Yours very truly

William Morris

108

FIGURE 108: William Morris: A letter to W. Scawen Blunt

This is an example of William Morris's ordinary handwriting, which forms an interesting contrast to the style he thought suitable for his manuscript book (No. 107).

VICTORIA & ALBERT MUSEUM
MS.L.2385–1954

FIGURE 109: John Jenkins: The art of writing reduced to a plain and easy system 1813

This work by Jenkins was the first of its kind to be published in America, and its title is very seductive. He based his system on the theory that the round-hand could be divided into six basic strokes of the pen and that having mastered these, anyone could write a good hand. Unfortunately he found that certain letters such as k *and* s *did not fit into his scheme, while* z *was omitted as unnecessary!*

VICTORIA & ALBERT MUSEUM
L.619–1916 21 × 23

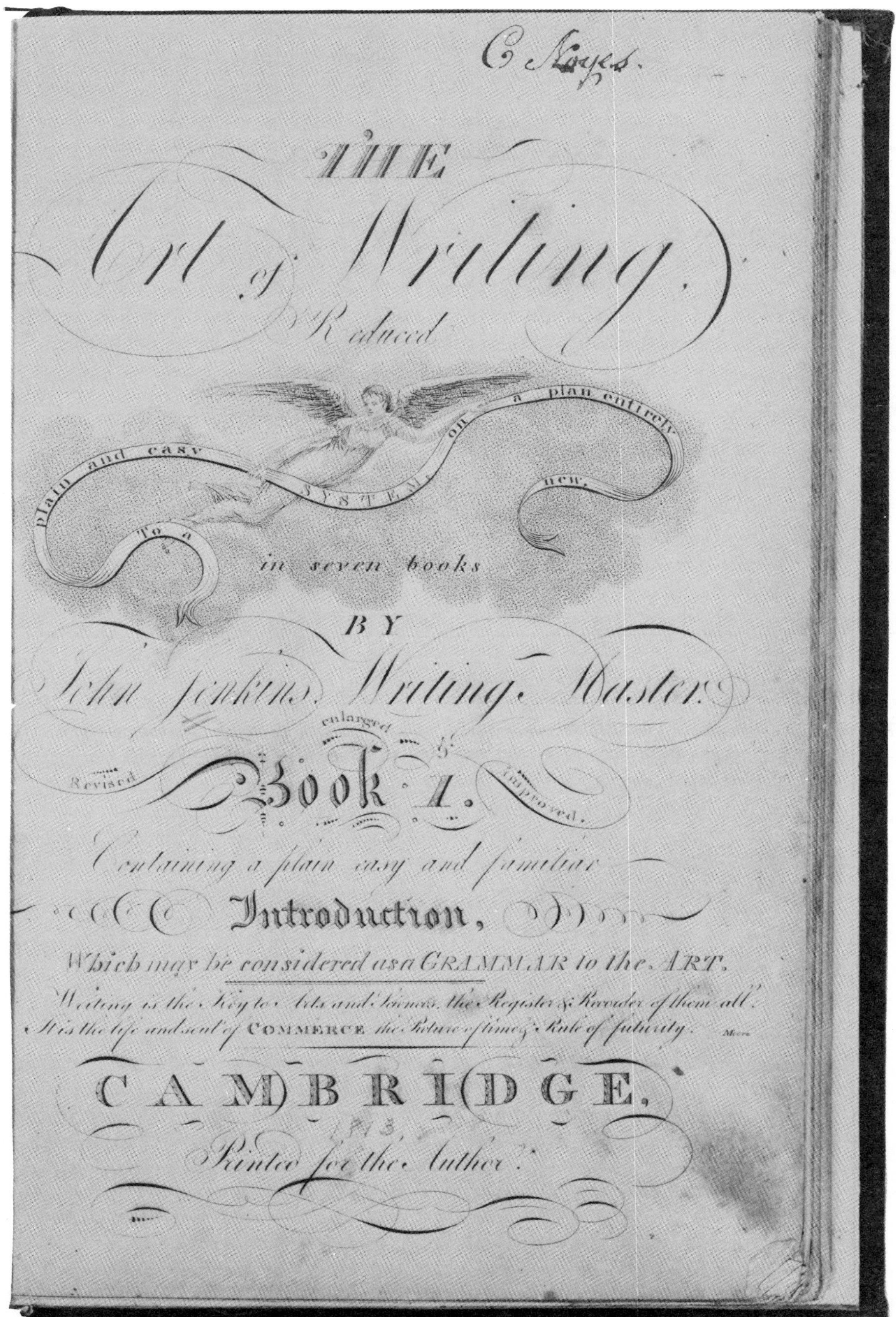

C Noyes

THE

Art of Writing,

Reduced

To a plain and easy SYSTEM on a plan entirely new,

in seven books

BY

John Jenkins, Writing-Master.

Revised enlarged & improved.

Book I.

Containing a plain easy and familiar

Introduction,

Which may be considered as a GRAMMAR to the ART.

Writing is the Key to Arts and Sciences, the Register & Recorder of them all. It is the life and soul of COMMERCE the Picture of time, & Rule of futurity. Moore

CAMBRIDGE,

1813,

Printed for the Author.

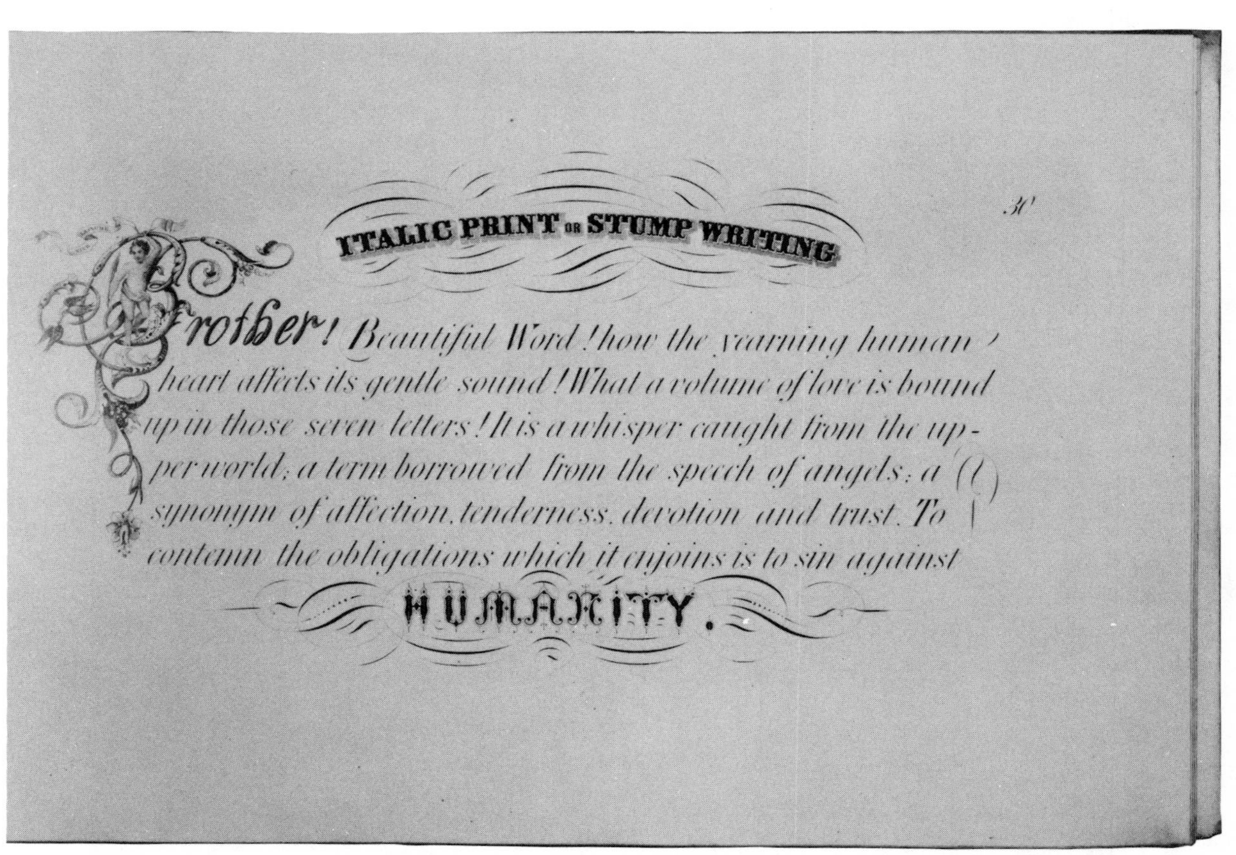

30

ITALIC PRINT OR STUMP WRITING

Brother! Beautiful Word! how the yearning human heart affects its gentle sound! What a volume of love is bound up in those seven letters! It is a whisper caught from the upper world; a term borrowed from the speech of angels; a synonym of affection, tenderness, devotion and trust. To contemn the obligations which it enjoins is to sin against

HUMANITY.

FIGURE 110: George J. Becker: Becker's ornamental penmanship c. 1855?

This work was published in Philadelphia and contains a variety of scripts. Although German and "Old English" hands predominate, Becker also included such items as "velvet letter" and "pearl letter."

VICTORIA & ALBERT MUSEUM L.616–1916 19.5×30

FIGURE 111: John D. Williams and S.S. Packard: Williams & Packard's original Gems of penmanship 1867

Williams was a teacher of handwriting at Packard's in New York, and published several works jointly with him. As can be seen from this example, the ornamental aspect of the work tends to overshadow the writing, which was the standard business hand, but rather weak.

VICTORIA & ALBERT MUSEUM L.610–1916 25.5 × 30

112

FIGURE 112: Platt Rogers Spencer: Spencerian key to practical penmanship 1866

The Spencerian system was one of the most widely used models in the United States. This particular work was published after his death by one of his sons, but Spencer himself had published many copybooks, concentrating mainly on business hands. Many of his examples derive from the work of another American, Benjamin Franklin Foster.

VICTORIA & ALBERT MUSEUM L.612–1916 20.5 × 13.5

FIGURE 113: G. A. Gaskell: The penman's hand-book, for penmen and students [etc.] 1883

This work includes practical examples "by the best American penmen," as well as complete alphabets, a history of writing, and other useful information, such as that shown here. This style of "copperplate" writing is frequently used for formal invitations today.

AUTHOR'S COLLECTION 27 × 21

It is the custom for the bride's parents to give the bride a Reception on her return to the city. The form is :

Mrs Charles L. Heatherstone,
Mrs Auguste Clarendon,
At Home,
Wednesday, November Eight,
from four until ten o'clock,
753 Fifth Avenue

If an Evening Reception, the form of invitation is :

Mr & Mrs Charles L. Heatherstone,
At Home,
Wednesday Evening, November Eight,
from nine until eleven o'clock,
753 Fifth Avenue

Enclosing also a card of

Mr & Mrs Auguste Clarendon

The form for Weddings at the residence is :

Mr & Mrs Charles L. Heatherstone
request your presence
at the marriage of their daughter,
Miss Georgia,
to
Mr. Auguste Clarendon,
on Tuesday Afternoon, October Eight, 1879,
at four o'clock,
753 Fifth Avenue

Diesen beyden Ehgatten, als conrad breneise ×× und seine eheliche Haus-Frau Maria ×× gebohrne ist eine ×× zur Welt gebohren, als:

Maria Breneisin ×× ist zur Welt gebohren, im Jahr unsers Herrn Jesu 177 den ten Tag augu ×× um 4 Uhr morgens ×× im Zeichen des Ist, weil alle Menschen in Sünden empfangen und gebohren, laut Christi Lehre alle Kindlein zu JEsu sollen gebracht werden, wie der Evangelist Marcus 10, v. 15. x. beschreibet, daß, wer das Reich GOttes nicht einpfähet als ein Kindlein, der wird nicht hinein kommen: mithin diese, durch die heilige Taufe in den Gnaden-Bund GOttes einverleibet, und von wilhelm ×× Pfarrer den ten Tag september getauft und genennet worden, wie oben gemeldt. Tauf-Zeugen sind valentin breneise und seine eheliche hausfrau × oben gemeldete maria breneisin ist gebohren und getauft worden, in America in der Provintz Pennsylvania, in lancaster Caunty in Taunschip geschrieben von mir Jacob otto

Wann wir kaum gebohren werden: Ist vom ersten Lebenstritt, bis ins kühle Grab der Erden, Nur ein kurtz gemessener Schritt. Ach mit jedem Augenblick! Gehet unser Kraft zurück, Und wir sind mit jedem Jahre, allzu reiff, zur Todtenbahre. Und wer weiß in welcher Stunde, uns die letzte Stimme weckt: Dann GOtt hat's mit seinem Munde, keinem Menschen noch entdeckt. Wer sein Haus nun wohl bestelt, geht mit Freuden aus der Welt. Da die Sicherheit hingegen; ewigs Sterben kan erregen. Geschrieben 1784.

114

FIGURE 114: Birth and baptismal certificate by Heinrich and Jacob Otto 1784

The German immigrants to the United States who settled in Pennsylvania continued the traditional styles of their homeland in their new country, but with greater modifications as time went on. Here we have a good example of the Pennsylvania Dutch (Deutsch) style applied to calligraphy. Part of the text in this example has been printed, using a typography based on traditional Gothic or "Fraktur" letters, and the rest has been written out by the calligrapher Jacob Otto.

FIGURE 115: Prayer, written out by Elisabeth Bordner "in Jahr unsers Herrn 1830"

A further example of Pennsylvania Dutch "Fraktur" script, showing how the Gothic quality of the writing became gradually modified through its prolonged contact with other American styles.

Haussegen oder die Engel des Morgens.

Auf Volk die Schatten sind vergangen, der Morgenröthe Glanz bricht an! Auf eh der Sonnenstralen Prangen, noch Sodoms Flur erleuchten kan, ermuntre dich aus deinem Schlafe, auf! höre hier des Höchsten Wort: den Augenblick verdirbt die Strafe, des höchsten diesen Sünden Ort. Du zauderst! hier gilt kein verweilen! Gott komt, der nach Verdienste lohnt das Land bebt schon von Donnerkeulen, dich einig hat der Herr verschont, reich mir die Hand, ich will dich leiten, steig diesen hohen Berg hinan! sieh nicht zurück auf keiner Seite, weil dich sonst niemand retten kan. Der Allmächtig Gott sey mit dir, der segne, erhalte, und beschütze dich im Zeitlichen und im Ewigen, durch unsern Herrn Jesum Christum. Amen.

Elisabeth Bordner

im Jahr unsers Herrn 1830.

115

Geburt und Tauf schein.

Diesen beiden Ehegatten. als . Wilhelm Portzeline und seine
Eheliche hausfrau Gertraut eine Geborne Zelerin ist ein Sohn zur
welt geboren den 7 ten Junius nachts um 11 uhr im jahr unseres herrn
1838 in Greenwood Taunschip junietka Caunty im Staat Pennsylvania
und erhielt durch die heilige Taufe den namen Benjamin durch den
Ehrwürdigen Prediger Frederich Seiberd. die Taufzeugen sind
Abraham Zeller und seine Ehefrau Nänzi.

Francis Portzline

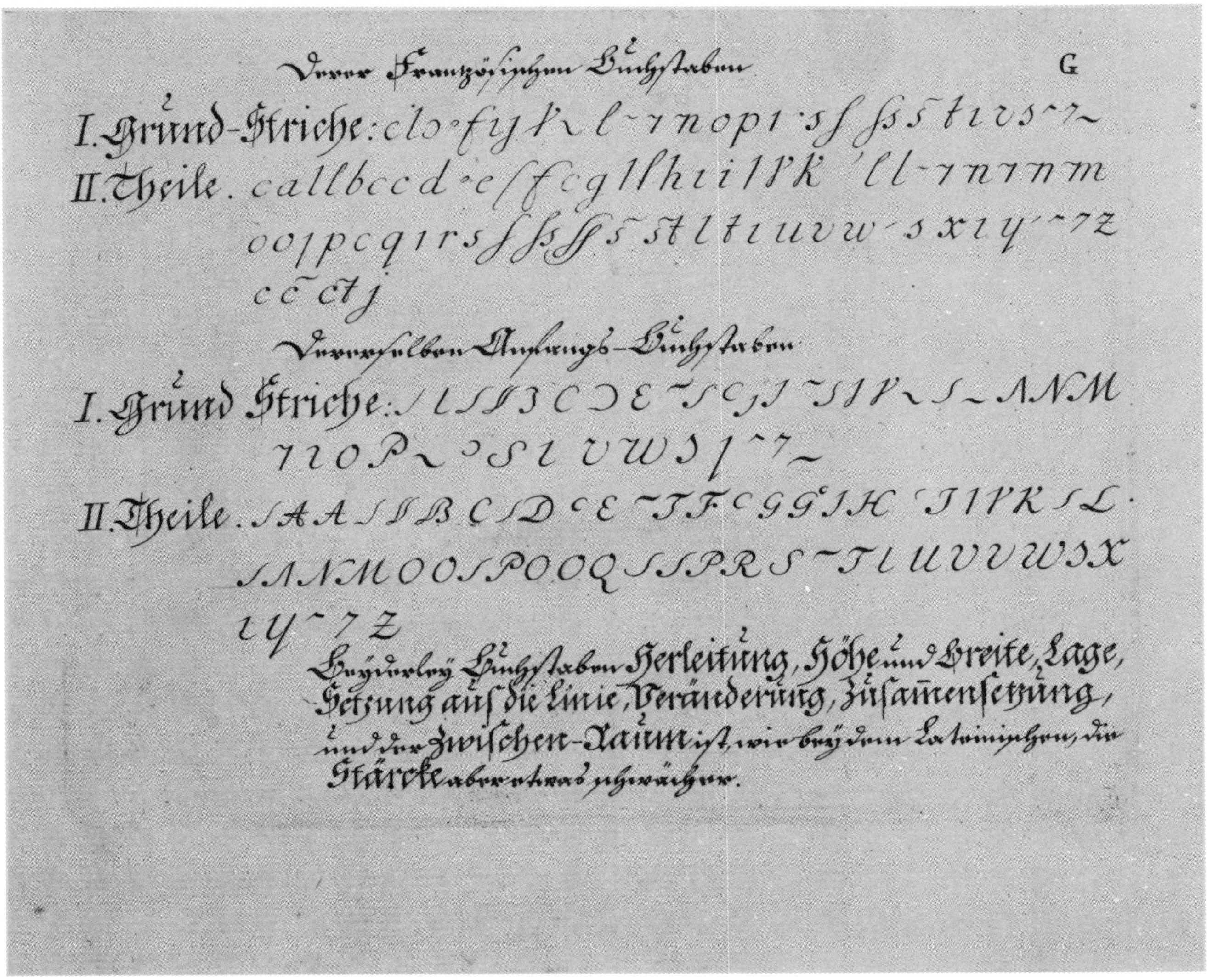

117

FIGURE 116: Birth and baptismal certificate written out by Francis Portzline 1838

This charming example of the Pennsylvania Dutch style shows how the same type of decoration could be used equally well on a variety of artifacts. The central European derivation of both script and ornament are very clear in this manuscript.

REPRODUCED BY PERMISSION OF THE PHILADELPHIA MUSEUM OF ART, GIFT OF J. STOGDELL STOKES, 28.10.89

FIGURE 117: Grundliche Unterweisung in der so nothig als nutzlichen Schreibe-Kunst [etc.] 1744

As this German copybook was aimed at merchants, among others, it included various west European scripts in addition to the contemporary German "Fraktur" script. This illustration shows how to form the French hand, which must have been quite difficult for those pupils more accustomed to the Gothic letters of their native script.

VICTORIA & ALBERT MUSEUM 21.ii.1833 17×21.5

118

FIGURE 118: J.G. Schwandner: Dissertatio epistolaris De calligraphiae 1756

This illustration shows one of a number of elaborate initial-letter pages from Schwandner's book. In this, the pen-formed letters appear more as a basis for the production of abstract patterns, something not unknown among today's practitioners.

VICTORIA & ALBERT MUSEUM CIRC.170–1972

FIGURE 119: Grant of nobility to Franz Anton Bihn 1764

This grant is dated 1764 and signed by the Empress Maria Theresa. Part of the text and the decoration is engraved and the other part has been done in pen-and-ink. But so closely does the handwritten part imitate the engraved that only a careful scrutiny of the original with a magnifying glass will show which is which. It certainly cannot be deduced from a photograph.

VICTORIA & ALBERT MUSEUM L.166-1923 36.5 × 31.5

minder die rothe Wax-Siegliing von nün an zü allen künftigen Zeiten in allen ünd jeden ritterlichen Sachen, ünd Geschäften zü Schimpf, ü: Ernst, in Stürmen, Schlachten, Streitten, Kämpfen, Türnieren, Gestechen, Gefechten, Ritterspielen, Feldzügen, Pannieren, Gezelten Aüfschlagen, Pettschaften, Kleinodien, Begräbnissen, Gemälden, aüch sonsten an allen Orten, ünd Enden nach ihren Ehren, Notdürften, Willen ünd Wohlgefallen sich gebraüchen, ü: geniessen, ünd dessen sich erfreüen können ü: mögen.

Und ergehet solchemnach an alle, ünd jede Khür-Fürsten, ünd Fürsten, geistlich ünd weltliche Prälaten, Grafen, Freÿe, Herren, Rittere, ünd Knechte Unser Gesinnen, ünd Begehren, an Unsere

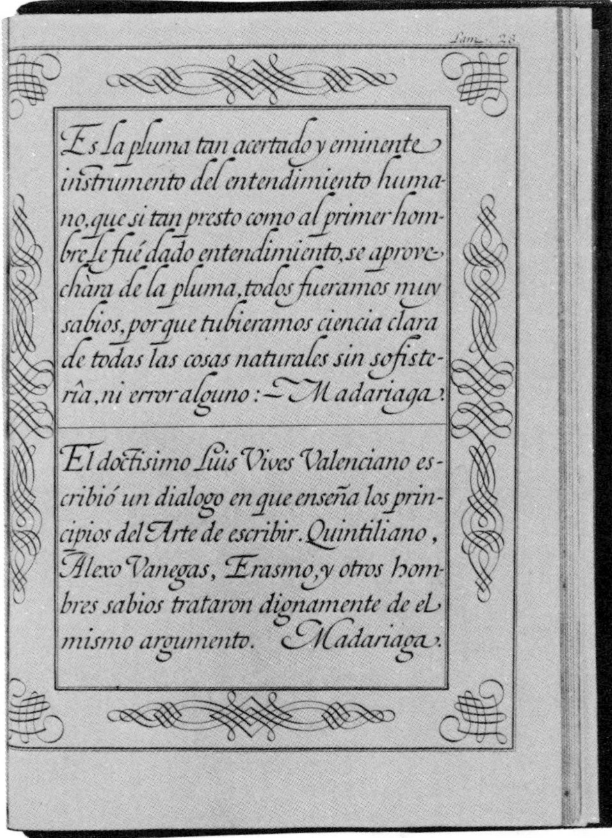

120

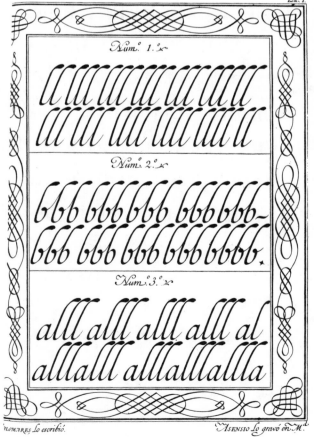

121

FIGURES 120 & 121: Francisco Xavier de Santiago y Palomares: Arte nueva de escribir inventada por el insigne maestro Pedro Diaz Morante, e ilustrada con muestras nuevas y varios discursos [etc.] 1776

Palomares was greatly influenced by the seventeenth-century Spanish writing master Diaz Morante, and he was also concerned about the decline in contemporary writing. His book was intended to revive the art of fine writing, and included examples from his own work as well as from other masters whom he admired. The second of the two illustrations from his book shows the type of practice he advocated in order to form the script he recommended.

VICTORIA & ALBERT MUSEUM L.1915–1913
30.5 × 21

FIGURE 122: Document appointing Manuel de Godoy, Prince de la Paz, Duke de la Alcudia, as governor of Teruel Spanish 1804

This is one of the simpler pages from a very elegant manuscript. Although written at the beginning of the nineteenth century, it looks back in the style of its writing to earlier centuries. It suggests that while Spanish calligraphy remained fairly static within the court circles from which this document came, it also retained the high standard lost in other countries. Beautifully decorated in color, with charming river scenes as backgrounds to the initial letters, and grisaille and rococo ornaments in the borders, the whole manuscript forms a striking contrast to the low level of work produced in other countries at the beginning of the nineteenth century.

VICTORIA & ALBERT MUSEUM
MS.L.4763–1978 30.5 × 20

PRINCIPE DE LA PAZ,

de que asistireis á los Ayuntamien-
tos que se celebren en ella la mayor
parte del año, segun está mandado,
pues os dispenso y relevo de esta cir-
cunstancia por lo respectivo á vuestra
persona, lo cual asi hecho, mando que
os hayan y tengan por tal REGI-
DOR DECANO Y PERPETUO
de la propia ciudad de TERUEL
con la preeminencia á todos los de-
mas Regidores, y en esta forma lo u-
sen con VOS en todo lo á él concer-
niente, y os guarden, y hagan guar-

FRIEDEN·WAS·DIESER·
ABER·SO·ANACLYPTA·
QUARCK·GEH·WEIB·JA
MÄDCHEN·PAUL·AXEN
UENUS· ·ZANCK
ZEPHYR·ÜBERMENSCH
RISOTTO·AUENTIUREN

123

124

FIGURES 123 & 124: Beispiele kunstlerischer Schrift. Herausgegeben von Rudolph v. Larisch 1900, 1906

By the end of the nineteenth century the Arts & Crafts Movement had encouraged artists to experiment in many art forms, among them typography and calligraphy. Inevitably their work reflected current artistic styles, as we see in the two examples illustrated here. They are taken from two of the portfolios issued in Vienna under the editorship of von Larisch—a project in which many western European artists participated. Walter Crane and C.R. Ashbee represented England and the work of well-known people like Alphonse Mucha was also included. These two examples are by Paul Burk of Darmstadt and Felix Valloton of Paris.

VICTORIA & ALBERT MUSEUM L.1052–1900, L.1541–1910 23×28

PAX DEI

quae superat omnem intellectum / servet corda vestra et mentes vestras in cognitione et amore Dei et Filii ejus / Jesu Christi Domini nostri: ET favor Omnipotentes Dei / Patris / Filii / et Spiritus Sancti / vobis adsit semperque vobiscum maneat:

AMEN

THE TWENTIETH CENTURY

ALTHOUGH handwriting had reached a very low ebb by the end of the nineteenth century, the seeds of renewal had already been sown. We have seen the interest shown by William Morris in the hand-produced book, and his own attempts to reproduce a nineteenth-century version of the medieval bookman's work. Two years after William Morris had completed his *Book of Verse* (Figure 107), there was born in England the man who was to become the father of twentieth-century calligraphy—Edward Johnston. It is an interesting fact that neither he nor the other major figure associated with the revival of calligraphy was originally destined for the field in which he was to make his name. Edward Johnston abandoned a medical career and Graily Hewitt a legal one in order to take up the study and practice of calligraphy. Edward Johnston was greatly encouraged in his chosen career by Sir Sydney Cockerell, who had been William Morris's secretary and thus formed a link between nineteenth- and twentieth-century calligraphers. Johnston did not just practice the art of fine writing, he also carefully studied the way in which the medieval scribe had formed his letters, and the tools he had used. As a result, he came to realize that the form of a letter was dependent on the instrument used to make it, and that an edged pen made thick and thin strokes by direction rather than pressure. Johnston also carefully considered the way in which the medieval scribe prepared his quill in order to give it the right shape, and the way he had held it in relation to the top of the writing paper. He put all

FIGURE 125: Edward Johnston: The order of the administration of the Lord's Supper or Holy Communion 1900

It was of course Edward Johnston who started the renaissance of calligraphy in the West. But this little manuscript is a very early work, and although the script shows its medieval source, it also indicates that Johnston as yet lacked the skill and confidence that his later work shows so clearly. The manuscript was decorated in red ink and (not very good) gold.

VICTORIA & ALBERT MUSEUM MS.L.131–1946 12×8.5

his discoveries, and his practical knowledge, into the book published in 1906, that he called *Writing & Illuminating, & Lettering*. This book is still in print today and remains the basic handbook for every calligrapher.

One of Edward Johnston's earliest pupils was William Graily Hewitt. The two "founding fathers" complement each other nicely, since Johnston's calligraphy was generally better than his gilding, while Graily Hewitt evolved an excellent modern method of gilding with gesso and gold leaf based on medieval practice—though his calligraphy was not always so good. Many of the scribes whose work is reproduced in this section of the present book were either pupils of one of these two men, or pupils of pupils, so that their skills have continued to be transmitted down to our own day. This transmission has not been confined to Britain alone, of course, but has spread throughout the continents where the western alphabet is used, with each country gradually transmuting the original style of the teachers into something approaching a new national style. This is particularly true of the United States, where the most exciting developments in modern calligraphy are taking place today.

But we have been talking about calligraphy—*fine* writing. Many people must have been quite unaware of this revolution in writing styles, since the schools continued for the most part to teach handwriting of the traditional kind. More recently, changed ideas about how children should be taught have rather downgraded the art (or craft) of writing; after all, there is very little call for it in modern life, beyond the need for an occasional signature, so why bother? But fortunately there have always been some people who have appreciated the need to improve the general standard of handwriting, and have been prepared to do something about it. One of the earliest in Britain was Mrs. Bridges, wife of the then Poet Laureate of that country, who in 1911 published *A New Handwriting for Teachers*. Later still came Marion Richardson, who gave her name to a form of writing that is still taught in some schools in the United Kingdom. We adults take it for granted that the handwritten and the printed letter may differ considerably in appearance, and forget the shock of incomprehension we received as children when we were confronted with our first personally addressed handwritten letter! "Print-script" acknowledged this fact, and was one of the hands taught to very young children during the 1930s. It was easy to learn, but difficult to progress from, since print-script letters did not easily form themselves into cursive letters at a later stage of the child's learning. It is for this reason that in recent decades the italic hand has often been taught in schools, since it makes the transition from individual letters to cursive forms much more easily.

The association of calligraphy with arts and crafts led to it being taught in colleges and schools of art, although, sadly, in Britain this subject has been discontinued. But one of the results of calligraphy becoming a formal art-school subject has been its increasing employment in advertisement art. It has become so familiar to most people in this form that much of the time we are unaware that the familiar signs of "Coca-Cola" or "Kelloggs," for example, are based on pen-written letters rather than printed ones. How many other examples can you see as you look around you?

The telephone and the typewriter may have helped to make writing redundant for most of us today, but that very fact seems to have stimulated more people to try to write better! Of course there has always been the professional scribe, who earns his or her living by practicing or teaching calligraphy. In Britain, for example, there is the Society of Scribes and Illuminators, founded in 1921, which ensures the maintenance of high professional standards, and which also has an enthusiastic and competent lay membership. In 1952 a Society for Italic Handwriting was also set up, with a journal that not only publishes scholarly articles on calligraphic subjects but also actively encourages the teaching of italic handwriting among non-professionals (including schools) by competitions and exhibitions. Similar bodies flourish elsewhere: the Fairbank Society in Canada, for example, takes its name from the great teaching pioneer Alfred Fairbank, whose manual and book of scripts are widely known and studied.

Just as in the nineteenth century there were technical developments that affected the style of writing, so in the twentieth century there have been technological advances. The most obvious one has been the advent of the ball-point pen, which is used by nearly everyone (scribes included!) at some time, and by most people all the time. Its advantages are obvious, its disadvantages less so. The ball-point flows easily and evenly over the writing surface, without any distinction of thicks and thins, and the result is a completely characterless script. It is not impossible to write well with a ball-point pen, but it is certainly much more difficult! After the ball-point came the felt-tip pen. This is much more like a brush than a pen point, and its effect on script has been quite different. For it does respond to the individual hand, and it gives the writer a freedom of movement to produce a much more fluid script. Many professional scribes have enjoyed using brush-made letters, especially in advertisement art, and the felt-tip gives the amateur calligrapher similar opportunities to experiment with exciting letter-forms and colors. But beware! The very ease with which the felt-tip pen flows over the writing surface can lead to a lack of discipline, which is always an essential attribute of a good script.

There is one other twentieth-century development which, while not affecting handwriting at the moment, may yet be pointing the way to the future of the art. During the period of nearly two thousand years that we have considered in the present book, the basic form of the alphabet has changed little; what has changed has been the way in which individual scribes or whole nations have chosen to write it. Now we have a new kind of alphabet: the computer alphabet. Although still based on the traditional Roman letters with which we began, there are in fact a number of radical differences. And who knows what the future may hold in the field of machine-readable letters? Perhaps we shall have a new calligraphic computer alphabet, too.

By the end of the twentieth century we find calligraphy treading two separate paths. On one side there is the professional aspect, ably supported by enthusiastic amateurs. On the other is mere writing, such as is taught, for the most part indifferently, in schools. Occasionally the two paths meet, when an enlightened teacher realizes that good handwriting is not just something that happens to every child, but that it needs practice and discipline. And children respond well to such good teaching, for calligraphy is very much an art for all. The materials needed are few and inexpensive; good work can be produced remarkably quickly; the results are visible to all on the humblest note or envelope; and however unskilled or unartistic the pupil may be—or of whatever age—patience and perseverance will usually be rewarded. What more can any man, woman or child want!

If you have read to the end of this book you are now probably eager to get to work. Do not look only at the examples illustrated here, but also look around you wherever you go, and relate what you have seen here to the many calligraphic forms that have been the inspiration of so much of the visual material of our daily life. Remember that the aim of all writing is to be *read*—and easily too—but that a good scribe will add beauty to legibility. Though the Johnston tradition may have become somewhat fossilized on one side of the Atlantic, many exciting developments are taking place in American calligraphy. Look them out for yourself!

FIGURE 126: Edward Johnston: Writing & Illuminating, & Lettering 1906

More than seventy years after it was published, this book is still the Bible for calligraphers. In it Johnston provided instruction on all aspects of the craft, and in particular the methods used by the early scribes and their adaptation to twentieth-century use. He included examples of many scripts, but this particular one forms an interesting parallel to the little prayer book of 1900 (figure 125).

VICTORIA & ALBERT MUSEUM L.4440–1959 18.5 × 12

SURELY THERE
IS A MINE FOR
SILVER
And a place for gold
which they refine.
Iron is taken out
of the earth,
And brass is mol-
ten out of the stone
Man setteth an end
to darkness,
And searcheth out
to the furthest
bound
The stones of thick
darkness and of
the shadow of death.
HE BREAKETH
open a shaft away
from where men
sojourn;
They are forgotten
of the foot that
passeth by;
They hang afar from
men, they swing
to and fro.

AS FOR The EARTH,
out of it cometh
bread:
And underneath it
is turned up as it
were by fire.
The stones thereof
are the place of
sapphires,
And it hath dust
of gold.
THAT PATH NO
BIRD OF PREY
KNOWETH,
Neither hath the
falcon's eye seen it:
The proud beasts
have not trodden it
Nor hath the fierce
lion passed thereby
hE PUTTETH FORTH
his hand upon
the flinty rock;
HE OVERTURNETH
the mountains
by the roots.
hE CUTTETH out

Black
& Red

enough, for diversity of Side Alleys: Unto which, the Two Covert Alleys of the Greene, may deliver you. But there must be, no Alleys with Hedges, at either End, of this great Inclosure: Not at the Hither-End, for letting your Prospect upon this Faire Hedge from the Greene; Nor at the Further End, for letting your Prospect from the Hedge, through the Arches, upon the Heath.

FOR the Ordering of the Ground, within the Great Hedge, I leave it to Variety of Device; Advising neverthelesse, that whatsoever forme you cast it into,

first it be not too Busie, or full of Worke. Wherein I, for my part, doe not like Images Cut out in Juniper, or other Garden stuffe: They be for Children. Little low Hedges, Round, like Welts, with some Pretty Pyramides, I like well: And in some Places, Faire Columnes upon Frames of Carpenters Worke. I would also have the Alleys, Spacious and Faire. You may have Closer Alleys upon the Side Grounds, but none in the Maine Garden. I wish also, in the very Mid-dle, a Faire Mount, with three Ascents, and Alleys, enough for foure to walke

FIGURE 127: Edward Johnston: Of gardens, by Francis Bacon 1911

This manuscript forms a great contrast to the prayer book of only ten years earlier (figure 125). The script now shows the elegance and competence associated with Johnston's work. It is written out in red and black ink, as can be seen from the illustration, and the contrasting inks form the only decoration.

VICTORIA & ALBERT MUSEUM MS.L.26–1945 15×11.5

ENJOY THE SEASON AND THE SAVINGS!

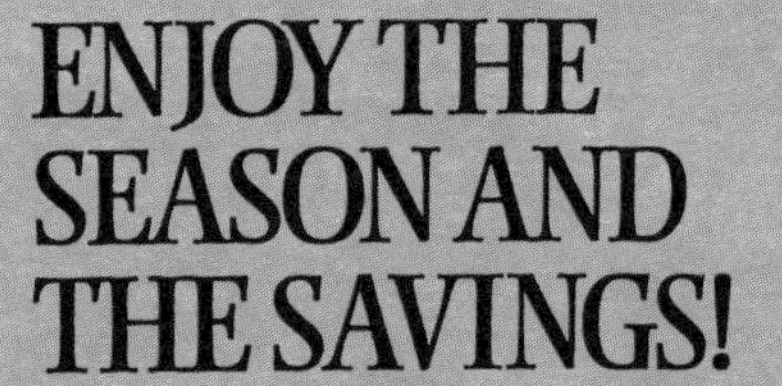

For a quality service experience at an attractive price, take a look at the enclosed coupons. You'll probably find one or more that meet your needs at this time.

We offer more than just the opportunity to save money, we also have the latest high tech diagnostic equipment, specially designed service tools and Ford and Motorcraft original equipment quality parts.

This season, enjoy the savings and the Quality Care that our dealership has to offer.

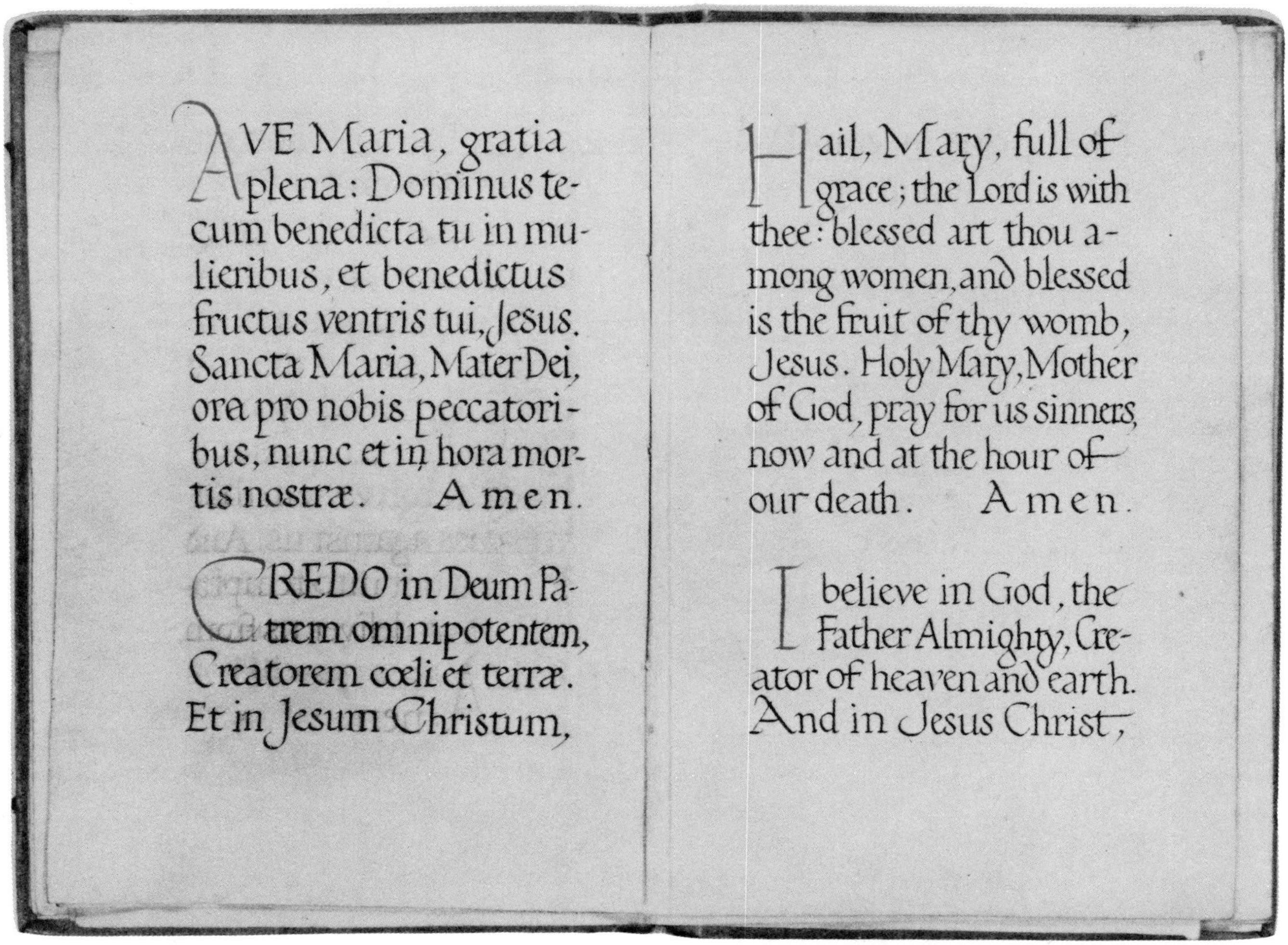

AVE Maria, gratia plena: Dominus tecum benedicta tu in mulieribus, et benedictus fructus ventris tui, Jesus. Sancta Maria, Mater Dei, ora pro nobis peccatoribus, nunc et in hora mortis nostræ. Amen.

CREDO in Deum Patrem omnipotentem, Creatorem cœli et terræ. Et in Jesum Christum,

Hail, Mary, full of grace; the Lord is with thee: blessed art thou among women, and blessed is the fruit of thy womb, Jesus. Holy Mary, Mother of God, pray for us sinners, now and at the hour of our death. Amen.

I believe in God, the Father Almighty, Creator of heaven and earth. And in Jesus Christ,

FIGURE 128: Edward Johnston: The Lord's Prayer, Hail Mary, and Apostle's Creed c. 1913

This little manuscript has an interesting history. It was written out by Johnston for Eric Gill, who later became better known for his carving, engraving, and typography; the manuscript shows signs of considerable use. It passed to members of the family on Gill's death and was eventually given to Heather Child, herself a noted calligrapher, as a token of her own devotion to the teaching of Edward Johnston. In 1977 Miss Child generously gave the manuscript to the Library of the Victoria and Albert Museum, which contains so many examples of Johnston's work.

VICTORIA & ALBERT MUSEUM MS.L.5316–1977 13×8

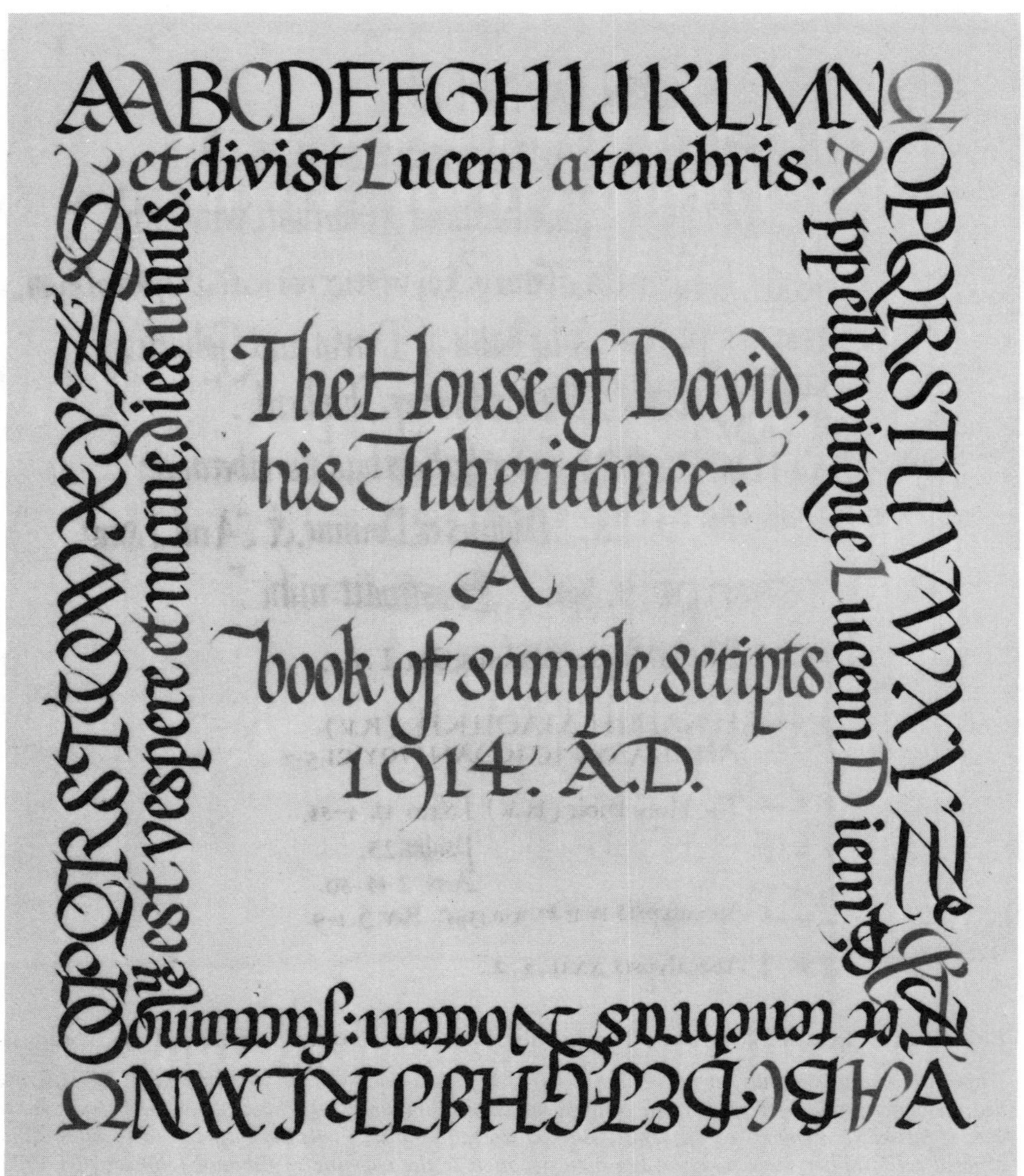

129

FIGURES 129, 130 & 131: Edward Johnston: The House of David, his inheritance: a book of sample scripts ' 1914

This manuscript was specially commissioned by Sir Sydney Cockerell for his own library; in 1959 he presented it to the Library of the Victoria and Albert Museum. This illustration shows the title page of the work and Johnston helpfully surrounds it with a complete alphabet! The manuscript actually contains a variety of scripts, as its title suggests, and the two following illustrations are taken from the same work. They show the "black italic" formed from his foundational hand, and his version of a modern uncial script (see figure 4).

VICTORIA & ALBERT MUSEUM MS.L.4391–1959 25×20

A Psalm of David. xxiij.

The LORD is my shepherd;
I shall not want.
He maketh me to lie down
in green pastures:
He leadeth me beside
the [1] still waters. 1. Heb. waters of rest.
He restoreth my soul:
He guideth me in the paths of
righteousness for his name's sake.
Yea, though I walk through the
valley of [2] the shadow of death,
I will fear no evil; 2. Or, deep darkness.

22

high dwelleth not in houses made
with hands; as saith the prophet,

The heaven is my
throne,
And the earth the foot-
stool of my feet:
What manner of house
will ye build me?
saith the Lord:
Or what is the place of
my rest?
Did not my hand make
all these things?

Acts.vij.44–50.

25

FIGURE 132: William Graily Hewitt: The Tempest, by William Shakespeare c. 1938

Graily Hewitt, like Edward Johnston, was one of the founding fathers of modern calligraphy. Although a fine calligrapher, his skill was at its best in illumination, in which he revived the skills of the medieval artist by gilding with gesso and gold leaf. He gathered round him a group of artists, one of whom was Ida Henstock, whose work adorns this manuscript.

VICTORIA & ALBERT MUSEUM
MS.L.1801–1946   30 × 20

FIGURE 133: William Graily Hewitt: The order of the administration of the Lord's Supper or Holy Communion c. 1935

This is quite a large manuscript and one of the finest examples of Graily Hewitt's work. The large letters are beautifully gilded, a fact that is not revealed by the illustration. Not only do the capital letters blend successfully with the smaller script, but the layout of the whole page is harmoniously contrived.

VICTORIA & ALBERT MUSEUM
MS.L.838–1953   38 × 26

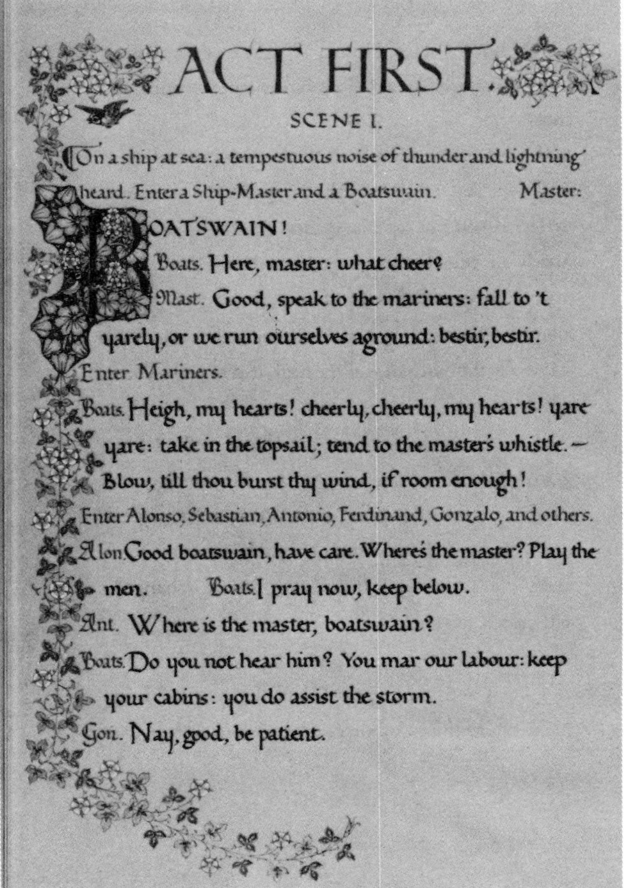

ACT FIRST.
SCENE I.
On a ship at sea: a tempestuous noise of thunder and lightning heard. Enter a Ship-Master and a Boatswain. Master:
BOATSWAIN!
Boats. Here, master: what cheer?
Mast. Good, speak to the mariners: fall to 't yarely, or we run ourselves aground: bestir, bestir.
Enter Mariners.
Boats. Heigh, my hearts! cheerly, cheerly, my hearts! yare yare: take in the topsail; tend to the master's whistle.— Blow, till thou burst thy wind, if room enough!
Enter Alonso, Sebastian, Antonio, Ferdinand, Gonzalo, and others.
Alon. Good boatswain, have care. Where's the master? Play the men.
Boats. I pray now, keep below.
Ant. Where is the master, boatswain?
Boats. Do you not hear him? You mar our labour: keep your cabins: you do assist the storm.
Gon. Nay, good, be patient.

132

before the people, & take the Cup into his hands, he shall say the Prayer of Consecration, as followeth.

ALMIGHTY GOD, OUR HEAVENLY FATHER, WHO OF THY tender mercy didst give thine only Son Jesus Christ to suffer death upon the cross for our redemption; who made there (by his one oblation of himself once offered) a full, perfect, and sufficient sacrifice, oblation, & satisfaction, for the sins of the whole world; & did institute, and in his holy Gospel command us to continue, a perpetual memory of that his precious death, until his coming again; Hear us, O merciful Father, we most humbly beseech thee; and grant that we receiving these thy creatures of bread and wine, according to thy Son our Saviour Jesus Christ's holy institution, in remembrance of his death and passion, may be partakers of his most blessed Body & Blood; who, in the same night that he was betrayed, took Bread; and, when he had given thanks, he brake it, and gave it to his disciples, saying, Take, eat,

THIS IS MY BODY

which is given for you. Do this in remembrance of me.

Likewise after supper he took the Cup; &, when he had given thanks, he gave it to them, saying, Drink ye all of this; for

THIS IS MY BLOOD OF THE NEW TESTAMENT,

which is shed for you and for many for the remission of sins: Do this, as oft as ye shall drink it, in remembrance of me. AMEN.

1. Here the Priest is to take the Paten into his hands.
2. And here to break the Bread.
3. And here to lay his hand upon all the Bread.
4. Here he is to take the Cup into his hand.
5. And here to lay his hand upon every vessel (be it Chalice or Flagon) in which there is any Wine to be consecrated.

133

Deo meo quamdiu sum.
Jucundum sit ei eloquium meum: ego vero delectabor in Domino.
Deficiant peccatores a terra, et iniqui ita ut non sint: benedic, anima mea, Domino.

CANTICUM TRIUM PUERORUM

BENEDICITE OMNIA OPERA DOMINI, DOMINO: LAUDATE ET SUPEREXALTATE EUM IN SECULA. BENEDICITE ANGELI DOMINI, DOMINO: BENEDICITE, CŒLI, DOMINO. BENEDICITE AQUÆ OMNES QUÆ SUPER CŒLOS SUNT, DOMINO BENEDICITE OMNES VIRTUTES DOMINI, DOMINO. Benedicite sol et luna, Domino: benedicite, stellæ cœli, Domino.

FIGURE 134: Louise Lessore (Mrs. Louise Powell): Psalms LXXXIV, CII, CIII. Canticum Trium Puerorum   1905

Louise Lessore was one of Edward Johnston's earliest pupils. She worked with Graily Hewitt and with Alfred Fairbank. In this manuscript she was both scribe and illuminator, and shows herself to be strongly influenced by medieval work, especially in the decoration of the large initial B (Benedicite).

VICTORIA & ALBERT MUSEUM
MS.L.4393–1959   24×16.5

FIGURE 135: Rudolph von Larisch: Unterricht in ornamentaler Schrift   1911

We have already seen examples of the influential portfolios published by von Larisch, and here is an example of his personal contribution to modern calligraphy. His appointment as a lecturer on lettering at the Vienna School of Arts & Crafts ensured for him in Austria the same sort of importance that Johnston had in England. This work was first published in 1905.

VICTORIA & ALBERT MUSEUM
L.825–1912   25×16

Jupiter und Apollo stritten,
welcher von ihnen der bes-
te Bogenschütze sei. Laß
uns die Probe tun! sagte
Apollo. - Er spannte seinen
Bogen und schoß somit-
ten in das bemerkte Ziel,
daß Jupiter keine Mög-
lichkeit sahe, ihn zu über-

24. 1/2 der Originalgröße. Vereinfachung einer bestimmten Buchstabenform. Stahlfeder.

Am andern Morgen fiel starker Schnee. Ein-
scharfer Ostwind fegte ihn über die Heide, über
die Marsch ins Meer. Wenn aber die Kleinen,
vom Winde gejagten Flocken einen Halt fanden und
war es auch nur ein Heidestrauch oder ein Maul

25. 3/4 der Originalgröße. Gewöhnliche Schreibschrift eines Kursteilnehmers. „Grenzen" der gewöhnlichen Schreibschrift.

wöhnliche Schreibschriften sehr dekorativ wirken können. ■

■ Bei solchen Schriften kann am ehesten eine Anlehnung an Vorbilder Platz greifen. Je mehr sich der ornamentale Schriftcharakter der gewöhnlichen Schreibschrift nähert, umso geringer ist die Gefahr, daß durch Kopiatur das Handschriftliche verloren geht. Selbst in den

135

1

Leo Paul Fenz

2

Ernst G. Hart & Co

3

4

Die Behandlung der Schrift in Kunst und Gewerbe.—Herausgeg. v.d. Bayerisch. Landesgewerbeanstalt Nürnberg.— Bearb. v. L.R. Spitzenpfeil.—

136

FEDERTECHNISCHE ÜBUNGEN

ABCDEFGHIJKLM
NOPQRSTUVWXYZ
abcdefghijklmnot
pqrsuvwxyz z.,;!?(/)

EINFÜHRUNG IN DIE TECHNIK D· BREITFEDER

1 2 3 4 5 6 7 8 9 0

DIE ALPHABETFORMEN DER MITTELSTUFE
TAFEL X

137

FIGURE 136: Lorenz Reinhard Spitzenpfeil: Die behandlung der Schrift in Kunst und Gewerbe 1911

Here we see the application of the new calligraphy to commercial purposes. In these examples the traditional German Gothic or "Fraktur" script has been modified by overtones of Art Nouveau lettering.

VICTORIA & ALBERT MUSEUM L.2253–1913
31 × 22.5

FIGURE 137: Paul Hulliger: Die neue Schrift 1927

This illustration comes from the second edition of a report by a commission considering the reform of handwriting in schools in Basel, Switzerland. It indicates how pupils should be taught in each of their school years. What sort of script do you get if you join up these letters?

VICTORIA & ALBERT MUSEUM L.19–1928
25 × 19

FIGURE 138: E.W. Baule: Scribtol. Anleitung zur Kunstschrift 1912

This book combined an advertisement for writing ink ("Scribtol") with a copybook. The ornamental writing is very much of its period and is certainly bold enough for use in advertisements. It is interesting in that at this period "Fraktur" or black-letters still prevailed in central Europe, although in order to reach a wider audience it was necessary to use the Roman alphabet, as here.

VICTORIA & ALBERT MUSEUM L.2423–1912
30 × 20

2

Führen Sie bitte
den Quellstift
leicht und ohne
nennenswer-
ten Druck

Gottlieb
Landerer's
photographisches Atelier
Amselgasse 5

Scribtol
Anleitung zur Kunstschrift
von E. W. BAULE
Verlag von Günther Wagner, Hannover u. Wien

most beautifully — with edges embroidered in white on the linen. She had dinner up in the bedroom with me (for I forgot to say, I am still kept in bed — but I am much better and am going to get up this afternoon for an hour or two. Poulticeing is finished & now I have got a belladonna plaster on my chest) and we had a long talk about everything — including the old subject — Latin services — how can children pray in Latin? I told her, among other things, that if you say "Glory be to the Father" etc. it means just as much as the English language can make the words mean (she agreed to that), but if you say "Gloria Patri et Filio & Spiritui Sancto" etc. it means as much as <u>the Church</u> means by the words.* That is their difficulty. They dont understand that there can be a church with divine authority to teach..... Well, then we had a tea-party in the bedroom. David J. was the only extra person (I didnt tell you, <u>he</u> gave me a splendid drawing of S. Peter — <u>very good indeed</u>) and Joan cut the birthday cake for me. At 5.30 grandma had to go to catch the 6.12 train & Petra walked to the top of Fellers Lane with her. (Mother has just brought me an extra cup of tea & some toast). In the evening after Complin Mr. P. & George M. came in & then David J. & then Uncle Charlie! So I am not exactly lonely — and I did have a most happy birthday xxxxxxxxxxxxx

This morning your letter of Sunday last has come & two most beautiful little drawings! Thank you again very much indeed my dear dear Elizabeth. We are all very much better, so you need not worry about us at all. Grippe is French for Influenza by the bye. xxxxxxxxxxxxxxxx

* You see English is a living language & so it has the right to make words mean what it likes — but that meaning changes with the years — But Latin is a "dead" language — so it depends on something else to give meaning — either most scholars or the living Church

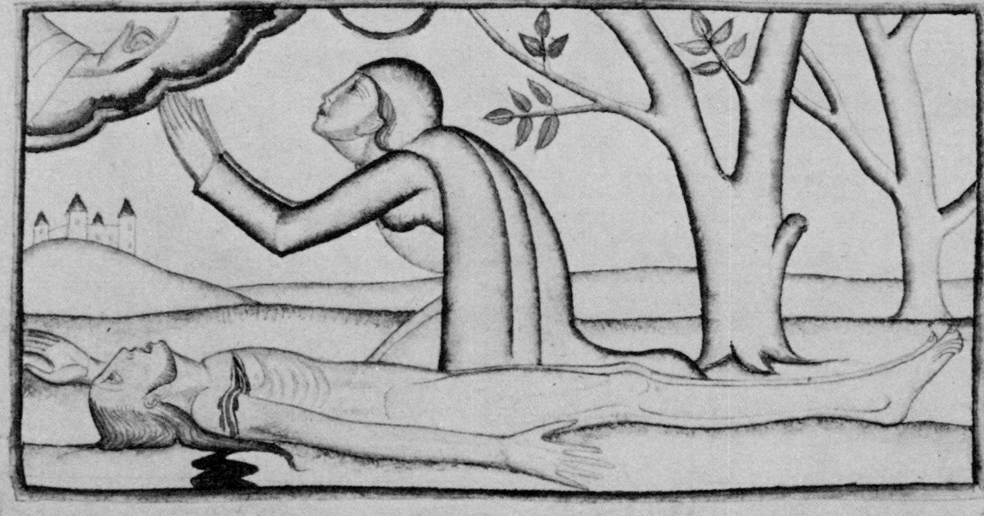

MARGARET of Cortona. She found her lover murdered and the sight of his corpse, the body she had embraced, showed her a figure of her own soul, disfigured by sin & dead to God. She immediately repented and gave herself to God & lived a life of heroic sanctity and miraculous friendship with our Lord
For Elizabeth
22 Feb 1932
E. P. T. G.

NO LONGER mourn for me when I am dead
Than you shall hear the surly sullen bell
Give warning to the world that I am fled
From this vile world, with vilest worms to dwell:
Nay, if you read this line, remember not
The hand that writ it, for I love you so,
That I in your sweet thoughts would be forgot,
If thinking on me then should make you woe.
O, if, I say, you look upon this verse
When I perhaps compounded am with clay,
Do not so much as my poor name rehearse,
But let your love even with my life decay;
Lest the wise world should look into your moan,
And mock you with me after I am gone.

THAT time of year thou mayst in me behold
When yellow leaves, or none, or few, do hang
Upon those boughs which shake against the cold,
Bare ruin'd choirs, where late the sweet birds sang.
In me thou see'st the twylight of such day
As after sunset fadeth in the west;
Which by and by black night doth take away,
Death's second self, that seals up all in rest.
In me thou see'st the glowing of such fire,
That on the ashes of his youth doth lie,
As the death-bed whereon it must expire,
Consumed with that which it was nourish'd by.
This thou perceivest, which makes thy love more strong,
To love that well which thou must leave ere long.

140

FIGURE 139: Eric Gill: Letter to his daughter Elizabeth, giving an account of his birthday celebration   1922

We have already seen the little manuscript that was made for Eric Gill by Edward Johnston, and which he evidently carried around with him. Here is Gill's ordinary handwriting, still quite elegant even in this hasty form—though a long way from the formality of his better-known lettering and typography.

VICTORIA & ALBERT MUSEUM   MS.L.3382–1957   25.5 × 19

FIGURE 140: Alfred Fairbank: Two sonnets by William Shakespeare   1929?

Alfred Fairbank played an important part in the revival and spread of the italic hand. He was not a professional scribe, working most of his life in a government office. Perhaps because he was not primarily concerned with earning his living as a calligrapher, he became well-known as a teacher: his writings and manuals have had a widespread influence on modern calligraphy, especially among schools and amateurs. A calligraphy society in Canada is named after him.

VICTORIA & ALBERT MUSEUM   MS.CIRC. 287–1929

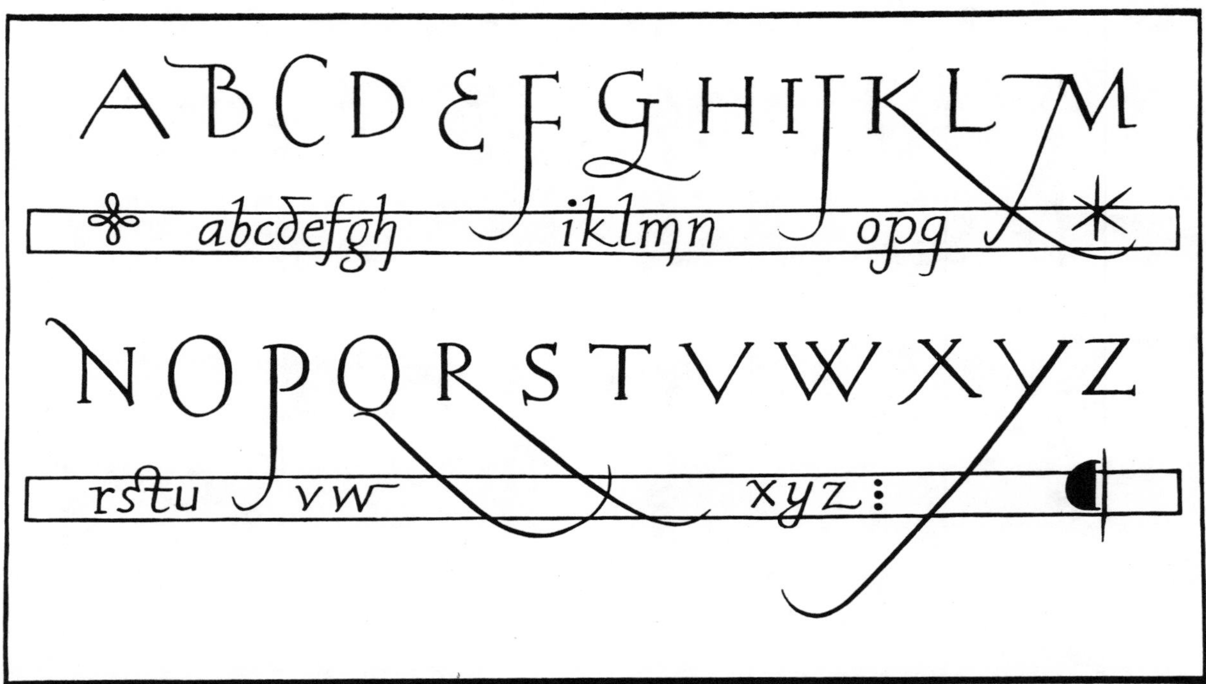

141

FIGURE 141: Rudolph Koch and Berthold Wolpe: Das ABC-Büchlein: Zeichnungen von Rudolph Koch und Berthold Wolpe. In Holz- und Metallschnitten von Fritz Kredel und Gustav Eichenauer 1934

Both Koch and Wolpe were well-known as typographers, and it is an interesting aspect of modern type forms that they have frequently been designed by people who are also practicing calligraphers. These letters certainly owe much to pen-made forms.

VICTORIA & ALBERT MUSEUM L.678–1936 15 × 23

FIGURE 142: Reynolds Stone: A book of lettering 1935

Reynolds Stone was known as a book illustrator and painter as well as a calligrapher. He had a very personal style of script, based on the Italian Renaissance hands, with modified flourishes. It looked particularly well cut in wood for small items such as bookplates.

VICTORIA & ALBERT MUSEUM L.699–1935 23 × 17.5

ABCDEFG

HIJKLM

NOPQRS

TUVW

XYZ

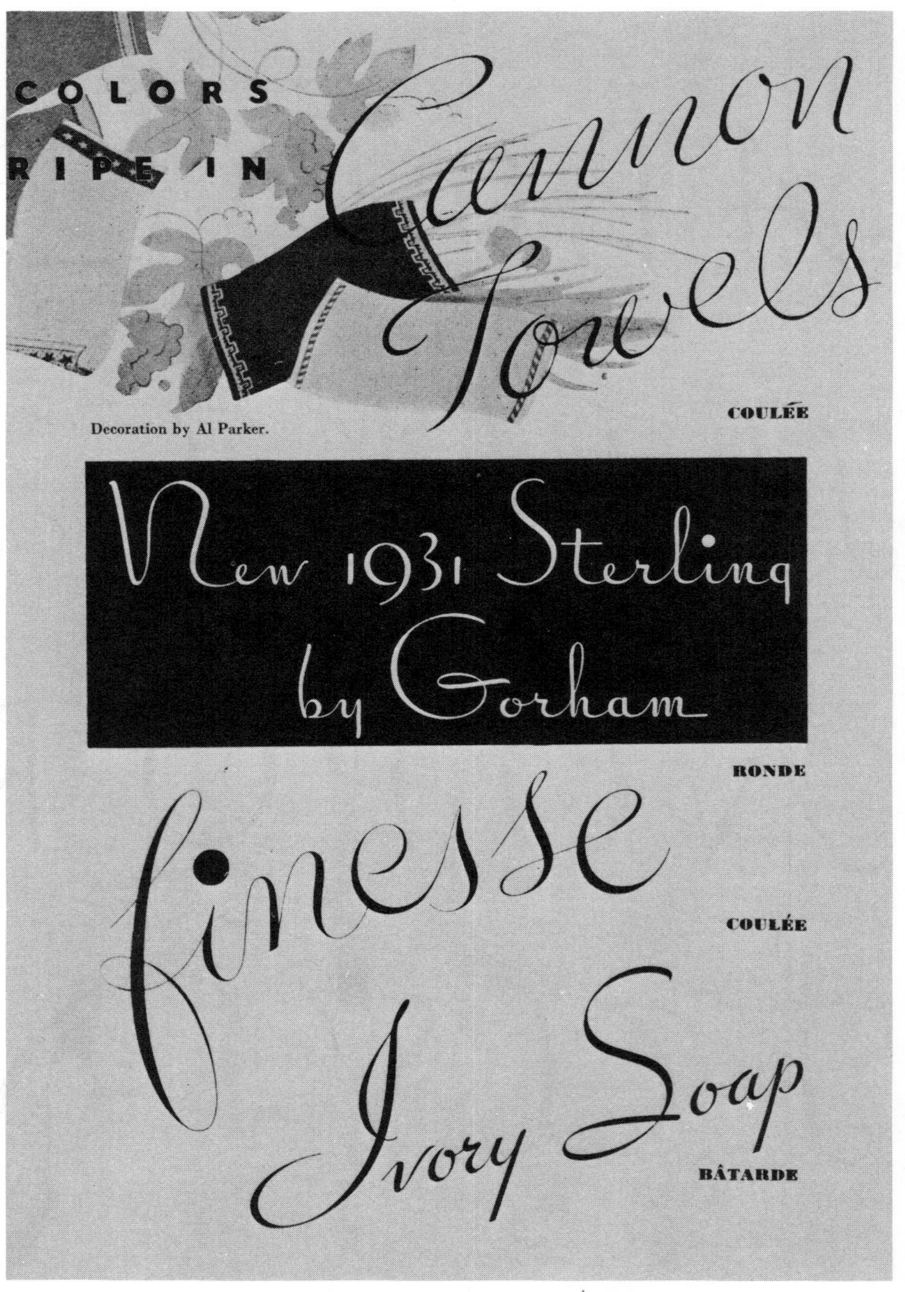

FIGURE 143: Tommy Thompson: The script letter, its form, construction and application. (One of the "How to Do It" series) 1939

Most of the examples we have seen in this book so far have been of formal scripts. Here is an example of calligraphy applied to advertising, a use that was to become increasingly important as the century progressed. While noting the fluid quality of the scripts, we see that the names given to them link them directly to the traditional sources on which they are based.

VICTORIA & ALBERT MUSEUM L.662–1940 24.5 × 19

IN FEBRUARY
IF THE DAYS BE CLEAR

The waking bee, still drowsy on the wing,
Will guess the opening of another year
And blunder out to seek another spring.
Crashing through winter sunlight's pallid gold,
His clumsiness sets catkins on the willow
Ashake like lambs' tails in the early fold.
But when the rimy afternoon turns cold
And undern squalls buffet the chilly fellow,
He'll seek the hive's warm waxen welcoming
And set about the chamber's classic mould.
And then pell-mell his harvest follows swift,
Blossom & borage, lime and balm & clover,
On Downs the thyme, on cliff the scantling thrift,
Everywhere bees go racing with the hours,
For every bee becomes a drunken lover
Standing upon his head to sup the flowers.

Taken from "The Land," by Victoria Sackville-West

Written out by Wendy Westover, December 1952

FIGURE 144: Wendy Westover: A passage from "The Land," by Victoria Sackville-West 1952

Wendy Westover studied calligraphy with Margaret Alexander, and she also studied lettering and letter-cutting with David Kindersley. It is not surprising therefore that the script in this work has a bold, almost sculptural, appearance. It is amusing to note that, like her medieval counterpart, she has made her letters smaller when it appeared that they would not all fit onto one line. How many times has she had to do this? Would the layout have been spoiled if she had let the poetic line spill over into two written lines?

VICTORIA & ALBERT MUSEUM MS. CIRC. 179–1953

V. Angelus domini nuntiavit Mariæ:
R. Et concepit de Spiritu Sancto:
Ave Maria, gratia plena. Dominus
tecum: benedicta tu in mulieribus. et
benedictus fructus ventris tui. Jesus
Sancta Maria, mater Dei. ora
pro nobis peccatoribus. nunc et in
hora mortis nostræ: Amen.
V. Ecce ancilla Domini:
R. Fiat mihi secundum verbum tuum:
Ave Maria
V. Et verbum caro factum est:
R. Et habitavit in nobis:
Ave Maria
V. Ora pro nobis Sancta Dei Genitrix:
R. Ut digni efficiamur promissionibus Christi:
Oremus
Gratiam tuam. quæsumus Domine. menti-
bus nostris infunde. ut qui angelo nuntiante.
Christi Filii tui Incarnationem cognovim-
us per Passionem eius et crucem ad Res-
urrectionis gloriam perducamur. Per eum
dem Christum Dominum nostrum. Amen.

145

FIGURE 145: Ruth Mary Wood: The Angelus 1953

The original manuscript is written out in red and black, and together with the interesting layout of the text, makes an attractive appearance. But appearances can be deceptive! When we come to look at the individual words we realize that, just as in some of the medieval scripts, the minims are so placed as to make the words difficult to read. Look at "nuntiavit" in the first line, and "Dominus" in the third. However, this fact also underlines the point that studying calligraphy from illustrations is never entirely satisfactory, since the definition is much clearer in the original.

VICTORIA & ALBERT MUSEUM
CIRC. 201–1953

FIGURE 146: John Woodcock: Quotations from "The Family Reunion," by T. S. Eliot 1953

The layout of verse is always a problem; see how John Woodcock has set about this passage. There is a change of script between the first five lines and the rest, the former being further united by the elongated capital letter "I" of the first word. Notice too the extra weight given to the initial letter "T" when there is a pause or break in the development of the theme.

VICTORIA & ALBERT MUSEUM
MS. CIRC. 169–1953

CHORUS

IN AN OLD HOUSE there is always listening, and more is heard than is spoken.
And what is spoken remains in the room, waiting for the future to hear it.
And whatever happens began in the past, and presses hard on the future.
The agony in the curtained bedroom, whether of birth or of dying,
Gathers in to itself all the voices of the past, and projects them into the future.

The treble voices on the lawn
The mowing of hay in summer
The dogs and the old pony
The stumble and the wail of little pain
The chopping of wood in autumn
And the singing in the kitchen
And the steps at night in the corridor
The moment of sudden loathing
And the season of stifled sorrow
The whisper, the transparent deception
The keeping up of appearances
The making the best of a bad job
All twined and tangled together, all are recorded.
There is no avoiding these things
And we know nothing of exorcism
And whether in Argos or England
There are certain inflexible laws
Unalterable, in the nature of music.
There is nothing at all to be done about it,
There is nothing to do about anything,
And now it is nearly time for the news
We must listen to the weather report
And the international catastrophes.

from "THE FAMILY REUNION" by T.S. Eliot O.M.

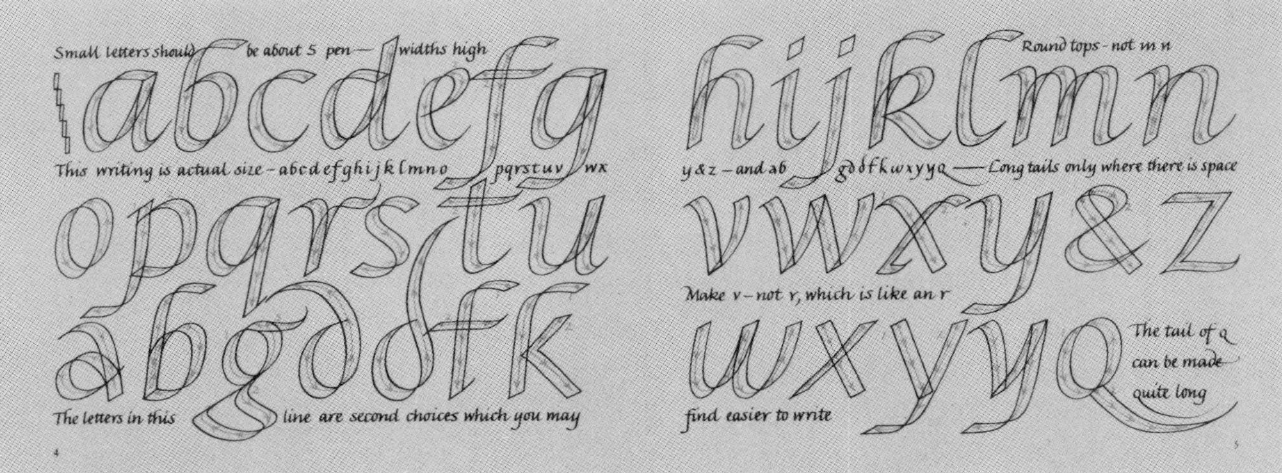

147

abcdefghij
klmnopqrs
ftuvwxyz

148

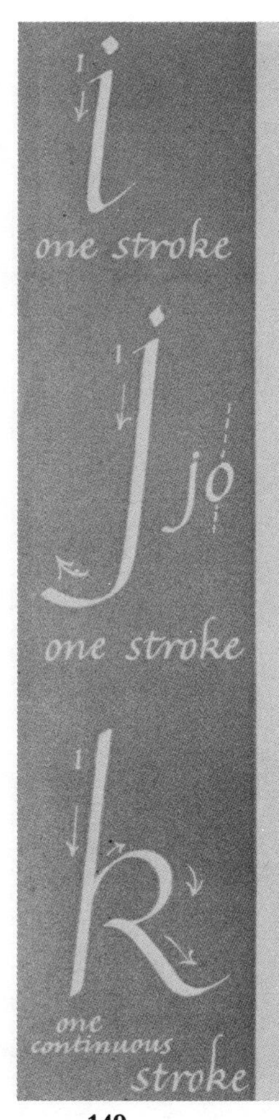

149

FIGURE 147: George L. Thomson: Better Handwriting 1954 (Puffin Picture Book 96)

Note the title! Also that the work was issued in a popular paperback edition. It is indicative of an interest in handwriting and a desire to produce something better than is possible with the ball-point pen. Thomson advocates the italic hand not only because he considers it more pleasing to the eye, but also because it is less likely to deteriorate when written at speed. Note how he has indicated the way the pen should flow when forming the letters.

VICTORIA & ALBERT MUSEUM L.2708–1954 18 × 22

FIGURE 148: Hans Burkardt: Pinselschriften 1958

Brush-stroke scripts like this one are frequently used in advertisement art today; they give a feeling of spontaneity which is lacking in more formal scripts. The modern felt-tip pen is especially suitable for copying this type of letter. Try it!

VICTORIA & ALBERT MUSEUM L.2136–1961 25.5 × 20

FIGURE 149: Irene Wellington: The Irene Wellington copybook 1957

We still need copybooks today, though we follow them less slavishly than our predecessors did. And today's masters still provide us with copies. Irene Wellington taught many of today's leading calligraphers.

VICTORIA & ALBERT MUSEUM L.3722–1957 18 × 23

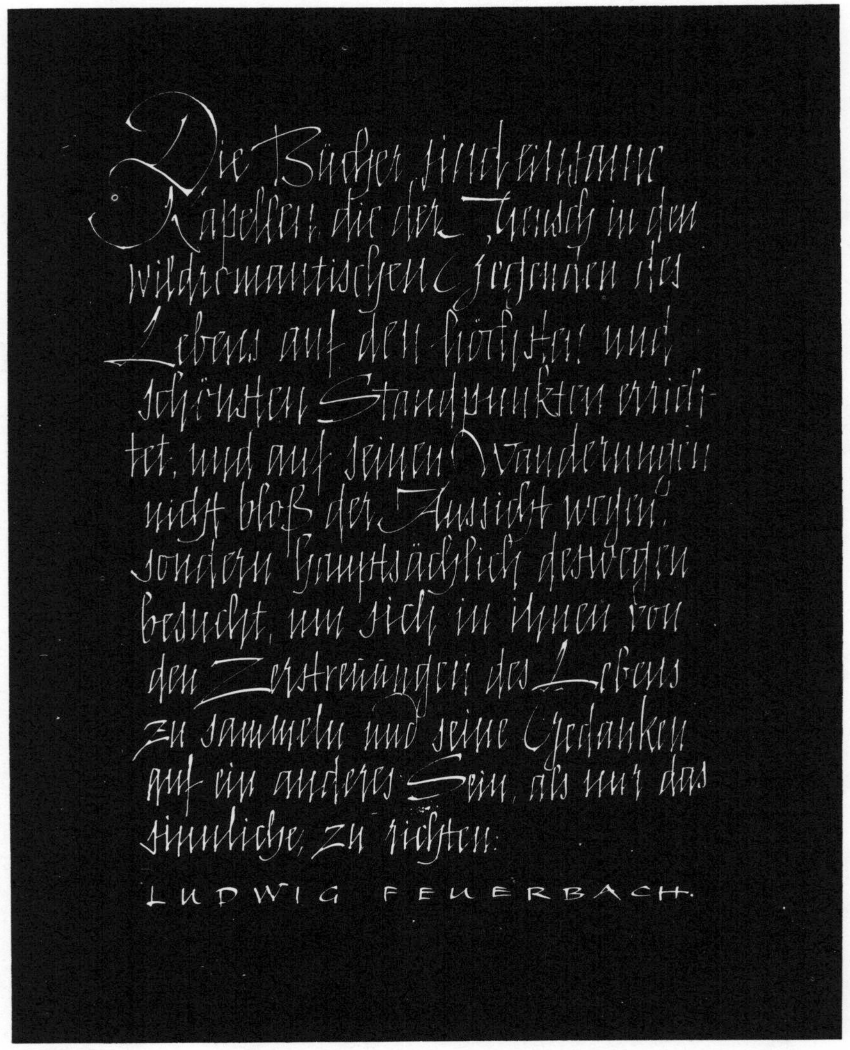

150

FIGURE 150: Friedrich Poppl: Quotation from Ludwig Feuerbach 1960

White-on-black examples go back to the earliest writing masters, and make an interesting change from the usual black script. Friedrich Poppl is a German calligrapher, and since we are perhaps less familiar with the words he has written, we have more chance to concentrate on the general appearance of this piece of writing, and the decorative pattern it makes on the paper.

VICTORIA & ALBERT MUSEUM MS.CIRC.164–1966

FIGURE 151: Herbert Lindgren: Circular greetings letter 1960

This amusing piece from Sweden has been written out in white ink on dark paper. It is not easy to keep the script even when it is written out in this circular form—try it yourself!

VICTORIA & ALBERT MUSEUM MS.CIRC.723–1966

Hej du tappre vandrare. Det var roligt att höra att Du kommit hem välbehållen. Jag förstår att det smakade gott med en festmåltid efter den resan. Tack för Ditt brev! Jag är mycket imponerad av Dina kunskaper i svenska språket. Synd att Du inte hade tillfälle att stanna här något längre. Med många hälsningar från oss på konstnärliga avdelningen genom vännen Herbert Lindgren

Stockholm den 18·10·1960

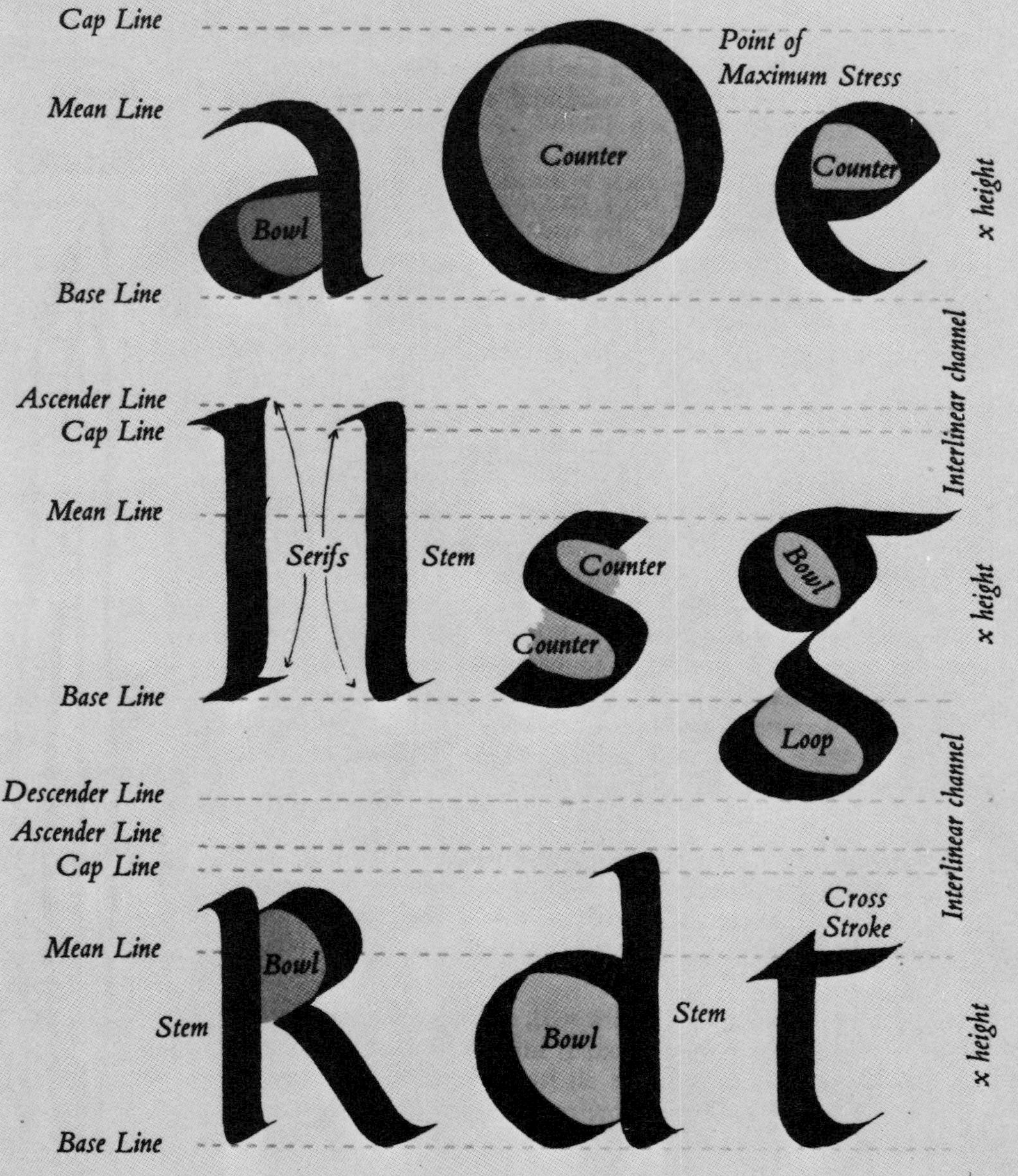
The Names of the Parts of a Letter
Cap Line
Point of
Maximum Stress
Mean Line
Counter
Counter
Bowl
x height
Base Line
Interlinear channel
Ascender Line
Cap Line
Mean Line
Serifs
Stem
Counter
Bowl
x height
Counter
Base Line
Loop
Descender Line
Ascender Line
Cap Line
Interlinear channel
Cross
Stroke
Mean Line
Bowl
Stem
Bowl
Stem
x height
Base Line
15

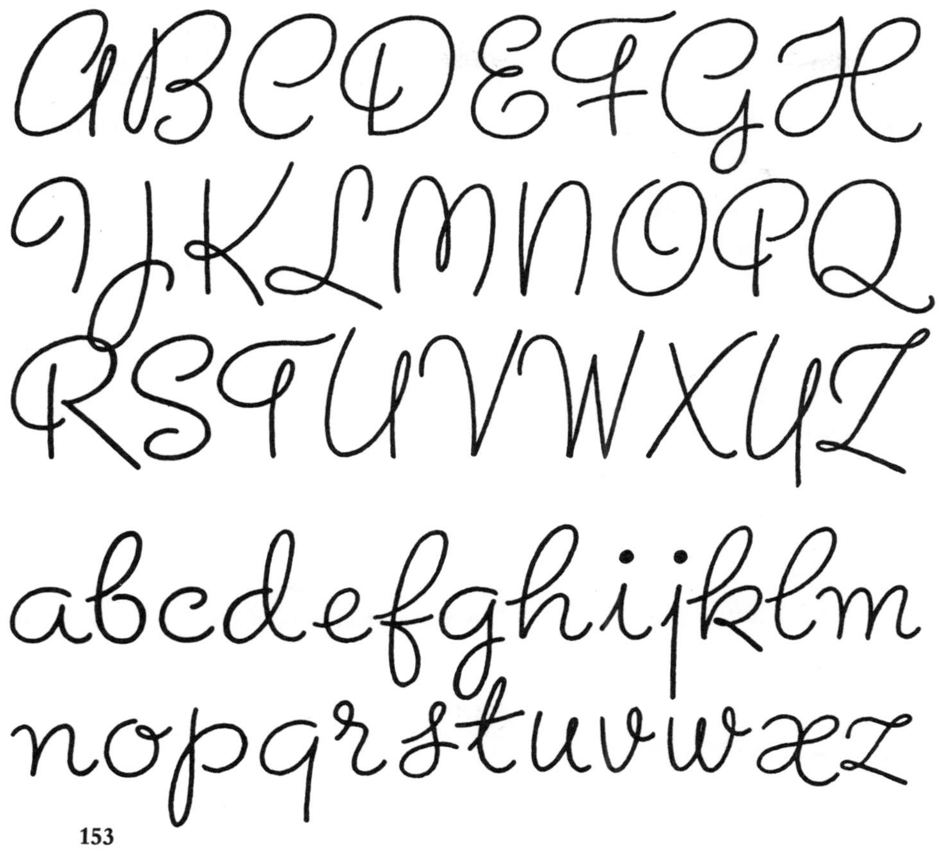

153

FIGURE 152: John R. Biggs: The craft of the pen 1961

John Biggs has written a number of books on calligraphy and typography. This particular illustration is useful because many writers on calligraphy (including the present one!) use technical terms for the parts of a letter without ever defining them. Not only does this explain the parts of a letter, but it also indicates clearly that letters are made up of parts, something we rarely think about when we come to actually write them.

VICTORIA & ALBERT MUSEUM L.3724–1961 22 × 15

FIGURE 153: M. Meijer: Script lettering. Revised edition 1964

This is the type of lettering used extensively in commercial art, and as the author says, it can vary between "a sense of urgency, and quiet elegance." Much of the work in this book was done with a brush, and hence it would be suitable for writing with the modern felt-tip pen.

VICTORIA & ALBERT MUSEUM L.2084–1964 25 × 19

THE BOOKE TO HIS READERS

Come hether you that much desire.
Rare flowers of dyvers landes
I represent the same to you.
Set downe unto your hands.
Presentinge them unto your vew
In perfect shape and faire :
And also teach to colour them.
Not missinge of a haire.
Vsinge such coulours as requires.
A master workeman will :
Not swarving thence in any case.
Declaringe there his skill.
Each flower his proper lineament
Presentes from top to toe :
And shewes both Roote, budd, blade, and stalke.
So as each doth growe.
Sparinge no paines, nor charge I have.
Each seasons flower te passe :
In winter, somer, springe and fall.
Vntill this compleate was.
Now use this same for thy delight.
Injoy it as thou wilt :
Of blotts and blurrs most carefully
Refraine, or else t'is spilt.

From 'A garden of Flowers' by Thomas Wood, the English version of the HORTUS FLORIDUS by Crispian van de Passe the younger, printed at Utrecht 1615.

154

FIGURE 154: Thomas Swindlehurst: From "A Garden of Flowers," by Thomas Wood 1965

Many medieval scribes adorned their manuscripts with flowers, even as this modern calligrapher has done. Note the shape of the work, and the way he has placed his text and illustrations within the frame he has chosen. Do you think it would have been better with a different layout, or is the artist right in doing it this way?

VICTORIA & ALBERT MUSEUM MS. CIRC. 193–1966

FIGURE 155: Karl Georg Hoefer: Pinselstudien 1962

This work is in the form of a folder and contains a great variety of alphabets. This illustration shows a set of formal square capitals, and also a pattern of flowing forms of the kind used in advertisement art. Here the letters of the alphabet have been used merely as a starting point for a decorative pattern.

VICTORIA & ALBERT MUSEUM MS. L. 136–1966 30 × 20

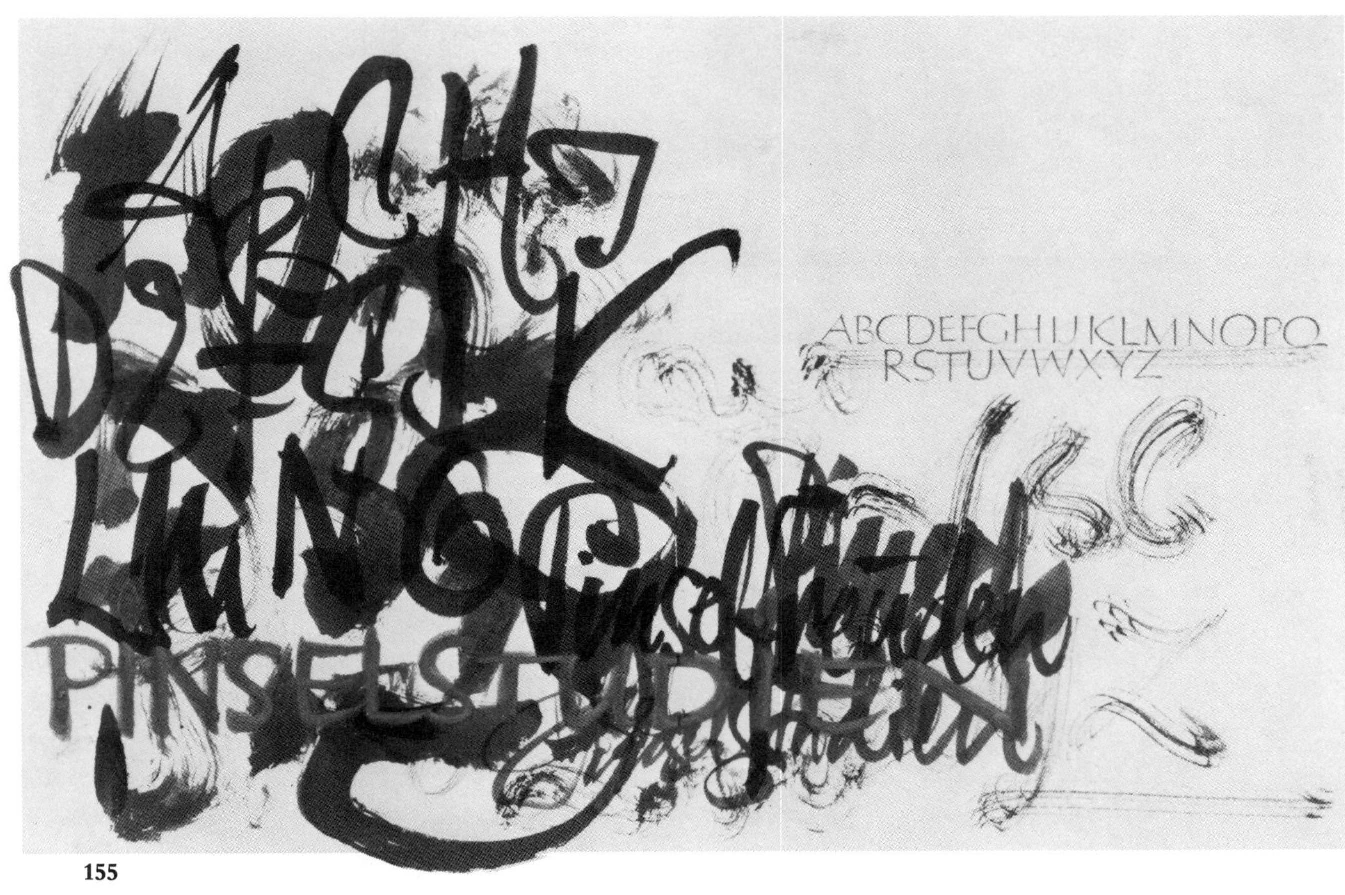

155

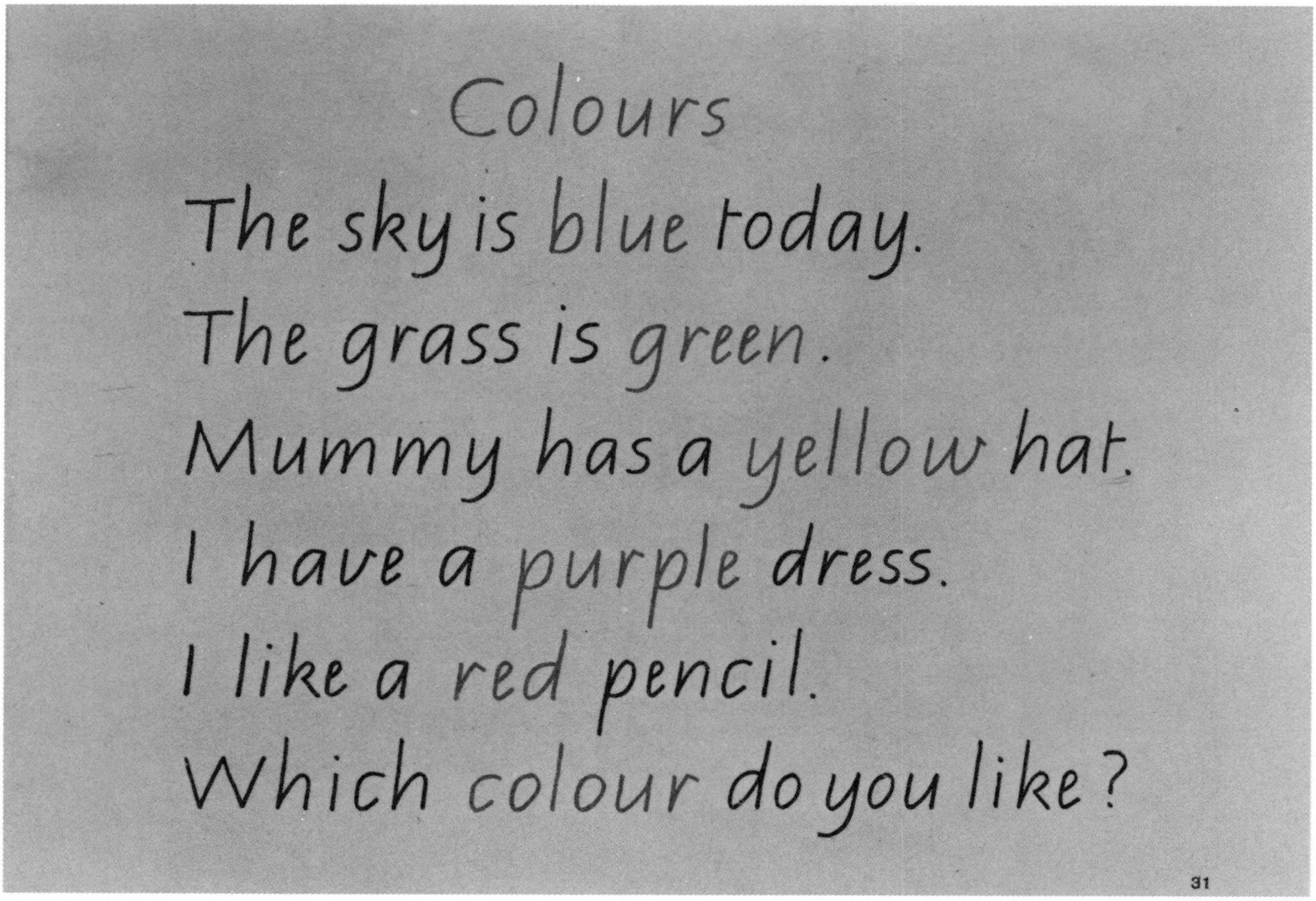

Colours

The sky is blue today.
The grass is green.
Mummy has a yellow hat.
I have a purple dress.
I like a red pencil.
Which colour do you like?

31

156

FIGURE 156: Tom Gourdie: The simple modern hand, Book I 1965

Tom Gourdie is a Scottish calligrapher and was a pupil of Irene Wellington (plate 149). He has done much to introduce italic writing in Scotland by his writings, exhibitions, and lectures. And this is a simple hand, suitable for the youngest pupil to begin with.

VICTORIA & ALBERT MUSEUM L.1030–1966 18 × 22

FIGURE 157: Joan Pilsbury: The Prelude, Book I, by William Wordsworth 1967

This is a very plain page of script, although Joan Pilsbury is well-known for her decorative maps. The script here is very fine and delicate, and is written in a very black ink on a white page; additional colored inks are used in the headings, but always with great restraint.

VICTORIA & ALBERT MUSEUM MS.L.5011–1970 24 × 16

OH THERE IS BLESSING
IN THIS GENTLE BREEZE,
A visitant that while it fans my cheek
Doth seem half-conscious of the joy it brings
From the green fields, and from yon azure sky.
Whate'er its mission, the soft breeze can come
To none more grateful than to me; escaped
From the vast city, where I long had pined
A discontented sojourner: now free
Free as a bird to settle where I will.
What dwelling shall receive me? in what vale
Shall be my harbour? underneath what grove
Shall I take up my home? and what clear stream
Shall with its murmur lull me into rest?
The earth is all before me. With a heart
Joyous, nor scared at its own liberty,
I look about; and should the chosen guide
Be nothing better than a wandering cloud,
I cannot miss my way. I breathe again!

Escape from the vast city

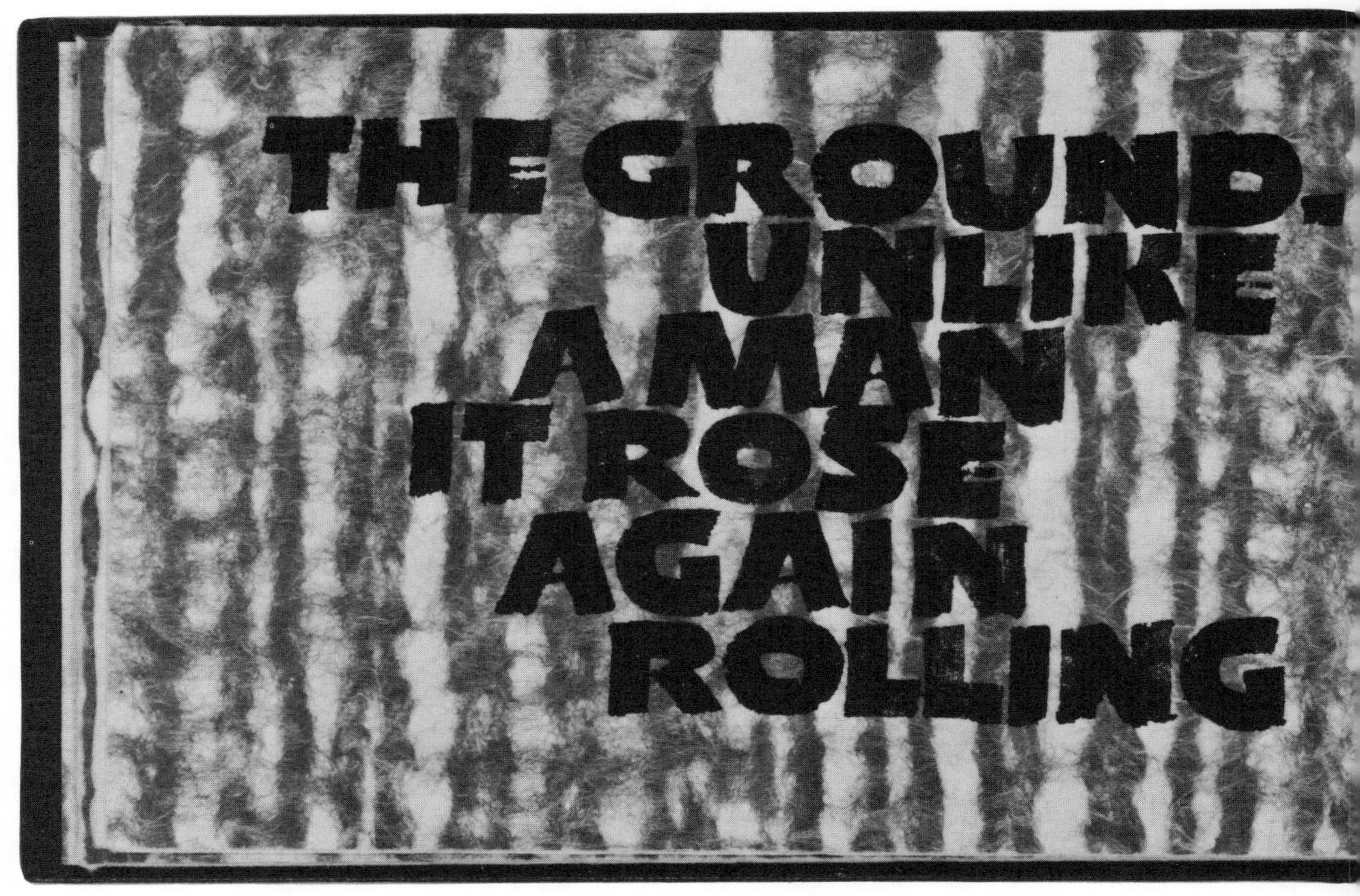

FIGURE 158: Pat Russell: The Term, by William Carlos Williams 1968

This example forms an interesting contrast to some of the more delicate scripts that we have seen elsewhere in this book, and of which Mrs. Russell is equally capable. However, a delicate script would have been quite out-of-place on this rough-textured and colored paper (it is brown and cream in the original manuscript), so she has chosen a thick bold form of lettering, which holds its own, and fittingly complements the book as a whole.

VICTORIA & ALBERT MUSEUM MS.L.2889–1970 10×16

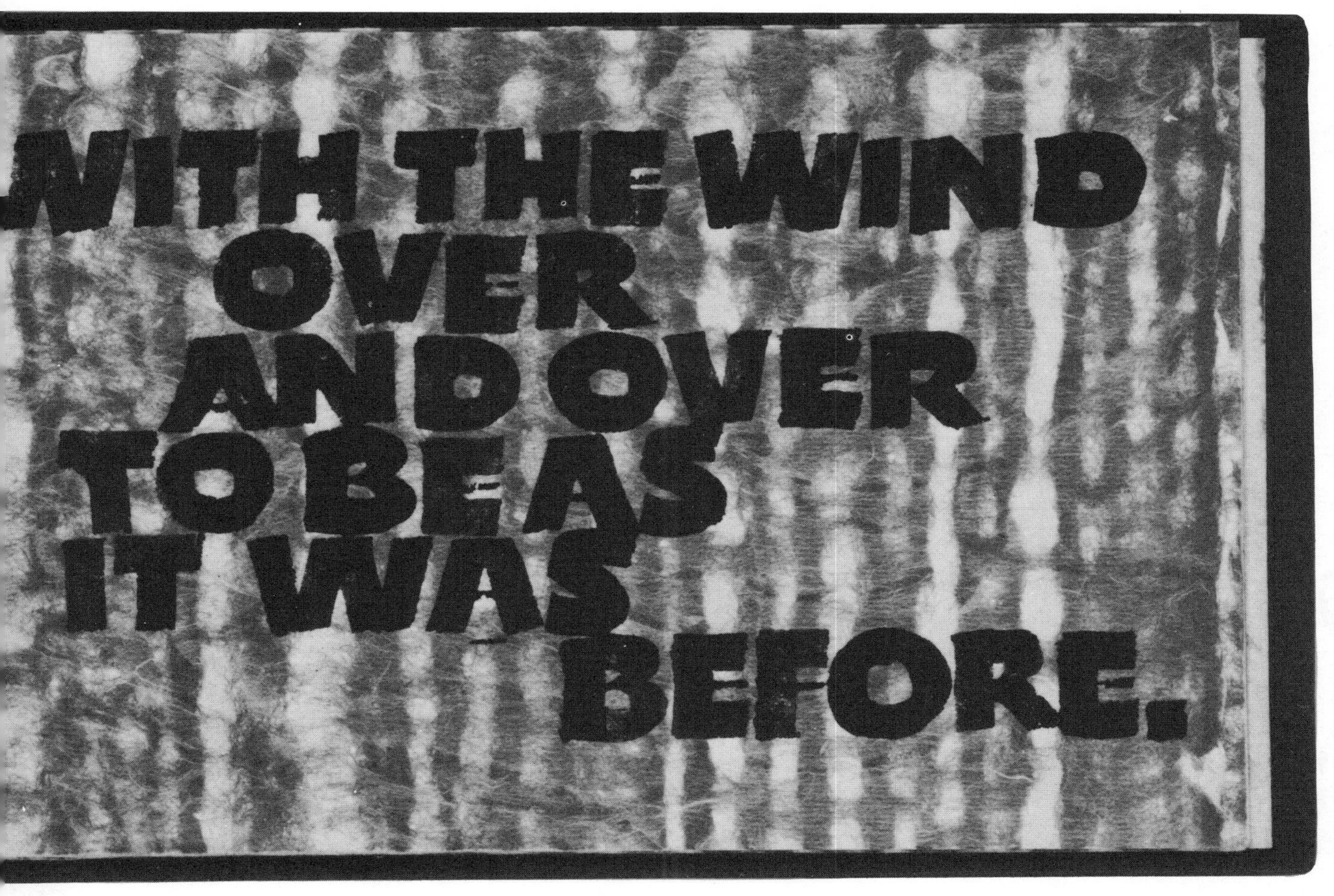
WITH THE WIND
OVER
AND OVER
TO BE AS
IT WAS
BEFORE.

THE·SINGING-BIRDS·OF·SELBORNE

From 'The Natural History of Selborne' by Rev. Gilbert White. Selected from the first and second Letters to the Hon. Daines Barrington, June 30th & Nov. 2nd 1769, on Singing-bir

Birds that sing in full song till after Midsummer

Woodlark	Alauda arborea	In January & continues to sing through all the summer and autumn.
Song-thrush	Turdus simpliciter dictus	In February and on to August: re-assume their song in Autumn.
Wren	Passer troglodytes	All the year: hard frost excepted
Red-breast	Rubecula	All the year: hard frost excepted
Hedge-sparrow	Curruca	Early in February, to July the 10th.
Yellow-hammer	Emberiza flava	Early in February and on through July to August the 21st.
Skylark	Alauda vulgaris	In February and on to October
Swallow	Hirundo domestica	From April to September
Black-cap	Atricapilla	Beginning of April, to July the 13th.
Titlark	Alauda pratorum	From middle of April to July the 16th
Blackbird	Merula vulgaris	Sometimes in February & March & so on to July 23rd: re-assumes in autumn
White-throat	Ficedulæ affinis	In April, and on to July the 23rd.
Goldfinch	Carduelis	April, and through to September 16th.
Greenfinch	Chloris	On to July and August 2nd.
Less Reed-sparrow	Passer arundinaceus minor	May, on to beginning of July
Common Linnet	Linaria vulgaris	Breeds and whistles on till August; re-assumes its note when they begin to congregate in October and again early before the flocks separate.

Birds that sing in the night — are but few

Nightingale	Luscinia	'In shadiest covert hid' – MILTON
Woodlark	Alauda arborea	Suspended in mid air
Less Reed-sparrow	Passer arundinaceus minor	Among reeds and willows

Birds that have somewhat of a note or song and yet are hardly to be called — Singing-birds

Golden-crowned Wren	Regulus cristatus	Its note as minute as its person; frequents the tops of high oaks and firs: the smallest British bird.
Small Willow-wren	Regulus non cristatus	Sings in March, and on to September
Largest Willow-wren	Regulus non cristatus	'Cantat voce stridula locustæ'; from end of April to August
Marsh Titmouse	Parus palustris	Haunts great woods: two harsh sharp notes
Grasshopper-lark	Alauda minima voce locustæ	Chirps all night; from the middle of April to the end of July
Martin	Hirundo agrestis	All the breeding time; from May to September
Bullfinch	Pyrrhula	
Bunting	Emberiza alba	From the end of January to July

Birds that cease to be in full song, and are usually silent at or before Midsummer

Middle Willow-wren	Regulus non cristatus	Middle of June; begins in April
Red-start	Ruticilla	Middle of June; begins in May
Chaffinch	Fringilla	Beginning of June; sings first in February
Nightingale	Luscinia	Middle of June; sings first in April

Birds that sing for a short time and very early in the Spring

Missel-bird	Turdus viscivorus	January the 2nd 1770, in February. Is called the Stormcock in Hampshire and Sussex, because its song is supposed to forebode windy wet weather; is the largest singing-bird we have
Great Titmouse or Ox-eye	Fringillago	In February, March, April; re-assumes for a short while in September

Birds that sing as they fly — are but few

Skylark	Alauda vulgaris	Rising, suspended, and falling
Titlark	Alauda pratorum	In its descent; also sitting on trees and walking on the ground
Woodlark	Alauda arborea	Suspended; in hot summer nights all night long
Blackbird	Merula vulgaris	Sometimes from bush to bush
White-throat	Ficedulæ affinis	Uses when singing on the wing odd jerks and gesticulations
Swallow	Hirundo domestica	In soft sunny weather
Wren	Passer troglodytes	Sometimes from bush to bush

159

FIGURE 159: Sheila M. Waters: The Singing Birds of Selbourne 1953

Mrs. Sheila Waters now lives and works in the United States, where she is better known for a quite different style of calligraphy. But it is interesting to see this delightful early work of hers and to compare it with her present output. We can thus see something of the directions taken by calligraphy today, especially in the United States.

VICTORIA & ALBERT MUSEUM MS.CIRC.167–1953

FIGURE 160: Sheila M. Waters: From the Book of Proverbs 1979

VICTORIA & ALBERT MUSEUM MS. CIRC. 167–1953

the soul of the slug-gard desir-eth, and hath no-thing
but the Soul of the DILIGENT shall be abundantly gratified
Chapter thirteen, Verse four
Sheila Waters·1978

160

CYDONIAN SPRING WITH HER ATTENDANT TRAIN,
MAELIDS & WATER-GIRLS,
STEPPING BENEATH A BOISTEROUS WIND FROM THRACE,
THROUGHOUT THIS SYLVAN PLACE
SPREADS THE BRIGHT TIPS,
& EVERY VINE-STOCK IS
CLAD IN NEW BRILLIANCIES.
AND WILD DESIRE
FALLS LIKE BLACK LIGHTNING.
O BEWILDERED HEART,
THOUGH EVERY BRANCH HAVE BACK WHAT LAST YEAR LOST,
SHE, WHO MOVED HERE AMID THE CYCLAMEN,
MOVES ONLY NOW A CLINGING TENUOUS GHOST.

161

FIGURE 161: Alison Urwick: From "The Spring," by Ezra Pound 1975

It is always difficult to get a good impression of a piece of calligraphy from a black-and-white photograph; that is especially true of this piece, where the scribe has not only varied the size of her letters but also the weight of color she has given them, in order to convey the sense of the passage. Alison Urwick says that the ideas for the letter forms were taken from a tomb of 1451 in Florence and from inscriptions in the Catacombs, but the result is something entirely modern.

VICTORIA & ALBERT MUSEUM MS.L.5436–1979

FIGURE 162: Ann Hechle: A calligraphic sampler 1979

This piece of calligraphy was specially commissioned by the Victoria and Albert Museum, London, but the choice of subject was left to the scribe. The sampler arose directly out of Miss Hechle's explanations in response to questions put to her during demonstration lessons by members of the public. In particular she has endeavored to show how different scripts can help to illuminate language and reflect the meaning of words. Study the sampler carefully, and then try out some experiments of a similar kind for yourself.

VICTORIA & ALBERT MUSEUM

alternative forms of
EACH STROKE HERE IS SINGLE
REFLECTS WIDTH OF PEN
flourished headings and ascenders:
R·O·M·A·N
CAPITAL LETTERS
·INSCRIPTIONAL·
WIDELY SPACED
CONDENSED
OLD FORMS OF CAPITALS REVIVED FOR CERTAIN USES
HIERARCHY OF SCRIPTS
sub head
Majuscules for headings & other important items, minuscule for main body of text. The longer the lines of writing, the more space is needed between them. Every context is unique
& the slithy toves
'twas brillig
condensed
daft·staff·half·laughed
absurd·word·stirred·bird
ate·eight·straight·gait
difficult to read
short lines can be neat
confusion · tongue-twisters · drama
BUILT UP LETTERS·FLOOD & IN
LINEAR
SEPARATE
compressed
SEQUENTIAL
gothic
Strange
Fantastic:
letters are illegible in the mass
italic branching arches
VERSALS
SIMPLE
decorative
alternatively in reverse
according to the flavour
of the text: A minuscule
has a more cursive and a
more informal character
WORDS ARE LIKE NOTES IN MUSIC
INTERLINEAR WRITING · AND
WHERE MEANING SUGGESTS IT:
TRANSLATIONS · DIALOGUE · ETC
QUO VADIS? · ORANGES · LEMONS
SAY THE BELLS OF ST CLEMENTS
Whither goest thou?
·O·P·E·N
UNCIALS · FLAT PEN ANGLE
RUGGED ROCKS
FOLLOW ROUND
PATTERNS
RAN
RASCAL
IN APPROPRIATE
THE RAGGED
EMBELLISHED
EVEN·UNEVEN
Ornate
ORNAMENTAL
fluid or static:
Words
alliteration
vowel assonance
end rhyme
I AM SOFT SIFT IN AN HOUR GLASS
THE DOWN-DUGGED GROUND-HUGGED GREY
All three bound together
even more complex still
counterpointed as below
STONES RING
LIKE EACH TUCKED STRING TELLS
EACH HUNG BELL'S
BOW SWUNG FINDS TONGUE TO FLING
OUT BROAD ITS NAME
narrative
narrative
crumpled horn
dog that worried
the rat that ate
THE HOUSE THAT JACK BUILT
DIFFERENT WAYS OF ILLUMINATING WORDS
TEMPO
rhythm & rhyme
stress
REGULAR METRE
Before the beginning of years
There came to the making of man
Time, with a gift of tears;
Grief, with a glass that ran;
Pleasure, with pain for leaven;
Summer, with flowers that fell;
Remembrance fallen from heaven,
And madness risen from hell.
a cock on a dung hill
crowing
to Lazarus the morning is vanity
IMAGERY
The Werberlonde Winde Wapped the
STARTLE
The SOUR SCYTHE CRINGE and the BLEAR SHARE COME
the poor sheep BACK · is the SHIPWRACK then a HARVEST
does TEMPEST carry the GRAIN for thee?
THE SEDGE HAS WITHER'D FROM THE LAKE
AND NO BIRDS SING
SPRUNG RHYTHM
current language

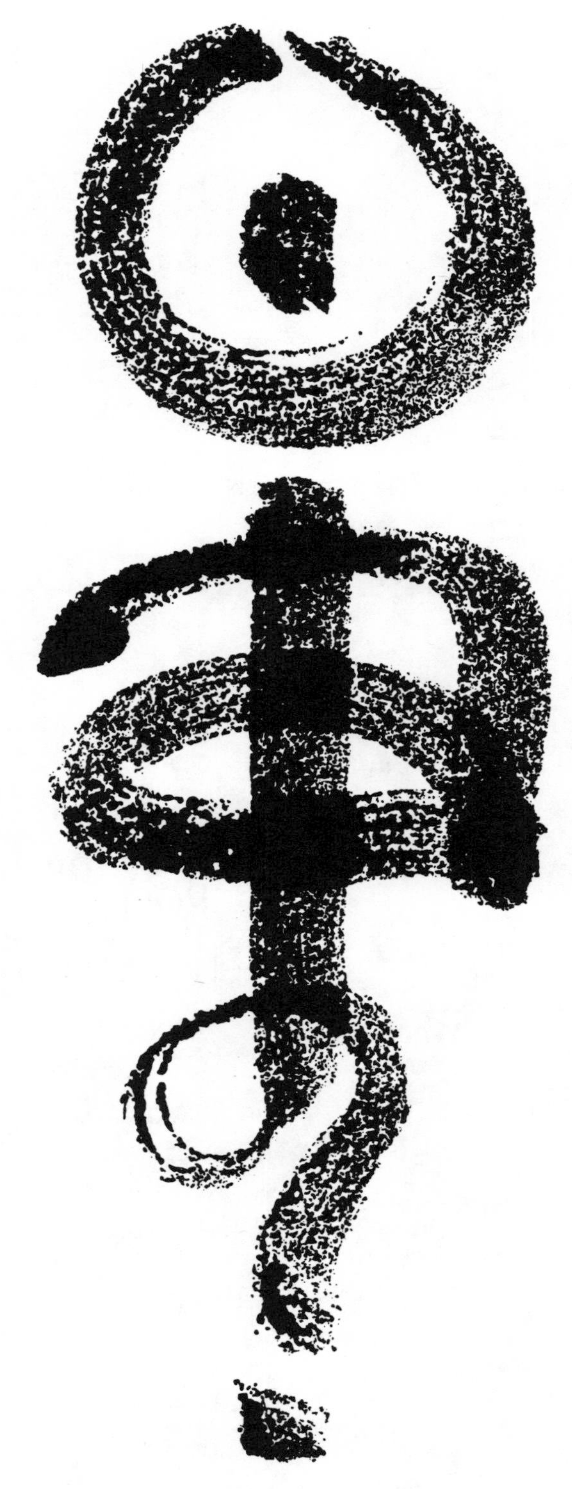

FIGURE 163: Ben Aalbers: O ja? Is that so? Ah bon? 1980?

This scribe, who works in The Netherlands, has used the letter forms of his phrase (O Ja?) to present an abstract image, while still conveying a sense of inquiry—see how the question mark dominates the design. Why not try your own hand at making similar links between phrases and their calligraphic expression?

AUTHOR'S COLLECTION 33 × 12

SNOWDROP
Galanthus nivalis
AMARYLLIDACEAE

The snowdrop is a native of Switzerland, Austria and Southern Europe. It was introduced to this country from Italy. It is sometimes called Fair Maid of February or Bulbous Violet. One of the first flowers of the year, it is also known as the emblem of Hope.

FIGURE 164: Betty Mayall: The snowdrop 1982

This is one of a set of small greeting cards that have been printed in black-and-white and then colored by the artist. Note the different styles of lettering she has used for the different parts of the text, and also the layout she has chosen. As with so many of the examples in this section, the illustration fails to do justice to the delicacy of the original design.

ARTIST'S COLLECTION 14.5 × 10.5

FIGURE 165: George Bickham: The universal penman 1743

This is an engraving taken from one of the pages of Bickham's splendid book, and it shows writers busily at work. In the middle we see a man using a pen knife to "mend" his quill, while his young assistant stands beside him with a further supply. These scenes must have been common in offices of the period.

VICTORIA & ALBERT MUSEUM 39×26

APPENDIX: WRITING IMPLEMENTS AND ACCESSORIES

THROUGHOUT the present book, the style of writing has been linked to the type of writing implements and materials in current use. This appendix is a summary of much of the information that has already been included in the various chapters, but has been brought together here for quick reference.

The commonest writing instrument used by the Romans was the reed pen, and it was used on papyrus; Roman books were usually kept in rolls or scrolls. But the Romans also made use of a metal stylus, especially when they wished to make quick or ephemeral jottings, which were usually done on wooden tablets covered with wax. The wax could be smoothed over and the surface re-used when the writing was no longer needed. Since this resembles the old school slate or blackboard, it is not surprising to find that wax tablets were the usual "notebooks" of the Roman schoolboy.

Vellum or parchment, which was made from the skins of animals, became more common during the Middle Ages, partly on account of the shortage of papyrus, and partly because of its greater durability. However, it was not a suitable material for making into rolls, nor were the Roman scroll books the easiest type for use by scholars. As a result the vellum codex, or modern-style book, gradually took the place of the earlier papyrus scroll. Although the reed pen still continued to be used, especially for certain parts of the text, the quill pen became the main writing implement and reigned supreme until the nineteenth century. Both vellum and quills needed a considerable amount of preparation before they could be used for writing. Vellum was usually supplied to the scribe more or less ready for use, though each writer would be prepared to improve or amend the surface before starting to work. But quills were normally prepared and mended (as they wore down) by the individual scribe himself, and methods of preparing the quill for use were frequently included in all the early copybooks.

Also included in the copybooks were recipes for ink. There were two kinds of ink. One was made from a combination of oak galls and iron salts, and this kind, known as *encaustum,* literally burnt into the writing surface; it tended to become brown with age. The other kind of ink was much blacker, but was inclined to flake off the surface, since it was composed of a suspension of carbon (such as lamp-black) in a mixture of gum and water. Many scribes made their own ink, with varying results, and it was not until 1834 that Henry Stephens set up the first ink factory in England, to produce, it was said, a non-corroding ink. But it was only with the discovery of aniline dyes in 1856 that a really satisfactory ink could be produced and supplied to all who needed it, thus at last obviating the need for the scribe to make his own.

With improved inks the steel pen was able to flourish, its nib uncorroded, and this pen directly affected the contemporary style of writing. A further development made during the last quarter of the nineteenth century was an improved version of the fountain pen. Many people had tried to invent a method to save the need to constantly replenish the ink supply when writing, and various kinds of reservoir pen had been tried out over the centuries. Many, and sometimes strange, were the types of fountain pen offered to the public before the style settled down to about four variants, each using a different method of filling the pen. But even the best fountain pen could hold only a limited amount of ink, and could not be compared with the next development, which was the ball-point pen. Although a patent had been taken out for a ball-point pen as early as 1895, in its present form it is the invention of two Hungarian brothers, Ladislao and Georg Biro, who first applied for patents in 1938. Its development was encouraged in the United States by defense experts who wanted a pen that would not leak at high altitudes, with a quick-drying ink, and that would be long-lasting. Today the ball-point pen is part of everyone's life, but its effect on calligraphy has been disastrous: it is too easy to use for it ever to produce stylish writing. A more recent development has been the felt-tip pen, and this is in fact much more like the old reed pen, for it can be used in a variety of ways to give character and style to handwriting.

For the most part, all the pens used in recent centuries have been made to write on paper rather than vellum, ever since paper mills began to become more widely established in the later Middle Ages. But the kind of paper that has been available has changed considerably. Until the nineteenth century, methods of producing paper changed little, and much of the preparation was done by hand. Inevitably in the nineteenth century the idea of mass-production was applied to papermaking as to many other things, thus making it cheaper and more consistent in quality. But not all paper is equally good, even today. The use of wood pulp in its manufacture, rather than the rags previously employed, has given rise to much poor quality material that quickly discolors and becomes brittle. Calligraphers watch out! One should choose writing paper with the same care as would be taken in choosing a pen, and it is worth noting that when professional scribes have a special piece of work to do, they frequently still prefer vellum.

Apart from the main items mentioned above, there were of course many more adjuncts to writing than such mere necessities. In the past the scribe also needed inkpots, pen knives, pounce pots, blotters—to name just a few. These are just some of the accessories that you as an interested calligrapher may like to think about, perhaps even collect. You should also look at contemporary prints and paintings, to see the various writing implements portrayed there, and to note how the people of the past sat, wrote, and held their pens. Then think how all this affected the writing of the period. Do such things have the same effect on your handwriting today? If not, what does?

For more information on the subject of this section see *Writing Implements and Accessories from the Roman Stylus to the Typewriter,* by J.I. Whalley (David & Charles, reprinted 1980).

Before you begin to Write, be accommodated with theſe neceſſary Impliments or Inſtruments. (*viz.*) 1. A choice *Pen-knife* of Razor-metal. 2. A *Hone*, and *Sallet-Oil*, wherewith to renew the Edge of your *Knife*. 3. Store of *Quills*, round, hard and clear, the Seconds in the Wings of Geeſe or Ravens. 4. Pure white, ſmooth grain'd, well gum'd Paper, or a Book made of ſuch, well preſſed. 5. The beſt *Ink* that you can poſſibly procure. 6. *Gum-ſandrick* beaten into Powder, ſearced, and tyed up in a fine Linen-cloth, wherewith pounce your Paper. 7. A flat *Ruler* for certainty, and a round one for diſpatch. 8. A ſmall pair of *Compaſſes*, wherewith to Rule double Lines at the firſt, and to keep your Lines equi-diſtant. 9. A choice *Black-lead Pen*. 10. *Indian Black-duſt*, or fine Sand, to throw on Letters written in haſte. 11. A ſmooth *Black Slate*, whereon to exerciſe the command of Hand in the expeditious producing of great Letters and Flouriſhes.

All theſe Accommodations will concern;
But moſt of all a willing mind to learn.

FIGURE 166: Edward Cocker: England's penmen 1703

This useful list for the would-be scribe was typical of the information frequently included in copybooks of all periods. Some of the instructions are still valid today!

VICTORIA & ALBERT MUSEUM

FIGURE 167: Denis Diderot: Enciclopédie; ou, dictionnaire des sciences, des arts, et des métiers 1751–1780

Vellum needs a lot of preparation before it can be used by the scribe, and methods of converting animal skins into writing material changed little over the centuries. This eighteenth-century engraving is taken from the Enciclopédie; ou, dictionnaire des sciences, des arts et des metiers *published by Diderot between 1751 and 1780, and shows the various stages in the preparation of vellum.*

FIGURE 168:

A further illustration from Diderot's Enciclopédie *showing the processes involved in papermaking before they were mechanized. It is still possible to buy handmade paper today, and many scribes prefer its texture.*

FIGURE 169: Tailpiece from "The Universal Penman," by George Bickham 1743

FIGURE 170:

An engraving from L'art d'éscrire *by C. Paillasson, 1783, which shows a selection of writing implements including a quill cutter or pen knife, a pounce pot, and inkstand which includes a bell for summoning the servant!*

VICTORIA & ALBERT MUSEUM L.1908–1911

FIGURE 171: Marchand: Nouveaux principes d'écriture italienne avec des exemples suivant l'ordre de Madame Maintenon pour les demoiselles de la Maison Royale de St. Louis établie a St. Cyr. Par le maître à écrire de Madame la Duchesse de Bourgogne Paris 1721

Many copybooks of all periods included an illustration showing how the pupil should sit and hold the pen. This is a particularly charming example, which is thought to show the young Duchess herself. The Italian hand was nearly always the one recommended for ladies—because it was supposed to be easier to learn!

VICTORIA & ALBERT MUSEUM L.2036–1978 19×25

have produced them. Thus, a *curve* which from the natural point of vision shows the rounding or *convex* surface is known as the *first* principle; a curve which shows the hollow or *concave* surface is the *second* principle; a combination of the two with the *convex* at the bottom and the *concave* at the top is the *third* principle; the reverse of this the *fourth* principle; and the *straight line*, in whatever position, the *fifth* principle.

A teacher who has these simple facts well grounded in the minds of his pupils has attained a leverage which can be used with astonishing results.

The advantage of adopting as the *principles* of writing simple lines, instead of combinations and complete letters, will be obvious to any thoughtful teacher; for not only can they be more readily and certainly acquired and retained by the pupil, but their constant recurrence and ready adjustment to practical ends, place the student so squarely and understandingly in the line of advancement, that progress is a natural result.

The *principles* once clearly fixed in the mind, their combinations into parts of letters, and thence into the letters complete, are easily enforced.

This will be shown in the model lessons which follow.

CLASS INSTRUCTION.

The time given to class instruction in writing, in schools where it is not taught as a specialty, is usually from a half to three-fourths of an hour to each lesson, with from two to five lessons per week. It is scarcely necessary to say that five lessons a week are preferable to less, even if the time for each lesson has to be shortened. A half-hour's class-drill, if no time is wasted, even if but three times a week, may be made productive of very gratifying results. When it is possible to do so, the writing hour should be fixed in the early part of the day, or before the pupil is worn out with application to study.

The use of copy-books with engraved copies and printed instruction has made it not only possible but feasible for any intelligent and faithful teacher to conduct the writing exercises with good success. Of course, in this, as in any study, the more conversant the teacher is with his subject, its applications and unfoldings, the better. It will be of great service to him to be able to exemplify the lessons upon the blackboard, and especially to point out characteristic faults. The use of charts, however, has made even this qualification not so essential as it would otherwise be.

It is, however, of the first importance that the class should be utterly under the teacher's control, and that everything should be done promptly and in order. This will necessitate movements in concert by proper signals. We shall not take up space in prescribing the methods of getting the classes in proper position for work, as it is presumed that the teacher is sufficiently master of his business to accomplish this task without special directions.

POSITION AT THE DESK.

COMMENCING THE WRITING EXERCISE.

We will suppose that the class is properly seated and in order; writing-books and pens lying properly on the desks; students sitting erect, with their eyes upon the teacher. The signals may be given either with a tap upon the bell or the word of command. The signals will be as follows:

1. *Open books.* The books should be opened at the copy and the attention of the class called to the lesson of the hour, with such general hints, blackboard illustrations, etc., as are deemed essential.
2. *Take position.* The students will simultaneously assume the position at the desk which is required of them when writing.
3. *Open inkstands.*
4. *Take pens.*
5. *Write.*

FIGURE 172: J.D. Williams and S.S. Packard: Guide to Williams & Packard's system of penmanship for teachers and adepts New York 1869

This sort of instruction continued in copybooks well into the nineteenth century. The teacher is supposed to instruct by a series of abrupt orders, which are given in the text below the picture.

VICTORIA & ALBERT MUSEUM L.611–1916 18.5×26.5

Glossary of Terms

Antiphoner Volume containing the choral parts of the Church Offices.

ascender Part of a letter which goes above the main body, e.g. *l, h*.

bastarda script A mixture of Gothic and cursive hands.

"black-letter" Gothic lettering, especially that used after the invention of printing.

Books of Hours Prayer books of private devotions for the use of laymen; especially popular in the fifteenth century.

cancellaresca Script used in the fifteenth and sixteenth centuries in the Papal chancellery.

Carolingian script Style of writing originating during the reign of the Emperor Charlemagne (742–814).

catchword The first word at the top of a page written at the bottom of the preceding one, usually intended to assist the binder in putting the book together.

chancery hand Script derived from that in use in the Papal Chancellery.

codex Manuscript with pages, in the form of the modern book.

command of hand See striking.

copperplate script Term used mainly of eighteenth and nineteenth century hands which were influenced by engraved rather than pen-made letters.

copybook A work containing a variety of scripts intended for the instruction of pupils.

copysheets A single sheet, sometimes decorated, containing examples of the pupil's writing ability.

cursive — A flowing script with letters joined together.

descender — Part of a letter which goes below the main body, e.g. *g*, *y*.

Fraktur — A form of the Gothic script which remained in use in Germany until the twentieth century.

Gradual — Volume containing the choral parts of the Mass.

graver — An engraving tool or burin, especially for use on copperplates.

humanist script — Script used by the early humanists, i.e. scholars of the Renaissance period who studied the culture of Greece and Rome.

italic script — Named after Italy, its country of origin, this script shows a pronounced slope to the right.

majuscules — Large capital letters based originally on Roman monumental lettering.

minuscules — Small, often cursive, letters.

papyrus — Reed grown mostly in the eastern Mediterranean and used to make writing material in Roman and early Christian times.

pen knife — Small knife used by scribes to prepare the quill for writing.

pricking — Prick marks in the margins of manuscripts were for guide lines to assist the scribe to keep his writing even.

Psalter — Volume containing the Psalms.

quill pen — In common use from Medieval times until the nineteenth century, the quill was formed from the feathers (Latin = *penna*) of goose, crow or raven.

rotunda — Name given to the form of the Gothic script in Italy.

square capitals — The monumental capital letters of Roman inscriptions.

striking — A method of decorating the early copybooks with fantastic shapes usually "by one entire stroke of the pen"—or so it was claimed!

stylus — Ancient metal writing instrument.

textura — Name given to the Gothic script.

vellum — Material prepared from the skins of animals for use as a writing material.

BIBLIOGRAPHY

Anderson, D. M.	*The Art of Written Forms*. New York: Holt, Rinehart & Winston, 1969
Gray, N.	*Lettering as Drawing*. London: Oxford University Press, 1971
Jackson, D.	*The Story of Writing*. London: Studio Vista/Parker Pen Company, 1980
Johnston, E.	*Writing & Illuminating, & Lettering*. London: J. Hogg, 1906
Lowe, E.	"Handwriting," in *The Legacy of the Middle Ages,* by C. G. Crump and E. F. Jacob. London: Oxford University Press, 1926
Nash, R.	*American Writing Masters and Copybooks: History and Bibliography through Colonial Times*. Boston: Colonial Society of Massachusetts, 1959
Nash, R.	*American Penmanship, 1800–1850: A History of Writing and a Bibliography of Copy Books from Jenkins to Spencer*. Worcester: American Antiquarian Society, 1969
Osley, A. S.	*Luminario: An Introduction to the Italian Writing Books of the Sixteenth and Seventeenth Centuries*. Nieuwkoop: Miland Publishers, 1972
Whalley, J. I.	*English Handwriting, 1540–1853*. London: Her Majesty's Stationery Office, 1969

EXHIBITION CATALOGUES

Two Thousand Years of Calligraphy: Catalog of an exhibition at the Walters Art Gallery, Baltimore, the Peabody Institute Library, and the Baltimore Museum of Art. Baltimore: Walters Art Gallery, 1965

The Universal Penman: a Survey of Western Calligraphy from the Roman Period to 1980. London: Her Majesty's Stationery Office and the Victoria and Albert Museum, 1980.

A more complete coverage of the material included in this book, together with additional illustrations and a detailed bibliography, will be found in *The Pen's Excellencie: a Pictorial History of Western Calligraphy,* by J.I. Whalley. New York: Taplinger Publishing Company, 1982 (paperback ed.)

INDEX

A

B

C

U

V

W

THIS BOOK IS SET IN

Mergenthaler Linotron 202 Bembo
by Jackson Typesetting Co. /Jackson, Michigan
and Ernie Brame Typecrafters/ Colorado
Concept and typographic design by Steven Lester
Page layout by Cheryl Craft
Calligraphy by Barbara Bash
It is printed on Publisher's Smooth Bright White
by McNaughton & Gunn/ Saline, Michigan
Cover design by Barbara Bash and Eje Wray